PRINCIPLES OF JUSTICE

Compiled by

TAFADZWA MAHACHI

TAFAPRINT

DISCLAIMER:

Concepts and philosophies contained in this book are a result of research and may not be true as times change but these are just but findings at the time of publication

Published by TafaPrint for Belvedere Teachers' College Debate Society.

3273 Parirenyatwa Drive, Kadoma, Zimbabwe

+263-736-255441

+263-771-318720

...we can and we will...

ISBN-13: 978-1537472348

ISBN-10: 1537472348

To our patrons **Mr. Mandizvidza & Mrs. Mbundure** *and our principal*, **Mrs. Mbofana** *for their limitless vision, uplifting encouragement and unwavering support…*

CONTENTS

ACKNOWLEDGMENTS

Our surefire gratitude is hereby expressed to the following:

Jack Murima, Tapiwa Matombo, James Kamphiriphiri and Wadzanai Kitchen Murima for making the fire of debate continue at Belvedere college.

Mr. Mandizvidza who has been running up and down to make sure all logistics are in order for us to grow as a debate society.

Mrs. Mbofana for her willingness to have us represent the school in numerous tournaments.

My sweetheart, Yolanda, who sang church hymns as I worked on this project.

1. ANCIENT POLITICAL PHILOSOPHY

Ancient political philosophy is understood here to mean ancient Greek and Roman thought from the classical period of Greek thought in the fifth century BCE to the end of the Roman empire in the West in the fifth century CE, excluding the rise of Christian ideas about politics during that period. Political philosophy as a genre was invented in this period by Plato and reinvented by Aristotle: it encompasses reflections on the origin of political institutions, the concepts used to interpret and organize political life such as justice and equality, the relation between the aims of ethics and the nature of politics, and the relative merits of different constitutional arrangements or regimes. Platonic models remained especially important for later authors throughout this period, even as the development of later "Hellenistic" schools of Greek philosophy, and distinctively Roman forms of philosophical adaptation, offered new frameworks for construing politics from a philosophical point of view.

1. The Scope of Ancient Political Philosophy
2. Politics and Philosophy in Ancient Greece
2.1 Politics and Justice
2.2 Politics, Justice, and Equality
2.3 Politics and Philosophy
3. Socrates and Plato
3.1 Socratic Ethics and Its Relation to Politics
3.2 Socrates' Trial: The Political Philosophy of Citizenship
3.3 The Defense of Justice in the Republic
3.4 The Definition of Political Knowledge in the Statesman
3.5 The "Second-Best" Regime of the Laws
4. Aristotle
4.1 Aristotle's Philosophical Method and Ethics
4.2 From Ethics to Politics by way of Law

1. The Scope of Ancient Political Philosophy

We find the etymological origins of both of our terms, "[the] political" and "philosophy", in ancient Greek: the former originally pertaining to the polis or city-state; the latter, as conceived by Plato and the subsequent tradition, being the practice of a particular kind of inquiry conceived as the "love of wisdom" (philosophia). These ideas were transmitted beyond the confines of the classical polis as the Greek city-states came under the suzerainty of larger kingdoms after an initial Macedonian conquest at the end of the fourth century B.C; those kingdoms in turn were eventually conquered and significantly assimilated by the Roman republic, later transmuted into an empire. Philosophers writing in Latin engaged self-consciously with the earlier and continuing traditions of writing about philosophy in Greek. In the case of political philosophy in particular, the ancient Greek classification (devised by Plato and adapted by Aristotle) of regimes or "constitutions" (politeia, singular)— in Aristotle's version, the three "good" regimes being monarchy, aristocracy, and a moderate form of democracy; and their three "perversions" being tyranny, oligarchy, and a bad form of democracy—continued to inform the discussion of politics in the context of the "mixed regime" of the Roman republic, held to combine elements of all three of the good regimes. Neither the transformation of the republic into an empire in the first-century BCE, nor the eventual abdication of the last pretenders to the Roman imperial throne in the Western part of the empire in 476 CE, prevented continued engagement with this Greek and Roman heritage of political philosophy among late antique and later medieval scholars and their successors writing in Latin, Arabic and Hebrew. Thus while all societies have had politics, and also organized reflection on politics, "ancient political philosophy" in this article refers to the plurality of discourses comprised in that Greek and Roman heritage.

Because the Greeks invented political philosophy in its technical sense, but it has had a long history since then, long past the time when the ancient models were accepted as defining the field and determining the "problems" to be considered, it is a mistake to approach their thought with a modern menu of expectations of what the subject will contain. At the same time, because the Greeks also invented other genres widely recognized today—among them, history, tragedy, comedy, and rhetoric— no understanding of their thought about politics can restrict itself to the genre of political philosophy alone. Some argue, for example, that Thucydides' elaboration of the nature of the political through his History of the fifth-century Peloponnesian Wars between leagues led by Athens and Sparta is more important and instructive than that issuing from Plato's philosophical dialogues (Geuss 2005). While that argument is contentious, it rests on an important broader point. "Politics" and what is "political" emerged as part of a widespread set of sociolinguistic practices, most notably and best documented in Athens, while "philosophy" was invented by a relatively small number of self-professed "philosophical" thinkers. Thus the invention of "political philosophy" as a genre can be understood as a deliberate challenge to existing practices, and conceptions, of "the political." The challenge was directed in particular, though not exclusively, to democratic practices in mid to late fifth century Athens, which was the polis both intellectually dominant and in many ways politically exemplary at the time, as well as bequeathing the lion's share of our surviving evidence from ancient Greece (Meier, 1990; on the evidence for ancient philosophy in general, see the entry on doxography for ancient philosophy).

This article therefore begins by surveying political practices and the reflective accounts to which they gave rise in the classical Greek period of the independent polis. It then turns to the thinkers who invented "political philosophy" par excellence: Socrates, Plato and Aristotle. It continues to Hellenistic Greek thinkers before considering the main currents and roles of political philosophy in the Roman republic. While offering a survey of certain developments in the Roman empire, it leaves aside the Christian Fathers, and in particular the great upheaval of thought effected by Augustine, who is the starting point for the SEP's treatment of medieval political philosophy. (See the entry on medieval political philosophy.) The article concludes with some reflections on how the nature of "ancient political philosophy" should, and should not, be understood.

2. Politics and Philosophy in Ancient Greece
2.1 Politics and Justice

The distinctive understanding of "politics" forged in Greece was marked by the historical emergence of the independent city-state[1] and the variety of regimes which it could harbor. Notwithstanding fantasies of a pre-political "Age of Kronos", the polis was widely understood as the acme of human civilization and the principal domain in which human fulfillment could be sought. The city was the domain of potential collaboration in leading the good life, though it was by the same token the domain of potential contestation should that pursuit come to be understood as pitting some against others. Political theorizing began in arguments about what politics was good for, who could participate in politics, and why, arguments which were tools in civic battles for ideological and material control as well as attempts to provide logical or architectonic frameworks for those battles.

Such conflicts were addressed by the idea of justice, which was fundamental to the city as it emerged from the archaic age, sometimes reflected in Homer, into the classical period. Justice was conceived by poets, lawgivers, and philosophers alike as the structure of civic bonds which were beneficial to all (rich and poor, powerful and weak alike) rather than an exploitation of some by others. Hesiod's late eighth-century epic poem Works and Days, for example, contrasts the brute strength with which a hawk can dominate a nightingale ("You are being held by one who is much stronger... I will make a meal of you, if I want, or let you go," lines 206–208), with the peace and plenty which flourishes wherever justice, such as rendering fair verdicts to foreigners, is preserved (lines 225–230).

4

So understood, justice defined the basis of equal citizenship and was said to be the requirement for human regimes to be acceptable to the gods. The ideal was that, with justice as a foundation, political life would enable its participants to flourish and to achieve the overarching human end of happiness (eudaimonia), expressing a civic form of virtue and pursuing happiness and success through the competitive forums of the city. Whether justice applied to the city's relation with other cities was a further and highly contested point, memorably debated in Thucydides' recounting of the "Melian Dialogue" in 416 BCE, in which emissaries of the Athenians debated the meaning of justice with the leaders of Melos, a city they were threatening with death and disaster should they fail to submit to Athenian domination (Thuc. V. 84–114).

2.2 Politics, Justice, and Equality

Justice, then, depended on treating equals equally, with only the equals being full citizens. Yet how should "the equal" be understood? This became the major political faultline of the Greek fifth century BCE. Oligarchical regimes considered only the kalokagathoi[2] —the elite and well-born, usually also wealthy landowners —to be full equals; democratic regimes treated the "many" (or some large proportion of them) as political equals of the elite "few," in the fullest democracies enfranchising all free- and native-born men.[3] Sparta, a unique political entity, still exemplified the same broad pattern in naming its citizens "the equals" (hoi homoioi).[4] The absence of slave status made one free but not necessarily a citizen. Slavery for its part was very little debated as a political question, serving to demarcate the domain of "politics" by contrast with it rather than being considered as a topic within it (see Garnsey 1996 for a full account including exceptions to that generalization). The exclusion of women from active citizenship in Athens was more consciously felt, giving rise to fantasies of female-dominated politics in Aristophanic comedy (Lysistrata, Assemblywomen) and to tortured reflection in many tragedies (consider the titles of Medea; Phaedra; Trojan Women).

Among equals, however defined, the space of the political was the space of participation in speech and decision concerning public affairs and actions. That invention of the political (what Meier 1990 calls The Greek Discovery of Politics) was the hallmark of the classical Greek world. Citizens, whether the few (usually the rich) or the many (including the poorer and perhaps the poorest free adult men), deliberated together as to how to conduct public affairs, sharing either by custom, by election, or by lot—the latter seen in Athens as the most democratic, though it was never the sole mechanism used in any Greek democracy—in the offices for carrying them out. Rhetoric played an important role especially, though not only, in democracies, where discursive norms shaped by the poor majority were hegemonic in public even over the rich (Ober 1989).

At the same time, politics was shaped by the legacy of archaic poetry and its heroic ethos and by the religious cults which included, alongside pan-Hellenic and familial rites, important practices distinct to each city-state. This was a polytheistic, rather than monotheistic, setting, in which religion was at least in large part a function of civic identity. It was a world innocent of modern bureaucracy and of the modern move to intellectual abstraction in defining the state: the entity we would call "Athens" in the abstract was called in its own day by the collective noun for its living and breathing citizens, "the Athenians." So if ancient political philosophy left out much that modern political philosophy would include (e.g., for the most part, the question of the justness of slavery), it also included much that the latter would tend to exclude: viewing an unquestioned civic religious cult, as well as the patterns of child-rearing, cultural stories expressed in music, epic, and drama, gender roles and sexual practices, military participation, as forming part of the "way of life" which constituted the politeia or "constitution" in its broadest sense (Lane 2014, 59–62). This broadest sense was initially most evident to the Athenians when they looked at the peculiar customs of Sparta, but Plato taught them to recognize that democratic Athens was as distinctive a regime (Schofield 2006: 31–43).

Most of the wise men (sophoi) and students of nature (physikoi) who appeared in this milieu thought within the same broad terms as the poets and orators. Justice was widely, if not universally, treated as a fundamental constituent of cosmic order. Some of the physikoi influenced political life, notably the Pythagoreans in southern Italy. Others held themselves aloof from political action while still identifying commonalities between nature and politics. However, this picture of broad consonance was rudely challenged in the mid to late fifth century BCE by a new kind of thinker and political agent, the professional teachers ("sophists"), who began to ask whether the laws and customs (nomos, singular; nomoi, plural) embodying political justice were truly a reflection of justice in nature (phusis), or merely an imposition of arbitrary human norms. Most of the sophists argued the latter, though they did so along a spectrum of interpretation (for which our evidence rests heavily on Plato, who portrays Socrates arguing with a considerable number of sophists): for Protagoras (as depicted in Plato's Protagoras), the human creation of political life was a cause of celebration of human virtues and practical abilities; for Thrasymachus (as depicted in Plato's Republic), it was a cause of condemnation, the powerful in any city imposing laws to serve their own interests. This nomos-phusis debate raised a fundamental challenge to the ordering intellectual assumptions of the polis, even though the sophists advertised themselves as teaching skills for success within it, a number of them being employed as diplomats by cities eager to exploit their rhetorical abilities. Socrates and Plato would respond to this challenge in shaping a new genre of "philosophy" which broke the mould of their predecessors. If Greek political thinkers presupposed justice, in the fifth and fourth centuries BCE many of them also increasingly problematized it.

2.3 Politics and Philosophy

In giving birth to philosophy, the polis also gave birth to a tension between what Aristotle would describe as two lives: the life of politics and the life of philosophy. A faultline between ethics and politics, so closely connected in an ancient culture preoccupied with flourishing (eudaimonia) and virtue (aretê), opened here. Should philosophers act politically (and if so, should they engage in ordinary politics in existing regimes, or work to establish new ones), or should they abstain from politics in order to live a life of pure contemplation? There was likewise a question as to whether philosophers should think politically: were human affairs worth thinking about in the broadest perspective opened by the study of nature and of the gods? In engaging with questions of rhetoric, virtue, knowledge, and justice, Socrates' philosophical life was engaged with the political even before his death (his trial and execution at the hands of the Athenian democratic regime) embattled him with it. But for his student Plato and Plato's student Aristotle, the practice and even the study of human affairs such as politics were less divine, and so less admirable, than the broader study of truth about the natural and the divine realms. Philosophy might have to address the political but its highest calling soared above it. If Socrates' political fate was part of the stimulus for Plato to invent a new metaphysics and epistemology in order to articulate an alternative realm of political possibility, Plato's dialogues show Socrates simultaneously asserting an independence for those disciplines from the bonds of the political alone.[5]

This distinctive Greek—and particularly Platonic – outlook must condition any historical understanding of the development of ancient political philosophy. While one influential approach to the history of political thought takes its bearings from what a thinker was trying to do in and by what he or she said or wrote, it is important to recognize that the founders of ancient political philosophy were in part trying to define a new space of doing as philosophizing, independent of ordinary political action. This is not to say that they did not also have ordinary political intentions, but rather to stress that the invention of political philosophy was also intended as a mode of reflection upon the value of ordinary political life.

3. Socrates and Plato

According to Cicero, Socrates (469–399 BCE) was the first to bring philosophy down from heaven, locating it in cities and even in homes (Tusc.V.10). A humbly born man who refused the lucrative mantle of the sophistic role as a professional teacher, yet attracted many of the most ambitious and aristocratic youth of Athens to accompany him in his questioning of them and their elders as to the nature of the virtues they claimed to possess or understand, he left no philosophical writings. We know him only through the surviving testimony of others, first the lampoons in Aristophanes' comic plays, and above all the dialogues written by his student Plato and his associate Xenophon (dialogues by others are known only by titles or fragments), and the remarks of Plato's student Aristotle, as well as other sources from after or long after his death (for a collection, see Giannantoni 1990). See the entry on Socrates.

3.1 Socratic Ethics and Its Relation to Politics

Socrates seems to have been the first philosopher to treat ethics – as opposed to cosmology and physics—as a distinct area of inquiry. Asserting in Plato's Apology that "the unexamined life is not worth living," he pressed for definitions of the virtues or excellences which were widely recognized and claimed by his fellows, but which they found difficult to explain. As depicted by Plato, the search for such definitions led invariably to a concern with knowledge of how best to live, as not only one of the conventional virtues (in the form of wisdom) but also as underpinning, even constituting, them all. That elevation of knowledge in turn led Socrates to militate against the practices of rhetoric and judgment which animated the political institutions of Athens—the law-courts, Assembly and Council. Instead he posited the existence, or at least the possibility, of political expertise, claiming (in Plato's Gorgias) to be the one person in Athens who at least tried to pursue such a true politikê technê (Grg. 521d). The notion of political knowledge limited to one or a few experts, as opposed to the embedded and networked knowledge produced and exercised by the whole demos of Athens in their judgments and deliberations, struck at the central premises of Athenian democracy and those of Greek politics more generally (in oligarchies, wealth rather than knowledge was the relevant criterion for rule; in tyrannies, sheer power). Thus the nature of Socrates' concern with ethics led him directly into a form of political philosophizing. The relation between politics and knowledge, the meaning of justice as a virtue, the value of the military courage which all Greek cities prized in their citizens, all seem to have been central topics of Socratic conversation.

3.2 Socrates' Trial: The Political Philosophy of Citizenship

That engagement with political philosophy was dramatically intensified when Socrates was, at the age of seventy, arraigned, tried, and sentenced to death by an Athenian court. Brought in the usual Athenian way by a group of his fellow citizens who took it upon themselves to prosecute him for the sake of the city, the charges against him were three-fold: not acknowledging the city's gods; introducing new gods; and corrupting the young (Apol. 24b). Each of these had a political dimension, given the civic control of central religious cults mentioned earlier, and the broad political importance of educating the young to take their place in the civic order. Timed a few years after a short-lived oligarchic coup in which several of Socrates' sometime associates (Critias, Charmides) participated, and after the ignominious Athenian defeat in the wars with Sparta which saw another earlier follower of Socrates (Alcibiades) turn traitor to Athens, the trial must be suspected of having served as a substitute for the prohibited political trials of the oligarchic partisans (such trials having been barred by a general amnesty passed in 403 BCE by the restored democracy; see Cartledge 2009, Ch.7).

Socrates' speeches in the court trial—literary versions of which were produced by Plato, Xenophon, and a number of other followers—forced him to confront directly the question of his role in an Athens defined by its democratic institutions and norms. Socrates had played his part as an ordinary citizen, allowing his name to go forward for selection by lot to serve on the Council, and serving in the army when required. But he had not engaged actively in "public affairs" (ta pragmata, Apol. 32e): he had not spoken in the Assembly (31c), nor, so far as we know, brought prosecutions or volunteered for selection for jury service in the law-courts. In Plato's account, after countering the religious accusations, Socrates acknowledged this abstention from public affairs but claimed to have had a more significant mission laid on him by the god Apollo when his oracle at Delphi declared that no man was wiser than Socrates: his mission was to stir up the city like a gadfly (30e), discussing virtue and related matters (38a), and benefiting each person by "trying to persuade him" to care for virtue rather than wealth for himself and for the city (36c-d). He went so far as to claim that as a civic benefactor, he deserved not death but the lifetime free meals commonly awarded to an Olympic champion (36e-37a). Socrates here depicts himself as a new kind of citizen, conceptualizing the public good in a new way and so serving it best through unprecedented actions in contrast to the conventionally defined paths of political contest and success (Villa 2001).

While depicting himself in his defense speeches in Plato's Apology as a new kind of virtuous citizen, Socrates makes three remarks which have in modern times been seized upon as indications of the principled limits which he might have put on the requirement to obey the law. The first two recalled political incidents: while serving on the Council, he had voted against an illegal proposal (32b-c); and under the short-lived oligarchical coup of "The Thirty", he had disobeyed an order of the ruling body to arrest a democratic partisan for execution (32c-d). The third is a hypothetical remark. If, he imagines, the jurors were to say to him, "we acquit you, but only on condition that you spend no more time on this investigation and do not practice philosophy, and if you are caught doing so you will die," his reply would be: "I will obey the god rather than you, and as long as I draw breath and am able, I shall not cease to practice philosophy" (both quotations excerpted from longer sentences, 29c-d). Particularly in Anglophone twentieth-century scholarship, these remarks have engendered a view of Socrates as endorsing civil disobedience in certain circumstances, and so have framed the question of civil disobedience and the grounds for political obligation as arising in Plato. A significant debate on these matters took shape in the United States in the 1960s and 1970s at the time of widespread civil disobedience relating to civil rights and the Vietnam War: see for example Konvitz 1964, Woozley 1972.

That debate has had to confront the fact that Socrates did not actually disobey his own death sentence with which his trial concluded: when the time came, he drank the poisonous hemlock prescribed. Before that moment, Plato imagines Socrates being visited in prison by his friend Crito (in a dialogue which bears his name), and urged to escape for the sake of his friends and family, a practice which was tolerated in Athens so long as the escapee fled into exile. Socrates is not persuaded by Crito's arguments. He begins his examination of them by recalling principles to which he and Crito had in the past agreed, including the principle that it is better to suffer injustice than to commit it (Cri. 47a-50a). He then goes on to ventriloquize a series of speeches which he ascribes to the "Laws of Athens" against escape.[6] These speeches articulate a set of special connections between Socrates and the Laws of Athens which, depending on one's reading, either flesh out the principle that it is better to suffer injustice than to do it (by dramatizing reasons on which it would unjust for Socrates to escape), or else stand in tension with that principle by invoking absolutist grounds that go beyond those that it would authorize (Harte 1999). On any reading, it is important to bear in mind that Socrates is choosing to obey a jury verdict that has commanded him to suffer what is arguably an injustice but not to commit one.

The "Laws of Athens" appeal to a kind of social contract made between themselves and Socrates. The contract is unequal: the "Laws" compare themselves to parents and slaveowners, and Socrates to child and slave. Obedience is owed because the "Laws" have provided the whole basis for Socrates' education and life in the city, a city in which he has notably chosen to remain, never traveling abroad except on military service. But the "Laws" also speak of the opportunity they afford to Socrates to "persuade or obey" them (51b; 51e-52a). The meaning of this clause and its relevance to civil disobedience is again much debated (Kraut 1984 remains a landmark). Nevertheless, the image of Socrates tried, convicted, and made to die (by his own hand) at the city's command has come to be the most vivid and powerful symbol of tension in the relationship between political philosophy and political authority.

3.3 The Defense of Justice in the Republic

The Crito depends upon a notion of justice and injustice which it never defines. In the Republic, by contrast, a dialogue in which Socrates is also the main character (and first-person narrator) but in which the views he advances go beyond the tight-knit pattern of debates in the dialogues discussed in section 3.1, Plato (424/3–348/7 BCE)[7] offers an account of justice linking the political to the psychological and justice to a higher understanding of true goodness. (See the entry on Plato.) The Republic is, with the Laws, an order of magnitude longer than any other Platonic dialogue. Readers today are likely to think of the Republic as the home par excellence of political philosophy. But that view has also been challenged by scholars who see it as primarily an ethical dialogue, driven by the question of why the individual should be just (Annas 1999). This section argues that the ethical and political concerns, and purposes, of the dialogue are inextricably intertwined.

Near the beginning of the dialogue, a challenge is launched by the character Thrasymachus, mentioned above, asserting that all actual cities define justice in the interest of the rulers. He takes this to mean that the ethical virtue of justice which their subjects are enjoined to cultivate—traditionally seen as the necessary bond among citizens and the justification for political rule—is in fact a distorted sham. (See the entry on Callicles and Thrasymachus.) The ethical question which Thrasymachus poses and which Plato's brothers Glaucon and Adeimantus reformulate—why should the individual be just if he or she can get away with not being just, when elevated above the demands of ordinary justice either by special power or good fortune?—thus already has a political correlate from the outset.

Socrates then launches a speculation as to the origins of cities: the city is held to have an existence independently of ethical concerns, coming into being for economic reasons and immediately needing to defend itself in war (and also to be able to make offensive war for economic gain). However, this origin already gives rise to a proto-ethical dimension, first insofar as the members of the primitive city each do their own work (the structure of what will emerge as the virtue of justice), which is fleshed out when political rulers are established who are able to use their wisdom to help their subjects maintain a psychological balance in their souls that approximates, if it does not fully embody, the virtues of moderation and justice and so enables them to enjoy a unified rather than a divided soul. The question of why the individual should be just, figured at the outset by the contrast with the putatively happy tyrant, is resolved eventually by demonstrating that the tyrant is at once maximally unjust and maximally unhappy.

That resolution rests on the division of the soul into three parts by which the Republic places moral psychology at the heart of political philosophy. Both soul and city are posited by Socrates in arguments in Books II-IV and VIII-IX, in particular, to have a tripartite structure when the soul is embodied in a living person. In the soul and city respectively, the rational part or class should rule; the spirited part or class should act to support the rule of that rational part; and the appetitive part of the soul and producing class in the city should accept being governed by it. Both soul and city are therefore in need of, and capable of exhibiting, four virtues (427e-444a). Two of these pertain to individual parts: the rational part being capable of wisdom, the spirited part of courage. Two however are defined by relations between the parts: moderation as the agreement of all three parts that reason should rule, justice as each part doing its own (this echoes, in a radically new context, a conservative Athenian suspicion of excessive democratic polupragmosunê or busybody interference).

The result is that justice is defined as primarily a condition of one's soul or city as a whole, not as any specific just action; yet if the soul or city is so ordered, the individual will have no cause to engage in the paradigmatically unjust action of pleonexia or grasping for more than one's fair share. A just soul will indeed reliably issue in traditionally just actions, such as refraining from theft, murder, and sacrilege (contra Sachs 1963, who argues that Plato has simply abandoned the usual domain of justice). But what makes its 'justice' count as such goes beyond these particular actions and omissions, lying in the health and orderliness of such a soul contrasted with the chaotic or even tyrannical character of an unjust soul (Burnyeat 2013). To be an effective agent at all, one must be just, moderate, courageous and wise. The just person enjoys psychic health, which is advantageous no matter how he is treated (fairly or unfairly) by gods and men; correspondingly, the just society enjoys civic unity, which is advantageous in being the fundamental way to avoid the assumed supreme evil of civil war. In contrast, all other cities are characterized as riven by civil war between the rich and the poor; none of them counts as a single, unified city at all (see Rep. 422e-423a, and more generally, Book VIII of that dialogue).

By treating these ethical and political questions as interrelated, and then going on to depict both an ideal political regime ("Kallipolis", the fine or beautiful city) in which they could be solved, and the imperfect regimes into which such an ideal regime will decay, the Republic lays out a novel and ambitious template for political philosophy: not only to interrogate the meaning of virtue and citizenship, but also to develop an ideal regime and an account of how and why such regimes may fail. That template will be followed by Aristotle's Politics, by Cicero's De Re Publica, and by Thomas More's Utopia, among other successors. In Plato's hands, however, this template included some specific political prescriptions to maintain the unity of the ideal city which most of his successors abhorred. In particular, Book V of the Republic suggests that a sufficiently unified regime can be achieved only by depriving its guardian-rulers of private property and of private families, instead making them live in austere communal conditions in which they are financially supported by their money-making subjects and allowed to procreate only when and with whom will best serve the city. Aristotle and Cicero would deplore what they construed as this abolition of private property, and even those following and radicalizing Plato on property (advocating the abolition of property for all the citizens, rather than only deprivation of it for the rulers, as would the sixteenth-century More), were generally opposed to if not scandalized by the suggestion of procreative communism.

The Republic initiates a further tradition in political philosophy by laying out a template for the integration of ethics and political philosophy into a comprehensive account of epistemology and metaphysics. By making the claim of the philosophers to rule depend on their knowledge of the good and of the other Platonic Forms (in conjunction with their moral character and tested practical experience), the dialogue vindicates the Socratic and Platonic thought that ruling well—what we might call "rule" proper – requires a rare form of expertise rather than lay judgment, rhetorical advice, or common knowledge. In the Republic, the knowledge required for rule is not specialized, but comprehensive: the knowledge of the good and the Forms is somehow to translate into an ability to make laws as well as the everyday decisions of rule. The rulers are philosophers who take turns over their lifetime in exercising collective political authority. They define their vocation as that of philosophizing, engaging in rule out of some sort of compulsion or necessity (see the entry on Plato's ethics and politics in the Republic). To that extent the Republic presents a paradox: if it is widely considered the first major work of political philosophy,[8] it is nevertheless a work in which there is no special content to political knowledge nor any special vocation for politics.

3.4 The Definition of Political Knowledge in the Statesman

In the Statesman, Plato turns his attention to precisely the topics identified at the end of the last section above. In a discussion led by an unnamed person, a philosopher visiting Athens from Elea, political expertise (harking back to the politikê technê met above with Socrates, sect. 3.1) is identified by separating it progressively by a set of distinctions from other forms of expertise. The discussion is interrupted but ultimately enriched by a story or myth in which politics is shown to be a matter of humans ruling other humans in place of living under divine guidance. That human expertise of statecraft is ultimately distinguished from its closest rivals—strikingly, the arts of rhetoric, generalship, and judging—by its knowledge of the correct timing (kairos) for the exercise and cessation of these other arts (Lane 1998). The statesman is wholly defined by the possession of that knowledge of when it is best to exercise the other arts and its exercise in binding the different groups of citizens together, a knowledge which depends on a broader philosophical grasp but which is peculiarly political. Here, political philosophy operates not just to assimilate politics to a broader metaphysical horizon but also to identify its specificity.

3.5 The "Second-Best" Regime of the Laws

The Laws, a work reported to have been still on wax tablets, and so presumably left unfinished, when Plato died (Diogenes Laertius III. 37), treats the specificity of politics as a matter not of distinct vocational expertise but of the requirements of a "second-best" (739a) city, one in which the ideal regime of Kallipolis requiring an absence of private property for the guardians is not followed. Here politics still aims at virtue, and at the virtue of all the citizens, but those citizens all play a part in holding civic offices; the ordinary activities of politics are shared, in what is described as a mixture of monarchy and democracy. That description would give rise to an idea of the "mixed regime" or "mixed constitution" which would become influential in its own right, as we shall see below (section 6).

Another influential aspect of the Laws is its concern with the nature of law itself as a topic proper to political philosophy. The Republic takes law in its stride as something the "founders" of Kallipolis (the dialogue's participants, primarily Socrates, Glaucon and Adeimantus) will employ; the Statesman analyzes law as a stubborn and imperfect substitute for the flexible deployment of expertise (293e-303c). While the Laws shares that notion of law per se as a brutish and stubborn commander, it recommends a "double" notion of law, in which each such command is prefaced with a persuasive account of its rationale, addressed to the citizens, who are expected to read and understand it (719b-723d, and passim). Some scholars have found that to be a distinctively democratic and liberal account of law (Bobonich 2002; see also the entry on Plato on utopia). That arguably goes too far in a proceduralist direction, given that the value of law remains its embodiment of reason or understanding (nous), so that while adding persuasive preludes is a better way to exercise the coercive force of law, no agreement on the basis of persuasion could justify laws which departed from the standard of nous. Nevertheless the emphasis on all citizens as eligible, and so presumptively capable, to hold offices, differs significantly from the Republic, where the only offices mentioned seem to be monopolized by the philosopher-rulers and the auxiliary guardians who assist them.[9] It develops at much more length the closing passages of the Statesman, which refer to the offices of rhetor, general and juryman which the citizens will hold (as they did in Athens). The Statesman however reserves a special extraordinary role (a higher office, or perhaps not an office as such) for the statesman whenever he is present in the city. The role of the Statesman's eponymous figure must therefore be distinguished from that of the "Nocturnal Council" in the Laws (which is actually to meet just before dawn), a body of citizens who are selected for wisdom and judiciousness and whose role is to review and revise the laws rather than (as in the Statesman) to override them when it is better to do so.

The Athenian Visitor, the protagonist in the Laws, presents the imagined new Cretan colony of Magnesia for which he and his Cretan and Spartan companions engage in legislating, as "second-best," (739a), in that it does not involve the community of women and children, and the absence of private property, for all citizens of a city (here advocating a more stringent standard than even that of Kallipolis in the Republic). Much literature on Plato's political philosophy has debated whether this turn to the "second-best" reflects a new form of realism on Plato's part about politics more generally, invoking other remarks by the Athenian which suggest that no one could ever be uniformly and reliably virtuous and immune to corruption, though this is not unequivocally stated. Has Plato in the Laws given up on his earlier idealism which rested on the possibility of the philosopher-king, or on the idea of the perfectly knowledgeable statesman? If so, should that be interpreted as disillusionment or pessimism on his part, or as a more democratic or liberal turn? These questions structure the broad debate about the meaning and trajectory of Platonic political philosophy (for an overview, compare Klosko 2006 to Schofield 2006).

4. Aristotle

The two Platonic themes of superior political knowledge and, expressed particularly in his Laws, political participation, also structure the political thought of Aristotle (384–322 BCE), who studied in Plato's Academy as a youth and researched there for many years thereafter. Living much of his life as a resident alien in Athens, with close familial ties to the extra-polis Macedonian court which would in his lifetime bring Athens under its sway, Aristotle at once thematized the fundamental perspective of the Greek citizenship of equals and at the same time acknowledged the claim to rule of anyone of truly superior political knowledge. While building on Plato's project of demarcating political expertise and depicting ideal as well as imperfect cities, the advances and new directions that Aristotle pioneered in political philosophy reflect disagreements with Plato in their wider philosophies, though these were also marked by some deep commonalities.

4.1 Aristotle's Philosophical Method and Ethics

Whereas Plato's philosophy continually sought a single or small set of unifying truths behind the veil of appearance, Aristotle's wide-ranging researches into what would now be considered the natural sciences, as well as in logic and other areas of inquiry, manifested respect for the opinions of "the many and the wise" as a starting-point for philosophical understanding. His approach likewise manifested appreciation of the multiplicity of forms of knowledge, in particular the cleavage between theoretical understanding of the world as it necessarily is, and practical knowledge of how to deliberate about acting in relation to whatever "could be otherwise." Uniting his accounts of phenomena as different as plants, animals, ethics and politics, was a teleological structure of explanation. Biological creatures work to fulfill the realization of their end or telos, a specific way of living a complete life characteristic of the plants or animals of their own kind, which is the distinctive purpose that defines their fundamental nature—just as human artifacts are designed and used for specific ends. Human action posits its own telos in light of which the nature of each action is intelligible, but these should ideally reflect the overall natural telos of humans as such.

Here arises a problem unique to humans. Whereas other animals have a single telos defining their nature (living the full life of a frog, including reproduction, being the sole telos of each frog, in the example used by Lear 1998), humans both have a distinctive human nature—arising from the unique capacity to use language to deliberate about how to act – and also share in the divine nature in their ability to use reason to understand the eternal and intelligible order of the world. Practical reason is the domain of ethics and politics, the uniquely human domain, but the political life is not necessarily the best life, compared with that devoted to the divinely shared human capacity for theoretical reason and contemplation (conmpare Nicomachean Ethics I with X.7–9).

4.2 From Ethics to Politics by way of Law
In considering practical reason to be the domain of both ethics and politics, Aristotle follows Plato in drawing no sharp line between those two domains (see on this point for ancient testimonies and modern arguments respectively, Bodéüs 1993: 22–24 and 59–63). In fact he closes his Nicomachean Ethics by remarking that for most people, the practice of ethics can only be ensured by their being governed by law, which combines necessity (compulsion) with reason. Because, for most people, the ethical life presupposes government by law, the student of ethics must become a student of political science, studying the science of legislation in light of the collection of constitutions assembled by Aristotle and his school in the Lyceum. All but one of the over one hundred items in this collection reported in antiquity have been lost: the analysis of the "Constitution of Athens" was recovered from a portion of a papyrus discovered in the nineteenth century. Aristotle's theoretical claims about

the nature of politics in the Politics must be understood against this backdrop. The legislator (for this is the standpoint adopted in the Politics, see the entry on Aristotle's political theory) needs to have a grasp of the nature of politics as such; an understanding of the major faultlines in the interpretation and practice of politics; and a grip on the structure and characteristics of the specific city for which he aims to legislate.

4.3 The Projects of the Politics

These requirements correspond to the three distinct projects which Malcolm Schofield (1999, ch.6) has proposed as a schema for reading the Politics: a "rational" model or regulative ideal of the nature of politics (Books I-III: most egalitarian); a "political" model in which factions contest the interpretation and application of the principles of the rational model (predominantly in Books III-V: in particular, the meaning of equality contested between democrats and oligarchs, as noted above (sect. 2.2) a characteristic faultline in Greek political life); and a "sociological" model of the functions needed for the city as an organism, which in Aristotle's hands excludes craftsmen and farmers from political participation based on lack of excellence and leisure respectively (canvassed at points in Books IV-VI and also in the description of the best regime in Books VII-VIII: least egalitarian, most hierarchical). Josiah Ober (1998) has controversially suggested a further project: that of political realization of the ideal virtuous regime of Books VII-VIII through Macedonian-led colonization of western Asia. Even if this suggestion is rejected, it reminds us that the standpoint of the legislator was not merely the appropriate standpoint to be adopted by the student of Aristotelian politics (as by the protagonists of Plato's Laws, legislating for a projected Cretan colony of Magnesia), but was also a recognized role in Greek political life: both in legend and in historical time, the founder-legislators of cities shaped their nomoi (both written laws and unwritten customs) in the context of selecting colonists, site, and officials for those cities to prosper.

The Politics begins in what Schofield, as seen above, would call rational-model mode, offering an analysis of the teleological ends of life and the human capacity for speech which together support one of its two most famous contentions: that "it is evident that the state is a creation of nature, and that man is by nature a political animal" (I.2, 1253a2–3). While for modern readers this sentence is resonant with democratic sentiments, for Aristotle it is an analytical claim. Necessary (though not sufficient) for humans to accomplish their full potential for virtuous life is their exercise of their capacity for deliberative reasoning in speech about actions taken at the highest and most complete level of the political community. As Hannah Arendt (1958) emphasizes, Aristotle's understanding of civic unity insists on respect for human plurality as the condition of political action; in Book II, he criticizes Plato's Kallipolis for interpreting the requirement of civic unity in so extreme a fashion as to have obliterated the properly political domain altogether (Nussbaum 1980). (Nevertheless, civic unity is still an aim of Aristotle's ideal virtuous regime, and a limited Platonic spirit survives in the common meals that this regime would offer to all citizens: VII.10.) However, since this potential for politics can only be fulfilled by those who are indeed capable of virtue, politics is most fully realized not by an arithmetically based democracy in which all who can be counted as individuals can vote, but rather by a regime in which citizenship is limited to all and only the (sufficiently) virtuous.

In another famous contention of the work—that "a citizen is one who shares in governing and being governed" (III.13, 1283b42–1284a1, often translated as "ruling and being ruled in turn"), the Greek dictum of citizenship among equals is presented as an analytical truth, leaving open how such equality is to be conceived in practice. The citizen "shares in the administration of justice, and in offices" (III.1, 1275a23–24). In defective regimes, the good citizen and the good man may come apart. The good citizen of a defective regime is one whose character suits the particular regime in question (whether oligarchic, or democratic, say) and equips him to support it loyally; hence he may be deformed or stunted by participation in offices defined on incorrect terms. In "the best state," however, the citizen is "one who is able and chooses to be governed and to govern with a view to the life of excellence" (III.13, 1284a1–3). In such a state, "the citizens must not lead the life of artisans or tradesmen, for such a life is ignoble and inimical to excellence" (VII.9, 1328b39–41, nor that of farmers, as political participation requires leisure. Here the limitations and exclusions among actual humans licensed by the principled formulation of the possibility—but need for actual realization—of human virtue become apparent.

Aristotle recognizes that there are other possible titles for political rule: "There is also a doubt as to what is to be the supreme power in the state:—Is it the multitude? Or the wealthy? Or the good? Or the one best man? Or a tyrant?" (III.10, 1281a11–13). He develops in particular detail the arguments that might be made on behalf of the many and the knowledgeable one respectively. The many can judge, as they did in Athenian dramatic audiences, juries, and the Assembly (where they "judged" the merits of a speaker's proposal). Aristotle uses the image of a collectively provided feast to illustrate the potential superiority of such collective judgement; how to interpret this image (whether as a potluck, Waldron 1995, Wilson 2011, Ober 2013, or in a more aggregative way, Bouchard 2011, Cammack 2013, Lane 2013) and other images that he uses is a matter of some renewed controversy. But the lesson Aristotle draws from this limits the role of the many to that of judging and electing to offices rather than to serving themselves in offices (III.11, 1281b31; Lane 2013). The many can contribute to virtuous decision-making in their collective capacity of judgment – presumably in assemblies and juries— but not as individual high officials.

In the contrasting case of the one supremely excellent person, Aristotle argues that such a person has, strictly speaking, no equals, and so cannot be made justly to take his turn in rule as one citizen among others. Instead it is right that such a person should rule:

If, however, there be some one person, or more than one, although not enough to make up the full complement of a state, whose excellence is so pre-eminent that the excellence or the political capacity of all the rest admit of no comparison with his or theirs, he or they can be no longer regarded as part of a state; for justice will not be done to the superior, if he is reckoned only as the equal of those who are so far inferior to him in excellence and in political capacity. Such a man may truly be deemed a god among men ....men like him should be kings in their state for life. (III.13, 1284a3–11...1284b32–34; cf. III.17, 1288a24–29)

Yet this argument is left at the hypothetical level of an alternative title for political rule, or better, of an alternative title for a form of rule that is not political. When Aristotle considers political rule as such, the formulation of mutual rule in turn by a large body of sufficiently virtuous citizens remains preeminent.

In the political model which begins to supplement the rational model from Book III onward, the major issue is conflict between rival factions over the basis for defining equality and so justice. In the Nicomachean Ethics, Book V, Aristotle had identified two types of equality: geometrical, or proportional to merit; and arithmetical, or proportional to mere numerical counting. In Politics III.9 he picks up this distinction and aligns it with the conflict between oligarchical and democratic justice. As he later puts it, "Democrats say that justice is that to which the majority agree, oligarchs that to which the wealthier class agree..." (VI.3, 1318a18–20), while truly aristocratic justice would enfranchise only those equal in virtue.

This attention to the actual political contentions of rival Greek groups leads into a discussion of the relative goodness and badness of imperfect regimes, modeled in part on Plato's Statesman. Whereas the Platonic text had distinguished monarchy from tyranny, aristocracy from oligarchy, and good from bad democracy on the basis of obedience to law (all these regimes being conceived as lacking the genuine political knowledge of the true statesman), Aristotle instead makes the dividing line the question of ruling in the common interest as opposed to ruling in the interest of a single faction. The "bad" democracy, for example, rules for the faction of the many as opposed to the faction of the few, whereas the "good" democracy—which Aristotle baptizes "polity"—rules in the common interest of all citizens.

To this political account of regimes, Aristotle adds an historical-sociological account which has much in common with the narrative of Athens offered in the Constitution of Athens compiled by his school. Democracy has historically taken on various forms in Athens, degenerating from an aboriginal democracy of non-meddling farmers (VI.4), through various intermediate forms to a democracy (seemingly that of contemporary fourth-century Athens) in which men rule, not laws. Yet this trajectory does not prevent him from asserting that in general democracy is "most tolerable" of the three perversions (IV.2, 1289b4–5) and noting that it at least involves the characteristic political liberty of ruling and being ruled in turn (VI.2). The sociological inquiry comes to a head when the question of some single "best" regime is replaced by a question about not what is "best" in the "ideal" sense, but the good constitution "that is easily attainable by all" (IV.1, 1288a37–39) and in practice best for most cities (IV.11). This Aristotle calls the middling regime: a political, because sociological, mean between oligarchy and democracy, in which the middle classes hold the preponderance of both wealth distribution and political power—hence it is attainable through reform of either an oligarchy or a democracy, the most prevalent constitutions among the Greeks. Strikingly, his example of such a regime is Sparta: presented as a case of a characteristically democratic distribution of education (among citizens only, of course) coupled with the characteristically aristocratic principle (but also a practice widely used in Greek democracies for some offices) of election to offices rather than selection by lot (IV.9).

4.4 Aristotle in Political Philosophy

"All modern discussions of citizenship as a noninstrumental good-in-itself are indebted, if only indirectly, to him [sc. Aristotle]" (Ober 1998: 290). The Politics emphasizes that "a state is not a mere society, having a common place, established for the prevention of mutual crime and for the sake of exchange" but is rather "a community of families and aggregations of families [sc. united] in well-being, for the sake of a perfect and self-sufficing life" (III.9, 1280b30-34, with square brackets added). It has been argued in this article that the final clause of that sentence is important: citizenship is a noninstrumental good-in-itself only so long as it does indeed aim at the telos of a perfect life. That is, while Aristotle indeed valued political participation, he saw it as an intrinsic good only insofar as it was an expression of virtue. Without virtue, participation was to be valued on the basis of expedience.

Nevertheless, Ober's observation rings true of the historical significance of Aristotle's political thought. The medieval rediscovery in the West of the full Greek texts of Aristotle's Ethics and Politics and their translation into Latin in the thirteenth century served as a basis for reconceiving civic life as valuable on the basis of reason independent of revelation. Thus 1260 – the date of William of Moerbeke's complete Latin translation of the Politics—symbolizes a fundamental turning point in political philosophy, one in which Aristotelian philosophy would be widely deployed within certain strands of thought of the Catholic Church, while also inspiring a wide range of philosophical movements and later becoming the target of others.

Modern debates over the meaning of Aristotle find him a precursor of or inspiration for a range of intellectual and political positions: Aristotle as a communitarian (MacIntyre 1984) vs. Aristotle as an exponent of class conflict (Yack 1993); Aristotle as a democrat, or at least as providing the basis for democracy (Frank 2005), vs. Aristotle in opposition to Athenian democracy in his day (Ober 1998). One interesting development has been the use of Aristotle to articulate an ethics of capability (Nussbaum 1993). In evaluating Aristotle's political thought, it is important to distinguish between modern democratic assumptions and his own starting points, many of which were in tension with the democracies of his own time.

5. Hellenistic Philosophies and Politics

Important developments in political thinking and practice took place under the Hellenistic kingdoms that supplanted Macedon in its suzerainty over the formerly independent Greek city-states. These included, for example, a genre of rhetorical letters addressed to rulers, and the important analysis of Greek and Roman constitutional change by the second-century Greek historian Polybius (Hahm 2000). This section will focus primarily on the implications for politics of the Epicurean and Stoic philosophical schools which, alongside others, emerged in this period. If the Cynics eschewed the city altogether, and the Epicureans eschewed active political participation for the most part, the skeptics adhering to the radical Pyrrhonist position allowed their adherents to live in an ordinary way but without inner assent or conviction to any doctrine, similarly not a stance supportive of active political engagement. Stoic arguments were more generally supportive of playing a part in political life, but in times of tyranny, some adherents inclined to withdrawal and contemplation, while others might incline to resistance; yet we see resistors to tyranny, as also active contributors to ordinary politics, among most of the other schools as well. As kingships flourished among the Hellenistic kingdoms and republican rule at Rome eventually transmuted into the principate, not only the value of political participation, but also the proper domains of politics (polis, empire, city of kosmopolitai or those seeing themselves as citizens of the world order as well as of particular political entities, were widely debated.

5.1 Persisting and New Schools

It should be stressed that in addition to the major movements of Epicureanism and Stoicism treated below, other schools also persisted and arose in this period. Those persisting included the Platonic Academy (transformed in a skeptical direction) and the Aristotelian Lyceum (the Peripatetic School). Newcomers, albeit tracing themselves to their own understanding of the figure of Socrates, included the Cynics and the Pyrrhonist skeptics.

The Cynics took their name from the Greek for "dog," referring to the animal-like life indifferent to social conventions which they pursued, carrying out all their bodily functions in full public view. While this generally led them to advocate what might be considered more an anti-politics than a politics, a provocative statement by their founder Diogenes of Sinope (c.404–323 BCE) – answering a query about his birthplace by asserting himself to be a "citizen of the world" (Diogenes Laertius, VI. 63) – would resonate with later Stoics and others developing a political philosophy of "cosmopolitanism" (see the entry on cosmopolitanism). Diogenes' indifference to political power was also reflected in his reported reply to the visiting world-conqueror Alexander the Great, asking him to request a boon: all the Cynic wanted was for the emperor to step out of his light (Diogenes Laertius, VI. 38). In their rejection of political and moral conventional opinion, the Cynics directly influenced the Stoics, yet they also have some parallels with the Epicureans and even with the skeptics.

One branch of ancient skepticism had its roots in Plato's Academy, which from the time of Arcesilaus' headship in the mid-260s BCE turned in a skeptical direction, arguing that there was no clear criterion of truth and so philosophers can only suspend judgment. While that was an "Academic" position within philosophical debate, a possible forebear (Pyrrho) had in the fourth century BCE putatively demonstrated the tranquility of mind which such a position could bring, by living a life seemingly without any investment in the truth of his beliefs (though the question of how, and how far, Pyrrho was guided by appearances would perplex later followers). (See the entry on Pyrrho.) From the first century BCE, a radical movement of "Pyrrhonist" skepticism was developed outside the Academy by Aenesidemus, followed about a century later by Agrippa, in a movement summed up for posterity in the second-century CE work of Sextus Empiricius (Outlines of Pyrrhonism) which would have a considerable influence on early modern philosophy. Meanwhile the milder "Academic" skepticism, allowing the inquirer to incline to one side or another though not to invest in full belief, had significant influence on first-century BCE figures such as Cicero. (See the entry on ancient skepticism.)

5.2 Epicureanism

Like the Cynics, the Epicureans were not primarily concerned with politics, though they offered a more complex evaluation of its origins and nature, and a more nuanced recognition of its instrumental value. Politics was not, for them, part of the good life or a fulfillment of human nature as it was for Aristotle. Reports of Epicurus' "Key Doctrines" (see the entry on Epicurus) include instead a contractarian view of justice for mutual protection from harm (reminiscent of Glaucon's initial proposal about justice in Republic Book II, which itself seems to echo the nomos-phusis debate among the sophists). Justice serves utility. "If someone makes a law and it does not happen to accord with the utility of social relationships, it no longer has the nature of justice" (KD 36, LS 22B). The greatest utility is that of tranquility or security, which is the naturally desired end or goal. Hence the social contract is not fortuitous or merely conventional or second-best: it arises from and meets a natural need. While, as Annas 1993: 298 argues, the individual agent will be disposed to justice as part of the path to tranquility properly understood ("The just <life> is most free from disturbance...", KD 36, LS 22B), nevertheless laws will be necessary to enforce obedience to the contract by most people.

The city serves a legitimate and necessary function in ensuring security. But this does not mean that an active public life is also a path to security. On the contrary, while many people will be attracted to the possible fortune and glory of such a life, and while cities need such people, the Epicurean wise man will on the whole refrain from active political participation. Instead the insecurities of life are best met by the formation of a community of friends. Friendships both secure us against risks and anxieties (more reliably than the hazards of a political career) and also provide pleasures and indeed joy: "The man of noble character is chiefly concerned with wisdom and friendship. Of these the former is a mortal good, but the latter is immortal" (Vatican Sayings 78, LS 22F (7)).

A sticking point for Epicurean ethics and politics is the justification for a further dimension of communal life: the willingness to sacrifice oneself for a friend, or to risk breaking the law for the greater good of one's fellow citizens (Sharples 1996: 122). That it is difficult to construct a compelling theoretical justification for such actions from Epicurean premises, which privilege obedience to law in order to avoid civic strife (as seen for example in Lucretius' poem De Rerum Natura, v.925–1157), did not prevent a number of Epicureans from undertaking such risky public service, among them more than one of the assassins of Julius Caesar (Sedley 1997; Fowler 1989 discusses a wide range of Roman Epicurean attitudes). A more modest but still striking example of Epicurean public service is the huge portico inscribed with Epicurean sayings and exegesis in second-century Oenoanda (in modern-day Turkey) by one Diogenes of that city (Smith 1992, 2003). Whether or not his fellow citizens appreciated the instruction, modern archaeologists and philosophers are grateful for this unparalleled source of knowledge of ancient philosophy.

5.3 Stoicism

While Epicurus' default stance for the sage was not to engage in politics except if "some special circumstance disturbs him," the Stoic Zeno (see the entry on Stoicism) held that such a person "will engage in politics unless something prevents it" (Seneca, De Otio 3.2, as translated and quoted in Sharples 1996: 124). Nevertheless, Stoics too had difficulty in justifying assassination of tyrants, insofar as civil war would be worse than even a monarchy flouting the law, as one Roman Stoic would say in rebuffing Junius Brutus' attempt to recruit him to the conspiracy to murder Caesar (Plut. Brut. 12. 3–4). As we shall see, a Stoic commitment to politics generally took it to be part of nature's rational plan for human happiness, though this was not incompatible with a Cynic tincture of questioning whether existing laws are truly in accordance with the natural law (Vogt 2008).

Both the founder of the school, Zeno, and the school's later head Chrysippus wrote works in the Platonic genre entitled Republic, neither of which survives in full. (So too, reportedly, had Diogenes the Cynic.) Zeno's was written as a young man, allegedly under Cynic influence, rejecting the use of money in the characteristic Cynic vein. His portrait of the republic combines the Stoic idea of a natural law by which human conduct is harmonized with cosmic order, with a classical vision of politics in which a Platonic ideal of friendship through communist and sexual bonding (more erotic than familial for Zeno) persists (Schofield 1991: 22–56). He seems to have adopted Plato's prescription for the community of women and children, and at least some aspects of his insistence on the potential civic equality of men and women and political irrelevance of their anatomical differences. Humans share many characteristics and tendencies with other animals, and their initial impulse to form into society is a social rather than strictly political one: they are animated by a tendency to associate with those akin to themselves (the Stoic notion of oikeiôsis). Such a social tendency is, according to what is reported of Chrysippus' lost treatise On Law, transformed into a political relationship by means of law (LS 67R). As for some tendencies in Platonism and Cynicism, such law might have to be radically different from existing laws if it is to be in full conformity with nature and reason. For Chrysippus, even certain forms of incest are said to have been "discredited without reason" (LS 67F): a comparison with animals would license them.

Plutarch's characterization of Zeno's Republic as prescribing that "we should regard all men as our fellow-citizens and local residents" (LS 67A) has often been read as prescribing cosmopolitanism: indeed Plutarch himself went so far as to take the aim of Zeno's treatise to have been fulfilled by the world-conquests of Alexander the Great (LS 67A), though this claim seems to have been a willful misunderstanding for his own purposes (Schofield 1991: 24, 104–11). But in fact, as in the case of Aristotle, the underlying kinship by nature establishes a potential only for a civic membership which is to be based solely on virtue. Thus it is reported that Zeno presented "only virtuous people in the Republic as citizens, friends, relations and free" (LS 67B). Especially for the early Stoics, the city remained an accepted arena both for political action—Stoic sages and scholars advising kings and serving in offices (LS 67W)—and for defining the nature of politics in terms of justice. However, over time later Stoics moved away from this classical concern with participation in specific cities, to a new ideal of a cosmic city in which all and only the wise are citizens. Malcolm Schofield (1991: 103) has argued that this development "mediates the transition from republicanism to natural law theory," so bequeathing a crucial resource to early modern thinkers who sought to construct new versions of the latter; under the emperors, Hellenistic theories of monarchy would also gain a new lease on life. Nevertheless, in the years of the Roman republic, the affinity between Stoic and republican ideas proved significant, as we will now see.

5.4 Hellenistic Philosophies and Roman Republican Politics
Roman fascination with Greek philosophy was catalyzed by the Athenian embassy of three leading philosophers sent to Rome to plead the legal case of their city in 156/155 BCE;[10] it would continue as late as the early sixth century CE, as seen especially in the life of the eminent

philosophical polymath and Roman senator under barbarian rule, Boethius. Roman aristocrats were especially attracted to the Stoic willingness to countenance the kingly and political lives alongside the scholarly one as equally preferable (LS 67W), beginning to study the Stoa seriously from the late second century BCE. The affinity between Stoicism and Roman republicanism was enhanced by the second-century Stoic teacher Panaetius, who seems to have argued that the Roman mos maiorum or ancient ways and customs were the best form of government, so burnishing philosophical principle with the ancestral piety dear to the Romans. Other Romans however were strongly attracted to Epicureanism or to Cynicism; some of these in both cases, however paradoxically, likewise played significant roles in political life. Thus the distinctive lineaments of the Roman republic, now to be described, were debated and interpreted by the philosophically minded in terms of Greek political theory.

While the founders of the city were said to be the legendary twins Romulus and Remus, Romans identified the origins of their distinctive liberty in the killing of a tyrannical king in 510 BCE, by the ancestor of the Junius Brutus who would eventually kill Julius Caesar. The position of king was replaced by two annually elected consuls, the royal council became the Senate, and popular assemblies were established to elect magistrates and pass the laws they proposed. By Cicero's time, this regime—self-identified as the S.P.Q.R., the "Senatus populusque Romanus" or "Senate and people of Rome"[11] – had become interpreted as the ideal form of the "mixed constitution" which had had a long if complicated and until then relatively minor history as an idea in the works of Thucydides, Plato, and Aristotle (Hahm 2009). An influential account of Rome as a mixed constitution, in this case combining the three classical regime forms of monarchy, aristocracy, and democracy, had already been given by the Greek historian Polybius, who referred to this as the distinction of powers (Histories 6.11–18; see von Fritz 1954). Cicero himself would refer to it as a system of checks and balances (compensatio, De rep. II. 57) with the language of "mixing" and "tempering" paramount, as observed by E.M. Atkins (2000: 491).

Each element of the constitution exercised a distinctive form of power. The elected consuls wielded imperium or executive power; the Senate enjoyed the power to deliberate and consent to specific policies; and the popular assemblies served as the source of authoritative law, also electing the magistrates and the popular tribunes who exercised veto powers over the Senate. An originally republican formula relating the consuls to the people as the source of authoritative law survives in a complete prescript of the Augustan period: "Titus Quinctius Crispinus [consul] lawfully asked the people, and the people lawfully resolved," as translated in Lintott 1999: 3). The perennial Greek contest between oligarchs and democrats had been tamed in Rome to allow a recognized security of role for the Senate, a group drawn from no lower than the minor ranks of aristocracy and typically rewarding birth as well as merit. Yet the tumultuous personal quest for office and influence led many aristocrats to seek support among the people, sometimes with radical measures of land reform which Cicero, among others, resolutely opposed. The theorizing of the proper role of aristocratic leadership and Senatorial independence, together with Platonic analogies for the requisite concord and harmony in the city, would become central themes of Cicero's political philosophy. ("What the musicians call harmony with respect to song is concord in the state, the tightest and best bond of safety in every republic; and that concord can never exist without justice," De rep. II.69.)

6. Cicero and the Roman Republic
6.1 Cicero: Life

Marcus Tullius Cicero (106–43 BCE) was the most famous "new man" of Roman politics, hailing from a minor provincial landowning family rather than the great clans of hereditary nobility. He rose to the office of consul and the Senatorial membership it conferred by his wits and audacity as a lawyer and orator in public prosecutions. His greatest moment as consul in 63 BCE came in exposing a conspiracy by Catiline; his brutal suppression of the conspiracy, executing Roman citizens without trial, would however tar his political legacy. He became an enemy of Julius Caesar (though accepting a pardon from him at the end of a stretch of civil wars in 47 BCE), seeing the assertion of rule by first Caesar and then Marc Antony as fatal to the republic. Having defended in his De officiis the murder of Caesar in 44 BCE, Cicero was himself murdered a year later by partisans of the then-ruling Triumvirate in which Antony figured.

The writings of Cicero were virtually canonized subsequent to his death as classic models of rhetoric and philosophy; as Richard Tuck (1990: 43) has remarked, "For fifteen hundred years, from the fourth century to the nineteenth, schoolchildren in Europe were exposed daily to two books. One was the Bible, and the other was the works of Cicero." His many speeches and letters are themselves of considerable political and often philosophical interest, while his philosophical writings—composed for the most part as a student of philosophy in Rome and Athens, and then in a brief period (46–44 BCE) when political developments led him to retreat from active public life – cover a wide range of topics of which politics is only a part. While Cicero would adhere to a moderate skepticism in general philosophical matters, he admired Panaetius and drew on a number of Stoic ideas in formulating his own ethical and political teachings. In particular, he emphasized the natural affinity for society and the existence of natural law. Here we will focus on his two writings modeled on Plato's, De re publica and De legibus (respectively On the Commonwealth and On the Laws), followed by his most important work of ethics, the De officiis (On Duties), which exercised particular influence on subsequent Western moral and political thought.

6.2 De re publica

De re publica was composed by Cicero between 54 and 51 BCE, a turbulent period of strife in Roman politics. Its dramatic setting is in 129 BCE at time of the crisis caused by Tiberius Gracchus, a consul who had championed a property redistribution law for the people and whom the Senate had suppressed as a threat to Roman civil order. All of it except the "Dream of Scipio" (Book VI) was lost from the Middle Ages onward; it has been reconstructed from references and excerpts in later authors, supplemented by a palimpsest of much of Books I-III discovered in 1819. Framed as a dialogue between Scipio Aemilianus, a hero of the anti-Gracchi resistance, and several others of his actual contemporaries, the dialogue has a discernible structure as identified by E.M. Atkins (2000: 490): Books I-II treat "the best condition of the res publica"; Books III-IV treat "justice and human nature", topics common to the best city and the best citizen; and Books V-VI treat the "best citizen' in the discussion of the statesman and in the Dream of Scipio.

While justice was for Cicero, as for the Greeks, the fundamental bond of the commonwealth, he offered distinctive and influential linked definitions of the res publica ("commonwealth", but literally the "public thing") as the res populi, the "property/thing of the people", and of a populus or "people" in turn as "an assemblage associated with one another by agreement on law [iuris consensu] and community of interest [utilitatis communione]" (both, I.39). This could be interpreted either as a strong normative claim –the people agree on law, also translatable as right or justice, and share a common interest – or in a weaker deflationary manner, in which the people nominally accept a common law and share a common conception of their self-interest which may or may not be in accord with justice.[12] Such ambiguity would be famously exploited by Augustine, who used Cicero's definition to argue that lacking justice, conflicted and divided republican Rome had been no commonwealth, before offering his own even weaker definition of a "people" as those united in (any) common love (City of God, II.21). In Cicero's own hands, the definitions were used to stress that the commonwealth was the property of the people, who entrusted it to the magistrates to be used for the common good (I.51–2), and that the "welfare of the people is the supreme law" ("salus populi suprema lex", De leg. III.8; this was a reference to a maxim in the ancient "Twelve Tables" compendium of Roman law). It followed too that just as Plato denied the title of a (single unified) regime to the imperfect regimes torn by civil discord, so Cicero inferred that corrupt regimes were not strictly speaking res publicae at all (III.43–48). The role of the statesman (rector rei publicae) is to aim at the happiness of the citizens, defined in a laxer way than most Greek philosophers would allow, as wealth, glory, and virtue all combined.

Cicero's spokesman Scipio adheres to Greek philosophical principles in declaring that "the commonwealth cannot possibly function without justice" (II.70), adhering to the standard abstract definition in an Aristotelian vein of justice as "giving each their due" (ius suum cuique tribuere). In Book III, two other dialogue participants present respectively the famous arguments given on one day for justice, and on the next day against justice, by the skeptical Greek philosopher and ambassador to Rome Carneades. Cicero's presentation reverses the order, no doubt to give justice the last word.

In Cicero's hands, Carneades' case against justice avails itself of the nomos/phusis contrast and of the kind of ambition for power expressed by Plato's character Callicles in the Gorgias. Justice is not natural, as it differs radically among different peoples; it conflicts with wisdom, which tells us "to rule over as many people as possible, to enjoy pleasures, to be powerful, to rule, to be a lord" (III.24b), and it is fatal for states and empires, which can't survive without injustice. The speech for justice avails itself in contrast of Stoic themes: "true law is right reason, consonant with nature"; there is "one eternal and unchangeable law" [i.e. what has come to be known as "natural law"] (III.33). This includes rule of the best over the weakest for the benefit of the latter (III.36): as in Plato's Republic, the justice of rulership is not exploitation but paternalistic benefit. And as in Plato's Book X, where the myth of Er supplies a revisionary religious justification for justice (it will help you to choose your next reincarnation well), so Cicero's Republic concludes with a dream recounted by Scipio Aemilianus about his even more eminent Roman ancestor, Scipio Africanus. The dream describes the divine order which both rewards humans for just service to their city (VI.13), and also puts human affairs in a cosmic perspective designed not to humble humans but to embolden them to care more for justice than for petty human advantage:

you must always look at these heavenly bodies and scorn what is human. What fame can you achieve in what men say, or what glory can you achieve that is worth seeking?" (VI.20)

In a dramatic rejection even of the traditional Roman motive of honor and glory as a motivation to virtue, the imagined elder statesman asks: "...and even the people who talk about us—how long will they do that?" (VI.21).

6.3 De legibus

De legibus, or On the Laws, is also written as a dialogue, but one set in Cicero's own day with himself, his brother, and closest friend as the interlocutors, gathered at his country estate of Arpinum. Probably begun after De re publica, it was likewise written in the years immediately before 51 BCE, and similarly survives only in piecemeal and fragmentary form. Books I-II treat natural law or ius naturae, with "Marcus" (Cicero himself) declaring that "law is the highest reason, rooted in nature" (I.18), and that men, bound to the gods by reason, are "born for justice" (I.28–32). However, "the corruption of bad habits...extinguishes...the sparks given by nature" (I.33) and can result in the formation of bad laws. Such iniquitous laws as those passed by tyrants are not just (I.42); nor is the title of law to be conferred upon "what bandits have agreed among themselves" (II.13).

In Books II-III, the speakers prescribe an ideal law code, based on but modifying Roman law; notably, for example, the institution of the tribunate is defended (III.16–17). As these prescriptions, and the circumstances of their writing (a temporary retreat from active politics), suggest, Cicero had a complex attitude to the Greek dilemma posing the lives of philosophy and of politics as opposed alternatives. He saw philosophy as a source of insight and perspective relevant to politics, but after his early studies, devoted himself to it primarily when temporarily debarred from more active pursuits: one might say that philosophy became, beyond its intrinsic value, a form of alternative public service when the forum was too dangerous for him to enter (for further reflection, see Baraz 2012).

6.4 De Officiis

"The De officiis, not the De re publica, is Cicero's Republic" (Long 1995: 240). A. A. Long's dictum is true not only in the sense that for Cicero, as for Plato and Aristotle, ethics was inseparable from politics. It is true also and more profoundly insofar as the De officiis takes as its subject the same subject as Plato's Republic, namely the apparent conflict between justice and individual advantage, and proposes broadly the same resolution, namely that the conflict is only ever apparent: violating one's ethical duties can never serve one's advantage so long as both are properly understood. Book I treats what is virtuous, or honestas; Book II treats what is advantageous, or utilitas; and Book III considers cases to show that any apparent conflict is illusory.

The most difficult case to resolve according to the overall argument of the book is that of advantage when understood as political ambition, driven by greatness of spirit in the pursuit of glory. As Cicero acknowledges, and as was especially true in the highest echelons of Roman society, "Men are led most of all to being overwhelmed by forgetfulness of justice when they slip into desiring positions of command or honour or glory" (I.26). The solution is for true glory to be gained only through the fulfillment of one's officia. Similar casuistry enables Cicero to resolve in accordance with his thesis a range of common cases where advantage might be sought at the expense of justice (in administering the estate of an orphan, for example, a common duty of eminent Romans). Yet such casuistry is always advanced within a context of celebration of justice and natural law: it is not simply that in fact justice never conflicts with advantage, but that justice properly understood is always to one's advantage as a human being.

As in Plato, a redefinition of the virtues plays a crucial role in the overall argument for the benefits of justice. For Cicero, the virtues are Romanized as officia or obligations of role or relationship, each attaching to someone in virtue of a distinct persona (as father, consul, neighbor, etc.). Some virtues are rooted in one's persona as a human being subject to natural law, others in the specific roles and customs of one's city. Four principal virtues are identified: wisdom; justice, resting on fides (good faith and credit) and respect for property; greatness of spirit; and decorum. Respect for property is a keystone of Cicero's political thought, here very far from the Platonism which subordinated property to civic harmony.

Strikingly, whereas tyrannicide might appear to be a difficult case for such an ethical code to confront, Cicero presents it – writing later in the year that Caesar was assassinated—as the straightforwardly ethically correct choice. Cicero couches his case in Stoic terms of naturalness and fellowship. His pivotal move is to deny that tyrants are party to the otherwise universal nature of human fellowship: "...there can be no fellowship between us and tyrants...just as some limbs are amputated if they are...harming other parts of the body, similarly if the wildness and monstrousness of a beast appears in human form, it must be removed from the common humanity...of the body" (Off. III.32: ostensibly about the tyrant Phalaris). Yet it has been observed that for the committing of tyrannicide, at least, Stoicism was not a strong or obvious support: if the wise are already free, and only the foolish are slaves, why should the Stoic risk his own life in killing a tyrant?[13] In extremis, Cicero prized the survival of the republic above all else, and so fashioned an eclectic justification, blending Stoic themes with Platonic imagery, for the elimination of its would-be destroyers.

7. Political Philosophy in the Roman Empire

Although Rome had an empire before Cicero died and remained technically a republic for centuries afterward, the transformation of the republic into an empire is standardly associated with the elevation of Octavian as princeps, literally the first citizen and the origin of our word 'prince', who was given the title of "Augustus" by the Senate in 27 BCE (among other novel titles and combinations of offices that he was variously accorded during his reign). Stoicism continued to exercise an important hold over many Roman political minds under the empire, drawing in part on the Hellenistic genre of advice to kings to which Stoics among others had contributed; Platonism too, and forms of Pythagoreanism, regained much sway. In the imperial era, important figures strongly (but in many cases not exclusively) shaped by Stoicism ranged from the philosopher Seneca—tutor and advisor to the first-century emperor Nero—to the second-century emperor, Marcus Aurelius, and the Stoic ex-slave Epictetus who taught and wrote around the turn of the first and second centuries CE. This article cannot explore the full ramifications of these philosophical developments under the Empire or their influence not only on pagan but also on Jewish and Christian thinkers. It also leaves aside the many and varied important contributions to political thought in Rome and its possessions made not by philosophers but by historians, including Livy, Sallust, Diodorus Siculus, Tacitus, and Suetonius.

7.1 Later Stoicism

If Cicero as a new man made senator had to contend with the competitive pressures of republican politics, Seneca (c. 3 BCE–65 CE), as a new man (from Spain) made senator a century later, had to contend with the problem of advising, and surviving, the poisonous politics of intimacy with the first man or princeps of the imperial period. Seneca too wrote essays in natural philosophy, as well as a De officiis (which is lost), and important collections of letters, including his distinctive "consolations" which would inaugurate a new philosophical genre (see the entry on Seneca). His most important surviving work for political philosophy is his De clementia ("On mercy"), addressed to the emperor Nero whom he served as tutor (in rhetoric, not in philosophy) and later in the official capacity of amicus or friend (Veyne 2003, vii, 19). Presenting itself as a "mirror" in which Nero could see himself and the consequences of his virtue (1.1.1), this text would become a fountainhead of the "mirror for princes" genre revived in the Renaissance.

For Seneca, Stoic philosophy can be best squared with politics if the ruler is supremely virtuous: in that case, the Stoic wise man is the king or prince. That still left a problem of squaring clemency or mercy, the distinctively Roman virtue (not corresponding exactly to any Greek word: Braund 2009, 33) that strict Stoic doctrine rejected as an emotionally induced deviation from justice. Appealing to the related Stoic virtue of philanthrôpia or love of humankind, Seneca refashioned the relationship between clemency and justice, claiming that being clement goes beyond the letter of the law but is paradoxically the highest justice (iustissimum, 2.7.3, following Braund 2009, 66–70). Clemency or mercy is so crucial a virtue because the single ruler has power derived from, and akin to, that of the gods; it is of the utmost importance that this power not be abused. In Seneca's hands, clemency constitutes a new expression of the Stoic conception of universal human fellowship while at the same time embodying the ruler's distinctive virtue (it had been one of "the four virtues attributed to Augustus on an honorific shield," as observed by Griffin 2000: 540). This clemency should also extend to slaves: Seneca concerned himself with their welfare, but his cosmopolitanism stopped short of advocating their manumission or the abolition of slavery (Griffin 1992: 256–85).

Seneca did not limit himself to the political function of advising rulers. Instead, he conceived the role of philosophy as benefiting people generally, in the widest sense of a cosmopolitan ethics and even politics. His De otio ("On Leisure") contrasts the single commonwealth embracing gods and men in a cosmic and cosmopolitan citizenship, with the ordinary multiple commonwealths to which the accidents of birth assign us (though these also rightly command allegiance) (4.1). Should such an ordinary regime turn lethal, the philosopher remains a citizen of the cosmic commonwealth and his serenity should remain intact. That fate befell Seneca himself in 65 CE, when Nero accused him of conspiring in a planned assassination of the emperor and ordered him to commit suicide. Seneca's suicide however reflected not so much political obedience as the belief, previously expressed in his writings (in particular De providentia and De ira, as well as his letters) that suicide is a supreme mark of freedom. No tyranny can so enslave us as to take away this freedom: a freedom to act based on the inner liberation of realizing that death and other worldly losses are in fact indifferent and irrelevant to happiness (Inwood 2005: 307–9).

Seneca was far from the only Stoic politically active in his day or in successive generations. Others like Thrasea Paetus and Barea Soranus under Nero, Helvidius Priscus under Vespasian, and Paconius Agrippinus under Tiberius, chose to defy those whom they saw as tyrannical rulers, becoming known as the so-called 'Stoic martyrs'. (On the varieties of

Stoicism under the principate, see the classic study of Brunt 2013, originally published in 1975.) Some Stoics spoke out against a wider range of customs that they took to be cruel or unfounded or otherwise irrational, most notably Musonius Rufus against such practices as the Athenians' holding of gladiatorial games in the same theatre of Dionysus where they celebrated religious festivals (assuming that it is indeed he who is described in Dio Chrysostom's Orationes XXXI, 122), and against the social convention of excluding women from philosophizing (for his fragments, see Lutz 1947). Yet if the fundamental analysis of living according to nature and reason, as developed by the later Stoic thinker Epictetus and reflected upon by the emperor Marcus Aurelius, remained an important touchstone for thinking about politics, and numerous Stoic-minded writers and orators played their parts in Roman political life, some fashioning the life of a philosopher itself into a distinctive form of what might be called non-political politics (Trapp 2007), it is also the case that these later Stoics made rather few detailed contributions to political philosophy.

7.2 Platonisms and Other Philosophies in the Empire

While the men of affairs in the Roman Senate and imperial court turned often (though not exclusively) to Stoicism, in the Greek centers of philosophy and among provincial Greek men of affairs Platonism remained an important framework for thinking about both ethics and politics, as did a related if somewhat shadowy form of Pythagoreanism which can be seen as a continuation of the genre of Hellenistic kingship treatises (Centrone 2000). The most important contributions made to political thought by the Platonist philosopher of the second-century AD, Plutarch (c.46 - c.120 CE), are his paired biographical lives of Greek and Roman statesmen, each with a comparison drawing political morals. Together with the histories of Thucydides, Livy and Sallust, these Lives instructed generations of students in the principles and perils of political ethics, and instituted the distinction between statesman and demagogue as we have come to know it today: with figures like the fifth-century BCE Athenian "Aristides the Just" embodying the ideal statesmen, in contrast to the Platonic view of all past and present statesmen as fatally flawed. Plutarch also made important contributions to political philosophy in the many essays collected in his volumes of Moralia.

Plutarch was a committed but in some ways revisionist Platonist. His attitude to public life was more Roman than Platonic (befitting the role in public affairs that he played in his own city): the political life was for him unproblematically noble, not inferior to the life of philosophy. Similarly, he revised the strict Platonic dictum that philosophers must rule by allowing that philosophers might rule merely in the sense of advising rulers, not of being rulers themselves. (In fact, this move had some Platonic pedigree in the Statesman's insistence that the science of statecraft is the same whether known and exercised by an advisor or by an actual ruler.) And he considered philosophy to be more of a character-building study than a source of knowledge of exact or politically relevant knowledge. Where statesmen were educated in philosophy, as for example in the Lives of Pericles, Cicero, Brutus, and Cato Minor, he treats this as valuable mainly because of the virtue—in particular, moderation and self-restraint—which it imparts to them (Van Raalte 2005). The study of philosophy serves as a sort of inoculation against greed and immoderate ambition. But it need not impart any particular substantive knowledge to the statesman (so competing philosophies could all be useful in shaping virtue: Anaxagaorean influence on Pericles, an eclectic mixture of Stoicism, Academic skepticism, and Platonism on Cicero; Stoicism on the younger Cato). Indeed, excessively rigid adherence to a philosophy could be deleterious, making a statesman rigid and inflexible. The younger Cato was defeated when he stood for the consulship because, Plutarch says, he experienced the same thing that happens to fruits that appear "out of season" (Phoc. 3.1). Like such fruits, he was admired, but "the weight and grandeur" of his virtue was "out of all proportion to the immediate times" (asummetron tois kathestōsi kairois, Phoc. 3.2–3).

Plutarch's political sympathies lay with monarchy. He treated the exemplary Greek or Roman statesman as inherently and ideally a kind of monarchical figure, even when functioning within a democratic or republican environment. "Aristocratic and kingly" was his praise for Pericles' type of true statesmanship (literally, his "politics" or "policy", politeia), once he has given up his initial recourse to demagogic methods (Per.14.2). Thus for all his admiration for Greek statesmen of the classical age, and his profound later influence on republican sentiments in Europe, Plutarch preferred monarchy as the best constitution and believed that he was following his master Plato in so doing. As John Dillon puts it, he held "that the accomplished statesman, like a first-rate musician, will be able to make the best of any of the three basic constitutions [monarchy, aristocracy, or democracy] that he is given to work on" (Dillon 1997). To quote Plutarch himself on this point from his fragmentary writing "On Monarchy, Democracy, and Oligarchy":

...if he [the statesman] is given the choice among governments, like so many tools, he would follow Plato's advice and choose no other than monarchy, the only one which is able to sustain that top note of virtue, high in the highest sense, and never let it be tuned down under compulsion or expediency. For the other forms of government in a certain sense, although controlled by the statesman, control him, and although carried along by him, carry him along, since he has no firmly established strength to oppose those from whom his strength is derived... (Peri mon. 827bc)

Plato's collective virtuous aristocracy (his philosopher-kings and -queens, in the plural; though contrast the singular figure identified in the Statesman) was transmuted by Plutarch into a monarchical ideal.

Later Platonic philosophers, known as Neoplatonists (see the entry on Plotinus), also focused primarily on ethics in the context of cosmology and theology, stressing the ascent of the soul to a disembodied pure understanding of the One. Yet they made room for the political virtues of the embodied soul as a first step in this process of divinization or "becoming like God" (O'Meara 2003). In working out the political implications of such views, Plato's Laws became an important model for theocratic political reform, especially as Neoplatonism became influential for a certain strand of Christian thinkers, in particular those able to absorb the translation of Greek texts into Arabic.

8. Conclusion

On a continuum of political rule stretching from the sheer domination of some over others on one extreme, to a vision of collaborative deliberation among equals for the sake of the good life on the other, many ancient Greek and Roman political philosophers clearly staked out the latter ground. The very idea of the city and the civic bond as rooted in justice was common ground across the spectrum of ancient political philosophy. Even the Epicureans saw society as rooted in justice, although understanding justice in turn as rooted in utility. (However, this generalization, like many about ancient philosophy, leaves the ancient skeptics and Cynics aside.) Philosophers taking this approach were not however ignorant of possible objections to it. The diagnosis of politics as domination has never been more powerfully advanced than by Plato's character Thrasymachus, nor has the attack on justice as a good life for the individual ever been as powerfully made as by Plato's character Callicles or the skeptic Carneades. The nostalgic view of ancient political philosophy as predicated on widely shared conceptions of human nature and the human good, before the splintering and fracturing of modernity, is an oversimplification.

It is true that those ancient visions of politics which rooted themselves in a commitment to ethical cultivation and the common good did not have to contend with the absolutist claims of rival versions of monotheistic religions. But the ancients did have to answer various forms of relativism, immoralism, and skepticism, contending with rival philosophical schools which disagreed profoundly with one another. If some of them chose to see politics as a domain of common benefit and a space for the cultivation of virtue, this was not because it had not occurred to them that it could be thought of otherwise, but in part because they had developed powerful philosophical systems to support this view. The experience and practices of the Greek poleis (the plural of polis) and the Roman res publica played important roles in shaping these approaches.

Plato and Aristotle can in many ways be seen as defending some fundamental tenets of Greek ethics (such as the value of justice), but doing so by means of advancing revisionist philosophical doctrines and distancing themselves from the ways in which those tenets were interpreted by the democratic institutions of their day. The range of ethical and political views which they, along with their Hellenistic successors, laid out, continue to define many of the fundamental choices for modern philosophy, despite the many important innovations in institutional form and intellectual approach which have been made since. Many of those innovations, indeed, came in response to a revival of the ancient skeptical and relativist challenges: challenges already known.

PRINCIPLES OF JUSTICE

2. CONTEMPORARY APPROACHES TO THE SOCIAL CONTRACT

The idea of the social contract goes back, in a recognizably modern form, to Thomas Hobbes; it was developed in different ways by John Locke, Jean-Jacques Rousseau, and Immanuel Kant. After Kant the idea largely fell into disrepute until it was resurrected by John Rawls. It is now at the heart of the work of a number of moral and political philosophers. The basic idea seems simple: in some way, the agreement (or consent) of all individuals subject to collectively enforced social arrangements shows that those arrangements have some normative property (they are legitimate, just, obligating, etc.). Even this vague basic idea, though, is anything but simple, and even this abstract rendering is objectionable in many ways. To explicate the idea of the social contract we analyze contractual approaches into five variables: (1) the nature of the contractual act; (2) the parties to the act; (3) what the parties are agreeing to; (4) the reasoning that leads to the agreement; (5) what the agreement is supposed to show.

1. The Contractual Act
1.1 Consent and Agreement
1.2 Hypothetical Agreements
1.3 The Importance of Actuality
2. Modeling the Parties
2.1 Non-moralized v. Moralized Parties
2.2 The Level of Idealization and Abstraction
3. The Object of Agreement
4. The Reasoning of the Parties
4.1 Bargaining
4.2 Aggregation
4.3 Equilibrium
5. What Does the Contract Show?
6. Conclusion: The Social Contract and Public Justification

1. The Contractual Act
1.1 Consent and Agreement
The traditional social contract views of Hobbes, Locke, and Rousseau crucially relied on the idea of consent. For Locke only "consent of Free-men" could make them members of government (Locke 1689, §117). Now in the hands of these theorists—and in much ordinary discourse—the idea of "consent" implies a normative power to bind oneself. When one reaches "the age of consent" one is empowered to make certain sorts of binding agreements—contracts. By putting consent at the center of their contracts these early modern contract theorists (1) were clearly supposing that individuals had basic normative powers over themselves before they entered into the social contract (a point that Hume [1741] stressed), and (2) brought the question of political obligation to the fore. If the parties have the power to bind themselves by exercising this normative power, then the upshot of the social contract was obligation. As Hobbes (1651, 81 [chap xiv,¶7) insisted, covenants bind; that is why they are "artificial chains" (1651, 138 [chap. xxi, ¶5). According to James Buchanan, the key development of recent social contract theory has been to distinguish the question of what generates political obligation (the key concern of the consent tradition in social contract thought) from the question of what constitutional orders or social institutions are mutually beneficial and stable over time (1965b). The nature of a person's duty to abide by the law or social rules is a matter of a morality as it pertains to individuals (Rawls 1999, 293ff), while the design and justification of political and social institutions is a question of public or social morality. Thus, on Buchanan's view a crucial feature of more recent contractual thought has been to refocus political philosophy on public or social morality rather than individual obligation.

Although contemporary social contract theorists still sometimes employ the language of consent, the core idea of contemporary social contract theory is agreement. "Social contract views work from the intuitive idea of agreement" (Freeman 2007a, 17). Now one can endorse or agree to a principle without that act of endorsement in any way binding one to obey. Social contract theorists as diverse as Freeman and Jan Narveson (1988, 148) see the act of agreement as indicating what reasons we have. Agreement is a "test" or a heuristic. The "role of unanimous collective agreement" is in showing "what we have reasons to do in our social and political relations" (Freeman 2007, 19). Thus understood the agreement is not itself a binding act—it is not a performative that somehow creates obligation—but is reason-revealing (Lessnoff 1986). If individuals are rational, what they agree to reflects the reasons they have. In contemporary contract theories such as Rawls's, the problem of justification takes center stage. Rawls's revival of social contract theory in A Theory of Justice thus did not base obligations on consent, though the apparatus of an "original agreement" persisted. The aim of the original position, Rawls announced (1999, 16), is to settle "the question of justification ... by working out a problem of deliberation."

The social contract in contemporary moral and political theory is an attempt, then, to solve a justificatory problem by converting it to a deliberative problem. At its heart is the "question of justification." As James Buchanan points out, "precepts for living together are not going to be handed down from on high" (1975, 3). Justifying social arrangements (showing that they have the requisite normative property, see §5 below) requires showing that all (suitably idealized) citizens have reasons favoring the arrangements. Now this would be an otiose requirement unless, to some extent, the reasons of citizens differed. If all citizens had precisely the same set of reasons there would be no point in showing what they all can agree to. The idea of a unanimous collective agreement only does justificatory work when the reasons of citizens can differ, and so it is an open question what everyone has reason to endorse—what everyone would agree to. Under conditions of reasonable pluralism, we cannot suppose that the reasoning of one member of the public is a proxy for everyone else's reasoning. Consequently, under reasonable pluralism the requirement that every member of the public has reason to endorse a social arrangement is not implied by one member doing so.

1.2 Hypothetical Agreements
Given that the problem of justification has taken center stage, the second aspect of contemporary social contract thinking appears to fall into place: its reliance on models of hypothetical agreement. The aim is to model the reasons of citizens, and so we ask what they would agree to under conditions in which their agreements would be expected to track their reasons. Contemporary contract theory is, characteristically, doubly hypothetical. Certainly, no prominent theorist thinks that questions of justification are settled by an actual survey of attitudes towards existing social arrangements, and are not settled until such a survey has been

carried out. The question, then, is not "Are these arrangements presently the object of an actual agreement among citizens?" (If this were the question, the answer would typically be "No".) The question, rather, is "Would these arrangements be the object of an agreement if citizens were surveyed?" Although both of the questions are, in some sense, susceptible to an empirical reading, only the latter is in play in present-day theorizing. The contract nowadays is always hypothetical in at least this first sense.

There is a reading of the (first-order) hypothetical question "Would the arrangements be the object of agreement if___" which, as indicated, is still resolutely empirical in some sense. This is the reading where what is required of the theorist is that she try to determine what an actual survey of actual citizens would reveal about their actual attitudes towards their system of social arrangements. (This is seldom done, of course; the theorist does it in her imagination. See, though, Klosko 2000). But there is another interpretation that is more widely accepted in the contemporary context. On this reading, the question is no longer a hypothetical question about actual reactions; it is, rather, a hypothetical question about hypothetical reactions—it is, as we have said, doubly hypothetical. Framing the question is the first hypothetical element: "Would it be the object of agreement if they were surveyed?" Framed by this question is the second hypothetical element, one which involves the citizens, who are no longer treated empirically, i.e. taken as given, but are, instead, themselves considered from a hypothetical point of view—as they would be if (typically) they were better informed or more impartial, etc. (see further §2.2 below). The question for most contemporary contract theorists, then, is, roughly:"If we surveyed the idealized surrogates of the actual citizens in this polity, what social arrangements would be the object of an agreement among them?"

Famously, Ronald Dworkin has objected that a (doubly) hypothetical agreement cannot bind any actual person. For the hypothetical analysis to make sense, it must be shown that hypothetical persons in the contract can agree to be bound by some principle P regulating social arrangements. Suppose that it could be shown that your surrogate (a better informed, more impartial version of you) would agree to P. What has that to do with you? Where this second-stage hypothetical analysis is employed, it seems to be proposed that you can be bound by agreements that others, different from you, would have made. While it might (though it needn't) be reasonable to suppose that you can be bound by agreements that you would yourself have entered into if given the opportunity, it seems crazy to think that you can be bound by agreements that, demonstrably, you wouldn't have made even if you had been asked. This criticism is decisive, however, only if the hypothetical social contract is supposed to invoke your normative power to self-bind via consent. That your surrogate employs his power to self-bind would not mean that you had employed your power. Again, though, the power to obligate oneself is not typically invoked in the contemporary social contract: the problem of deliberation is supposed to help us make headway on the problem of justification. So the question for contemporary hypothetical contract theories is whether the hypothetical agreement of your surrogate tracks your reasons to accept social arrangements, a very different issue.

1.3 The Importance of Actuality
It is almost a commonplace today that contemporary social contract theory relies on hypothetical, not actual, agreement. As we have seen, in one sense this is certainly the case. However, in many ways the "hypothetical/actual" divide is artificial: the hypothetical agreement is meant to model, and provide the basis for, actual agreement. Understanding contemporary social contract theory is best achieved, not through insisting on the distinction between actual and hypothetical contracts, but by grasping the interplay of the hypothetical and the actual.

The key here is Rawls's (1996, 28) distinction among the perspectives of:

you and me
the parties to the deliberative model
persons in a well-ordered society
The agreement of the parties in the deliberative model is certainly hypothetical in the two-fold sense we have analyzed: a hypothetical agreement among hypothetical parties. But the point of the deliberative model is to help us (i.e., "you and me") solve our justificatory problem— what social arrangements we can all accept as "free persons who have no authority over one another" (Rawls 1958, 33). The parties' deliberations and the conditions under which they deliberate, then, model our actual convictions about justice and justification. As Rawls says (1999, 514), the reasoning of the hypothetical parties matters to us because "the

conditions embodied in the description of this situation are ones that we do in fact accept." Unless the hypothetical models the actual, the upshot of the hypothetical could not provide us with reasons. Gerald Gaus describes something like this process as a "testing conception" of the social contract (2011a, 425). We use the hypothetical deliberative device of the contract to "test" our social institutions. In this way, the contemporary social contract is meant to be a model of the justificatory situation that all individuals face. The hypothetical and abstracted (see §2) nature of the contract is needed to highlight the relevant features of the parties to show what reasons they have.

Freeman has recently stressed the way in which focusing on the third perspective—of citizens in a well ordered society— shows the importance of actual agreement in Rawls's contract theory. On Freeman's interpretation, the social contract must meet the condition of publicity. Freeman (2007b:15) writes:

Rawls distinguishes three levels of publicity: first, the publicity of principles of justice; second, the publicity of the general beliefs in light of which first principles of justice can be accepted ("that is, the theory of human nature and of social institutions generally)"; and, third, the publicity of the complete justification of the public conception of justice as it would be on its own terms. All three levels, Rawls contends, are exemplified in a well-ordered society. This is the "full publicity" condition.

A justified contract must meet the full publicity condition: its complete justification must be capable of being actually accepted by members of a well-ordered society. The hypothetical agreement itself provides only what Rawls (1996, 386) calls a "pro tanto" or "so far as it goes" justification of the principles of justice. "Full justification" is achieved only when actual "people endorse and will liberal justice for the particular (and often conflicting) reasons implicit in the reasonable comprehensive doctrines they hold" (Freeman 2007b, 19). Thus understood, Rawls's concern with the stability of justice as fairness, which motivated the move to political liberalism, is itself a question of justification (Weithman, 2010). Only if the principles of justice are stable in this way are they fully justified. Rawls's concern with stability and publicity is not, however, idiosyncratic and is shared by all contemporary contract theorists. It is significant that even theorists such as James Buchanan (2000 [1975], 26-27), David Gauthier (1986, 348), and Ken Binmore (2005, 5-7)—who are so different from

Rawls in other respects—share his concern with stability.

2. Modeling the Parties
2.1 Non-moralized v. Moralized Parties

How the contract theorist models the parties to the hypothetical agreement, then, is determined by our (actual) justificatory problem, and what is relevant to solving it. A major divide among contemporary social contract theories thus involves defining the justificatory problem. A distinction is often drawn between the Hobbesian ("contractarian") and Kantian ("contractualist") interpretations of the justificatory problem. These categories are imprecise, and there is often as much difference within these two approaches as between them, yet, nevertheless, the distinction is useful in isolating some key disputes in contemporary social contract theory. Among those "contractarians" who—very roughly—can be called followers of Hobbes, the crucial justificatory task is, as David Gauthier puts it, to resolve the "foundational crisis" of morality:

From the standpoint of the agent, moral considerations present themselves as constraining his choices and action, in ways independent of his desires, aims, and interests....And so we ask, what reason can a person have for recognizing and accepting a constraint that is independent of his desires and interests? ... [W]hat justifies paying attention to morality, rather than dismissing it as an appendage of outworn beliefs? (Gauthier 1991, 16)

If our justificatory problem is not simply what morality requires, but whether morality ought to be paid attention to, or instead dismissed as a superstition based on outmoded metaphysical theories, then obviously the parties to the agreement must not employ moral judgments in their reasoning. Another version of this concern is Gregory Kavka's (1984) description of the project to reconcile morality with prudence. On both these accounts, the aim of the contract is to show that commitment to morality is an effective way to further one's non-moral aims and interests. The justificatory problem is the problem of satisfactorily answering the question "why be moral?" This "contractarian" project is reductionist in a pretty straightforward sense: it derives moral reasons from non-moral ones. Or, to use Rawls's terminology, it attempts to generate the reasonable out of the rational (1996, 53).

This approach is appealing for several reasons. First, insofar as we doubt that moral reasons are genuine or motivationally effective, such a reductionist strategy promises to ground morality on the prosaic requirements of instrumentalist practical rationality. The justificatory question "why be moral?" is transformed into the less troubling question "why be rational?" Second, even if we recognize that moral reasons are, in some sense, genuine, contractarians like Kavka also want to show that prudent individuals, not independently motivated by morality would have reason to reflectively endorse morality. Furthermore, if we have reason to suspect that some segment of the population is, in fact, knavish then we have good defensive reasons based on stability to build our social institutions and morality so as to restrain those who are only motivated by prudence, even if we suspect that most persons are not so motivated. Anticipating concerns about evolutionary stability (see §4 below) Geoffrey Brennan and James Buchanan argue that a version of Gresham's law holds in political and social institutions that "bad behavior drives out good and that all persons will be led themselves by even the presence of a few self-seekers to adopt self-interested behavior" (2008 [1985], 68). We need not think people are mostly self-seeking to think that social institutions and morality should be justified to and restrain those who are.

On the other hand, "contractualists," such as John Rawls, John Harsanyi (1977), Thomas Scanlon (1998), Stephen Darwall (2006), and Nicholas Southwood (2010) attribute ethical or political values to the deliberative parties, as well as a much more substantive, non-instrumentalist form of practical reasoning. The kinds of surrogates that model the justificatory problem of 'you and me' are already so situated that their deliberations will be framed by ethico-political considerations. The agents' deliberations are not, as with the Hobbesian theorists, carried out in purely prudential or instrumentalist terms, but they are subject to the 'veil of ignorance' or other substantive conditions. Here the core justificatory problem is not whether the very idea of moral and political constraints makes sense, but what sorts of moral or political principles meet certain basic moral demands, such as treating all as free and equal moral persons, or not subjecting any person to the will or judgment of another (Reiman 1990, chap. 1). This approach, then, is non-reductionist in the sense that not all of morality is derived from the non-moral. Many of the concerns with this approach to contract theory are related to the particular idealization of the parties that the substantive conception of practical rationality in the contract procedure requires.

2.2 The Level of Idealization and Abstraction

The core idea of social contract theories, we have been stressing, is that the deliberation of the parties is supposed to model the justificatory problem of "you and me." Now this pulls social contract theories in two opposing directions. On the one hand, if the deliberations of the hypothetical parties are to model our problem and their conclusions are to be of relevance to us, the parties must be similar to us. The closer the parties are to "you and me" the better their deliberations will model you and me, and be of relevance to us. On the other hand, the point of contract theories is to make headway on our justificatory problem by constructing parties that are idealizations of you and me, suggesting that some idealization is necessary and salutary. To recognize that some forms of idealization are problematic does not imply that we should embrace what Gaus has called "justificatory populism" that every person in a society must actually assent to the social and moral institutions in question (Gaus 1996, 130-131). Such a standard would take us back to the older social contract tradition based on direct consent. But, as we saw in §1, modern contract theories are concerned with appeals to our reason, not our self-binding power of consent.

Despite possible problems, there are two important motivations behind idealization of the deliberative parties. First, you and I, as we now are, may be confused about what considerations are relevant to our justificatory problem. We have biases and false beliefs; to make progress on solving our problem of justification we wish, as far as possible, to see what the result would be if we only reasoned correctly from sound and relevant premises. So in constructing the hypothetical parties we wish to idealize them in this way. Ideal deliberation theorists like Habermas (1985) and Southwood (2010), in their different ways, are deeply concerned with this reason for idealization. On the face of it, such idealization does not seem especially troublesome, since our ultimate concern is with what is justified, and so we want the deliberations of the parties to track good reasons. But if we idealize too far from citizens as they presently are— suppose we posit that they are fully rational in the sense that they know all the implications of all their beliefs and have perfect information—their deliberations may not help much in solving our justificatory problems. For example, suppose that hyper-rational and perfectly informed parties would have no religious beliefs, so they would not be concerned with freedom of religion or the role of religion of political decision making. But our problem is that, among tolerably reasonable but far from perfectly rational citizens, pluralism of religious belief is inescapable. Consequently to gain insight into the justificatory problem among citizens of limited rationality, the parties must model our imperfect rationality.

Secondly, social contract theories are pulled towards idealized and abstracted representations of the parties in order to render the choice situation determinate. This goal of determinacy, however, can have the effect of eliminating the pluralism of the parties that was the original impetus for contracting in the first place. In his Lectures on the History of Political Philosophy Rawls tells us that "a normalization of interests attributed to the parties" is "common to social contract doctrines" and it is necessary to unify the perspectives of the different parties so as to construct a "shared point of view" (2007, 226). Here Rawls seems to be suggesting that to achieve determinacy in the contract procedure it is necessary to "normalize" the perspectives of the parties.

The problem, however, is this. Suppose that the parties to the contract closely model you and me, and so they have diverse bases for their deliberations— religious, secular, perfectionist, and so on. In this case it is hard to see how the contract theorist can get a determinate result. Just as you and I disagree, so will the parties. Social contract theorists have sought to generate a determinate result by modeling the parties in a very abstracted way, supposing that they are all centrally concerned with promoting their conception of the good, and insuring that they reason in the same way. Rawls (1999, 121) acknowledges that his restrictions on particular information in the original position are necessary to achieve a determinate result. If we exclude "knowledge of those contingencies which set men at odds ... " then since "everyone is equally rational and similarly situated, each is convinced by the same arguments"(Rawls 1999, 17, 120).

Gaus (2011a, 36-47) has recently argued that a determinative result can only be generated by an implausibly high degree of abstraction, in which the basic pluralism of evaluative standards—the core of our justificatory problem—is abstracted away. Thus, on Gaus's view, modelings of the parties that make them anything approaching representations of you and me will only be able to generate a non-singleton set of eligible social contracts. The parties might agree that some social contracts are better than none, but they will disagree on their ordering of possible social contracts. This conclusion, refined and developed in (Gaus 2011a, Part Two) connects the traditional problem of indeterminacy in the contract procedure with the contemporary, technical problem of equilibrium selection in games (see Vanderschraaf, 2005). A topic we will explore more in §4 below.

It is possible, however, that determinacy may actually require diversity in the perspective of the deliberative parties in a way that Rawls and others like Harsanyi didn't expect. The reason for this is simple, the proof is somewhat complex. Normalizing the perspectives of the parties assumes that there is one stable point of view that has all of the relevant information necessary for generating a stable and determinate set of social rules. There is no reason, antecedently, to think that such a perspective can be found, however. Instead, if we recognize that there are epistemic gains to be had from a "division of cognitive labor" there is reason to prefer a diverse rather than normalized idealization of the parties to the contract (see Weisberg and Muldoon, 2009 and Muldoon 2009). There is reason to conclude that if we wish to discover social contracts that best achieve a set of interrelated normative desiderata (e.g., liberty, equality, welfare, etc.), a deliberative process that draws on a diversity of perspectives will outperform one based on a strict normalization of perspectives (Gaus 2011b). James Buchanan goes even further, eliminating all idealization and normalization of the parties (2000 [1975], 221-222). Although, insofar as Buchanan and other contractarians model the parties as guided solely by the reasoning characteristic of Homo Economicus there is some idealization of the parties in terms of their practical rationality.

3. The Object of Agreement
Social contract theories differ about the object of the contract. In the traditional contract theories of Hobbes and Locke the contract was about the terms of political association. In particular, the problem was the grounds and limits of citizen's obligation to obey the state. In his early formulation, Rawls's parties deliberated about "common practices" (1958). In his later statement of his view Rawls took the object of agreement to be principles of justice to regulate "the basic structure:"

The basic structure is understood as the way in which the major social institutions fit together into one system, and how they assign fundamental rights and duties and shape the division of advantages that arises through social cooperation. Thus the political constitution, the legally enforced forms of property, and the organization of the economy, and the nature of the family, all belong to the basic structure. (Rawls 1996, 258)

For Rawls, as for most contemporary contract theorists, the object of agreement is not, at least directly, the grounds of political obligation, but the principles of justice that regulate the basic institutions of society. Freeman (2007a: 23), perhaps the preeminent student of Rawls, focuses on "the social role of norms in public life." James Buchanan is concerned with justifying constitutional orders of social and political institutions (2000[1975]). Gauthier (1986), Scanlon (1998), Darwall (2006), Southwood (2010), and Gaus (2011a) employ the contract device to justify inter-personal moral claims. The common thread that runs through all of these contemporary accounts is an idea at the heart of the contract theory, namely that rules and constraints, at whatever level, must be justified to those whom they apply. There is some debate over how to understand this condition (see Gauthier 2003) but some version of it underlies the desire for agreement inherent in the idea of the social contract.

The level at which the object of the contract is described is apt to affect the outcome of the agreement. "A striking feature of Hobbes' view," Russell Hardin points out, "is that it is a relative assessment of whole states of affairs. Life under one form of government versus life under anarchy" (2003, 43). Hobbes could plausibly argue that everyone would agree to the social contract because "life under government" is, from the perspective of everyone, better than "life under anarchy." However, if a Hobbesian sought to divide the contract up into, say, more fine-grained agreements about the various functions of government, she is apt to find that agreement would not be forthcoming on many functions. As we "zoom in" (Lister, 2010) on more fine-grained functions of government, the contract is apt to become more limited. If the parties are simply considering whether government is better than anarchy, they will opt for just about any government (including one that funds the arts); if they are considering whether to have a government that funds the arts or one that doesn't, it is easy to see how they may not agree on the former. In a similar way, if the parties are deliberating about entire moral codes, there may be wide agreement that all the moral codes, overall, are in everyone's interests; if we "zoom in" in specific rights and duties, we are apt to get a very different answer.

The point is that the level of agreement on the object of the contract will likely be very different depending on how concretely the contract itself is specified. One way to specify the alternative to the contract so as to make the choice situation more determinate is to think of the alternative to the contract not as an idealized "state of nature" but rather as the status quo. Both Binmore (2005, 5) and Gaus (2011a, 424-446) suggest that the contract procedure can be used as a device to test different sets of rules against the status quo. This is one way to incorporate the insight from Buchanan that when we theorize:

We start from here, from where we are, and not from some idealized world peopled by beings with a different history and utopian institutions. Some appreciation of the status quo is essential before discussion can begin about the prospects for improvements. (2000 [1975], xv)

Binmore, for instance, argues that we should think of the status quo as analogous to the state of nature in traditional contract theories. He makes this explicit in his representation of the contract device as a bargaining problem, making the disagreement point of the bargain (the equivalent of the state of nature) the status quo (2205, 25). To some, this identification of the state of nature with the status quo may seem unduly conservative, but this may be a mistake. Recall that Hardin's complaint against contract theories is that they, in effect, rig the game in favor of a particular outcome by making the disagreement point or state of nature so horrible that almost any alternative will look attractive in comparison. By making the disagreement point the status quo instead of the Hobbesian state of nature, however, agreement will be harder to achieve because, presumably, many will find the status quo attractive. Whether or not this will lead to conservative outcomes depends on the alternatives that are put up against the status quo. It also depends on the nature of the status quo. Each starting point will present new challenges and will likely result in different points of agreement.

Another way to avoid ambiguity is the determination of the object of agreement is to follow Buchanan and, arguably, Gauthier in developing a two-stage contract theory. Buchanan divides his contract procedure into two stages: the constitutional and post-constitutional. The object of the constitutional stage is to develop a system of constraints that will allow individuals to peacefully co-exist, what Buchanan calls the "protective state" (2000 [1975]). The state of nature, for Buchanan, is characterized by both predation and defense. The amount of time one can engage in productive enterprises is decreased because of the need to defend the fruits of those enterprises against those who would rely on predation rather than production. We have reason to contract, according to Buchanan, in order to increase the overall ability of everyone to produce by limiting the need for defense by constraining the ability to engage in predation. Once the solution to the predation-production conflict has been solved by the constitutional contract, members of society also realize that if all contributed to production of various public goods, the productive possibility of society would be similarly increased. This second, post-constitutional stage, involves what Buchanan calls the "productive state". Each stage is logically distinct though there are causal relationships between changes made at one stage and the efficacy and stability of the solution at the later stage. The distinction between the two stages is analogous to the traditional distinction between commutative and distributive justice. Although these two are often bound up together in contemporary contract theory, one of Buchanan's novel contributions is to suggest that there are theoretical gains to separating these distinct objects of agreement.

4. The Reasoning of the Parties
Suppose we have identified the object of the parties' deliberations: practice, norms, basic institutions, moral codes, etc. Now social contract theories fundamentally differ in whether the parties reason differently or the same. As we have seen (§2.2) in Rawls's contract everyone reasons the same: the collective choice problem is reduced to the choice of one individual. Any one person's decision is a proxy for everyone else. In social contracts of this sort, the description of the parties (their motivation, the conditions under which they choose) does all the work: once we have fully specified the reasoning of one party, the contract has been identified.

The alternative view is that, even after we have specified the parties (including their rationality, values and information), they continue to disagree in their rankings of possible social contracts. On this view, the contract only has a determinate result if there is some uniquely rational or correct way to commensurate the different rankings of each individual to yield a social choice (D'Agostino, 2003). We can distinguish three different commensuration mechanisms.

4.1 Bargaining

As Rawls recognized in his 1958 essay "Justice as Fairness" one way for parties to resolve their disagreements is to employ bargaining solutions, such as that proposed by R.B. Braithwaite (1955). Rawls himself rejected bargaining solutions to the social contract since, in his opinion, such solutions rely on threat advantage and "to each according to his threat advantage is hardly a principle of fairness" (Rawls 1958, 58n). Gauthier, however, famously pursued this approach, building his Morals by Agreement on the Kalai-Smorodinsky bargaining solution (see also Gaus 1990, Ch. IX). Binmore (2005) has recently advanced a version of social contract theory that relies on the Nash bargaining solution, as does Muldoon (2009) while Moehler (2010) relies on a "stabilized" Nash bargaining solution. In addition to Rawls's concern about threat advantage, a drawback of all such approaches is the multiplicity of bargaining solutions, which can significantly differ. Although the Nash solution is most favored today, it can have counter-intuitive implications. Furthermore, there are many who argue that bargaining solutions are inherently indeterminate and so the only way to achieve determinacy is to introduce unrealistic or controversial assumptions (Sugden, 1990, 1991). Similar problems also exist for equilibrium selection in games (see Vanderschraaf 2005 and Harsanyi and Selten 1988) Although appealing to a bargaining solution can give determinacy to a social contract, it does so at the cost of appealing to a controversial commensuration mechanism.

4.2 Aggregation

We might distinguish bargaining from aggregation solutions. Rather than seeking an outcome that (as, roughly, the Kalai-Smorodinsky solution does) splits the difference between various claims, we might seek to aggregate the individual rankings into an overall social choice. Arrow's theorem and related problems with social choice rules casts doubt on any claim that one specific way of aggregating is uniquely rational: all have their shortcomings (Gaus 2008, chap. 5). Harsanyi (1977, chaps. 1 and 2; 1982) develops a contractual theory much like Rawls's. Reasoning behind a veil of ignorance in which people do not know their post-contract identities, he supposes that rational contractors will assume it is equally probable that they will be any specific person. Moreover, he argues that contractors can agree on interpersonal utility comparisons, and so they will opt for a contract that aggregates utility at the highest average (see also Mueller 2003, chap. 26). This, of course, depends on the supposition that there is a non-controversial metric that allows us to aggregate the parties' utility functions. Binmore (2005) follows Harsanyi and Amartya Sen (2009, Chap. 13) in arguing that interpersonal comparisons can be made for the purposes of aggregation, at least some of the time. One of the problems with this approach, however, is that if the interpersonal comparisons are incomplete they will not be able to produce a complete social ordering. As Sén points out, this will lead to a maximal set of alternatives where no alternative is dominated by any other within the set but also where no particular alternative is optimal (Sen, 1997). Instead of solving the aggregation problem, then, interpersonal comparisons may only be able to reduce the set of alternatives without being able to complete the ordering of alternatives.

4.3 Equilibrium

There is a long tradition of thinking of the social contract as a kind of equilibrium. Within this tradition, however, the tendency is to see the social contract as some kind of equilibrium solution to a prisoner's dilemma type situation (see Gauthier, 1986 and Buchanan, 2000 [1975]). Brian Skyrms (1996, 2004) suggests a different approach. Suppose that we have a contractual negotiation in which there are two parties, ordering four possible "social contracts":

both Alf and Betty hunt stag
both hunt hare;
Alf hunts stag, Betty hunts hare;
Alf hunts hare, Betty hunts stag.
Let 3 be the best outcome, and let 1 be the worst in each person's ranking (Alf's ranking is first in each pair). We thus get Figure 1

ALF
Hunt Stag   Hunt Hare
BETTY   Hunt Stag
3,3
2,1
Hunt Hare
1,2

2,2

Figure 1: A Stag Hunt

The Stag Hunt, Skyrms argues, "should be a focal point for social contract theory" (2004, 4). The issue in the Stag Hunt is not whether we fight or not, but whether we cooperate and gain, or each go our separate ways. There are two Nash equilibria in this game: both hunting stag and both hunting hare. Alf and Betty, should they find themselves at one of these equilibria, will stick to it if each consults only his or her own ranking of options. In a Nash equilibrium, no individual has a reason to defect. Of course the contract in which they both hunt stag is a better contract: it is Pareto superior to that in which they both hunt hare. The Hare equilibrium is, however, risk superior in that it is a safer bet. Skyrms argues that the theory of iterated games can show not simply that our parties will arrive at a social contract, but how they can come to arrive at the cooperative, mutually beneficial contract. If we have a chance to play repeated games, Skyrms holds, we can learn from Hume about the "shadow of the future": "I learn to do a service to another, without bearing him any real kindness; because I foresee, that he will return my service, in expectation of another of the same kind, and in order to maintain the same correspondence of good offices with me and with others" (Skyrms 2004, 5). Sugden, along different lines, also suggests that repeated interactions, what he calls "experience" is essential to the determination of which norms of social interaction actually hold over time (1986).

The problem with equilibrium solutions is that, as in the stag hunt game, many games have multiple equilibria. The problem then becomes how to select one unique equilibrium from a set of possible ones. The problem is compounded by the controversies over equilibrium refinement concepts (see Harsanyi and Selten 1988). Many refinements have been suggested but, as in bargaining theory, all are controversial to one degree or another. One of the interesting developments in social contract theory spurred by game theorists such as Skyrms and Binmore is the appeal to evolutionary game theory as a way to solve the commensuration and equilibrium selection problem (Vanderschraaf 2005). What cannot be solved by appeal to reason (because there simply is no determinate solution) may be solved by repeated interactions among rational parties. The work of theorists such as Skyrms and Binmore also blurs the line between justification and explanation. Their analyses shed light both on the justificatory problem—what are the characteristics of a cooperative social order that people freely follow?—while also explaining how such orders may come about.

The use of evolutionary game theory and evolutionary techniques is a burgeoning and exciting area of contract theory. One of the many questions that arise, however, is that of why, and if so under what circumstances, we should endorse the output of evolutionary procedures. Should one equilibrium be preferred to another merely because it was the output of an evolutionary procedure? Surely we would want reasons independent of history for reflectively endorsing some equilibrium. This problem highlights the concern that social contracts that are the product of evolutionary procedures will not meet the publicity condition (§1.3) in the right kind of way. If the publicity condition seems harder to meet, the evolutionary approach provides a powerful and dynamic way to understand stability. Following Maynard Smith, we can see stability as being an evolutionarily stable strategy equilibrium or an ESS (1982). Basically this is the idea that an equilibrium in an evolutionary game where successful strategies replicate at higher rates is stable if the equilibrium composition of the population in terms of strategies is not susceptible to invasion by a mutant strategy. An ESS is an application of the Nash equilibrium concept to populations. A population is evolutionarily stable when a mutant strategy is not a better response to the population than the current mix of strategies in the population. This gives a formal interpretation of Rawls's conception of "inherent stability" and to Buchanan's notion that social contracts should be able to withstand subversion by a sub-population of knaves. This new conception of stability combined with the dynamic nature of evolutionary games provides interesting new ways for the social contract theorist to model the output of the contract.

5. What Does the Contract Show?
Suppose, then, that we have arrived at some social contract. Depending on the initial justificatory problem, it will specify principles (P) that have some normative property (N)— such as justice, morality, authority, obligation, legitimacy, mutual benefit, and so on. But, supposing that the contract has generated principle P with the relevant normative property N, precisely what is shown by the fact that P was generated through the contractual device?

Throughout we have been distinguishing the justificatory problem from the deliberative model. Now the strongest that could be claimed for a contractual argument is that the outcome of the deliberative model is constitutive of both the correct solution of the justificatory problem and that P has N. On this "constructivist" reading of the outcome of the deliberative model, there is no independent and determinate external justification that P has N that the contractual device is intended to approximate, but, rather, that P is the outcome of the deliberative model is the truth-maker for "P has N". Rawls, along with Gauthier and Buchanan, were attracted to such a reading. Rawls (1999, 104) describes the argument from the original position as invoking "pure procedural justice"—the deliberative situation is so set up that whatever principles it generates are, by the fact of their generation, just. But though Rawls sometimes seemed attracted to this strong interpretation, his considered position is that the outcome of the deliberative model is indicative (not constitutive) of the correct solution to "the question of justification" (1999, 16). We might say that the deliberative model is evidence of the proper answer to the question of justification. However, this is still consistent with Rawls's "constructivism" because the answer to the justificatory problem is constitutive of P's having N. So we might say that Rawls's two principles are just—simply because they are in reflective equilibrium with the considered judgments of you and me, and that they would be chosen in the original position is indicative of this.

The weakest interpretation of the contract is that the contractual result is simply indicative of the correct answer to the justificatory problem, which itself is simply indicative of the fact that P has N. One could be a "realist," maintaining that whether P has N is a fact that holds whether or not the contract device generates principle P with N, and independently of whether the correct answer to our justificatory problem (i.e., what we can justify to each other) is that P has N. There is still room for contractualism here, but not "constructivism." Some, for example, have argued that T.M. Scanlon's theory is actually based on a sort of natural rights theory, where these rights are prior to the contract (Mack 2007). Even if this is correct, Scanlon can be a sort of social contract theorist. The diversity of possible approaches within social contract theory indicates the variety of different uses to which social contract theory can be applied.

6. Conclusion: The Social Contract and Public Justification
The social contract theories of Hobbes, Locke and Rousseau all stressed

that the justification of the state depends on showing that everyone would, in some way, consent to it. By relying on consent, social contract theory seemed to suppose a voluntarist conception of political justice and obligation: what is just depends on what people choose to agree to—what they will. Only in Kant (1797) does it become clear that consent is not fundamental to a social contract view: we have a duty to agree to act according to the idea of the "original contract." Rawls's revival of social contract theory in A Theory of Justice did not base obligations on consent, though the apparatus of an "original agreement" persisted as a way to help solve the problem of justification. As the question of public justification takes center stage (we might say as contractualist liberalism becomes justificatory liberalism), it becomes clear that posing the problem of justification in terms of a deliberative or a bargaining problem is a heuristic: the real issue is "the problem of justification"—what principles can be justified to all reasonable citizens or persons.

THE SOCIAL CONTRACT

3. THE GROUNDS OF MORAL STATUS

An entity has moral status if and only if it or its interests morally matter to some degree for the entity's own sake, such that it can be wronged. For instance, an animal may be said to have moral status if its suffering is at least somewhat morally bad, on account of this animal itself and regardless of the consequences for other beings, and acting unjustifiably against its interests is not only wrong, but wrongs the animal. Others owe it to the animal to avoid acting in this way. Some philosophers think of moral status as coming in degrees, reserving the notion of full moral status (FMS) for the highest degree of status.

Sometimes the term "moral standing" rather than "moral status" is used, but typically these terms have the same meaning. Some philosophers employ the language of "moral considerability" but this term is extremely ambiguous. Some use it as an alternate expression for "moral status" which is understood to come in degrees. In other cases the phrase is used to mean FMS. Act Utilitarians employ yet a third notion of moral considerability, which is a matter of having one's interests (e.g., the intensity, duration, etc. of one's pleasure or pain) factored into the calculus to determine which action minimizes the bad and maximizes the good. To avoid these ambiguities, this entry will use the terminology of "moral status" and "FMS."

After reviewing which entities have been thought to have moral status and what is involved in having FMS, as opposed to a lesser degree of moral status, this article will survey different views of the grounds of moral status as well as the arguments for attributing a particular degree of moral status on the basis of those grounds.

1. For Which Entities Does the Question of Moral Status Arise?

A variety of applied ethics debates regarding how certain beings – human beings, non-human animals, and even ecosystems – should be treated hinge on theoretical questions about their moral status and the grounds of that moral status. It is these theoretical questions that are the focus of this entry, but a quick survey of the applied ethics debates helpfully allows us to identify which entities have been thought to have moral status.

It is usually taken for granted that all adult cognitively unimpaired human beings have FMS. Of course, historically the moral status of people falling into a group perceived as "other," such as foreigners, racial minorities, women, the physically disabled, etc. has been routinely denied. Either they were not seen as having any moral status, or if they were granted some status, it was not FMS. However, accounting for their status does not pose much of a theoretical challenge (see section 4.1) and nowadays their status is rarely explicitly and directly denied on principled moral grounds.

By contrast, constructing plausible theories that account for the moral status of other human beings—not only the degree of their status, but in some cases also whether they have it at all—is more challenging (see section 4). Debates about disability rights and the permissibility of eugenics rest in part on theoretical disagreements about the moral status of cognitively impaired humans. These issues include controversies regarding the treatment of cognitively disabled infants, such as the practice of allowing infants with Down syndrome to die. Debates concerning abortion, stem cell research (see the entry on the ethics of stem cell research), and the question of what to do with unused frozen embryos from in vitro fertilization also rest on the theoretical question of the moral status of extremely underdeveloped human beings at various stages of development: zygote, embryo, fetus (see section 4.2). The moral status of both underdeveloped and cognitively impaired human beings is often taken to be at issue when it comes to the use of pre-implantation genetic diagnosis and amniocentesis. In addition, medical advances that prolong life, as well as debates about euthanasia, have led people to question the moral status of humans incapable of consciousness, such as those in a persistent vegetative state and anencephalic babies (born without the higher brain).

Humans are not the only beings about whom we might ask if they have moral status, and if so, to what degree. The moral status of animals is also of concern. Debates regarding the treatment of livestock (e.g., raising calves for veal, burning off the beaks of chickens, etc.), management of wild animals (e.g., killing wolves to protect livestock, killing deer in response to their overpopulation, etc.), and the creation and design of zoos rest, in part, on the moral status of domesticated and wild animals. In some cases the ethical question of an animal's treatment arises because of the discovery of their cognitive sophistication (e.g., dolphins, elephants, and great apes), which is taken to have a bearing on the theoretical issue of their moral status.

We have already noted that, while there are disagreements from one culture to another, and even within a single culture, both historically and at any given time, there is also significant agreement at least among non-philosophers that all cognitively unimpaired human adults have the highest degree of moral status. But, in addition, non-philosophers in principle, if not always in practice, accept the same view regarding all cognitively unimpaired human infants and severely cognitively impaired human beings (as we will use this term, it excludes those incapable of consciousness). That is, they hold that infants and the severely impaired, whether their impairment is intellectual or emotional, not merely have higher moral status than most animals but have FMS. By contrast, there is no such consensus about the moral status of human fetuses, humans incapable of consciousness, and even sophisticated animals like great apes.

Nonetheless, providing an adequate theory to account for the FMS of unimpaired infants and cognitively impaired human beings without attributing the same status to most animals has proven very difficult. In fact, our survey in section 4 suggests that this challenge has not been met by any of the existing accounts of the grounds of moral status. Some philosophers have, as a result, questioned or even abandoned this seemingly commonsense view, including the aspect that holds all adult cognitively unimpaired human beings have FMS (see the end of section 4.1).

It is important to note that questions of moral status – having it at all as well as the degree to which it is had – arise not only for human or non-human sentient individuals, but also for any living being/entity (such as a tree), as well as for entire species and ecosystems and non-living entities, such as mountains or a natural landscape (see the entry on environmental ethics).

In section 4 we will discuss how a range of humans (developed, and in various stages of underdevelopment, unimpaired and impaired), non-human animals, species, and ecosystems fare with respect to various accounts of the grounds of moral status.

2. What Is Full Moral Status (FMS)?

In this section we will discuss what having FMS amounts to, since with respect to this highest degree of moral status the literature is the most developed and detailed. Those with FMS are often called "moral persons." Standardly, FMS is understood to involve (i) a very stringent moral presumption against interfering with the being in various ways — destroying the being, experimenting upon it, directly causing its suffering, etc. While the strong presumption against interfering is the main aspect of FMS, some philosophers include as part of FMS (ii) a strong, but not necessarily stringent, reason to aid and (iii) a strong reason to treat fairly.

2.1 Stringent Presumption against Interference

All who employ the concept of FMS agree that, under most circumstances, we are morally prohibited from interfering in various ways with a being with FMS even for the sake of another valued creature and its interests, or for the sake of any other value, such as art, justice, or world peace. For instance, we are prohibited from killing a being with FMS for the sake of saving one or several other such beings. Some philosophers discuss this presumption using the terminology of duties; others use the terminology of rights and focus mainly on the right not to be killed (e.g., Feinberg 1980, pp. 98–104).

Note that FMS is not typically considered to preclude paternalistic interference. A seven-year-old human being is typically granted FMS (as we will see below) but it is nevertheless permissible to treat her paternalistically in some respects (see the entry on paternalism).

The moral presumption against interfering with a being with FMS, as it is typically understood, has at least these features:

It is a particularly strong moral reason against interfering, regardless of whether this interference results in harm. This strong reason can be overridden only in special circumstances and might altogether silence many types of conflicting reasons. For example, while pleasure is a legitimate reason for action in numerous circumstances (e.g., when choosing a leisure activity), the fact that someone might receive pleasure from killing a being with FMS is altogether removed from consideration as a reason for this action.

Despite its strength, the presumption not to interfere with beings with FMS may be overridden, perhaps, for example, when the lives of a very large number of others are at stake. But, crucially, even when the presumption is legitimately overridden in such special circumstances a moral residue remains, so that, for example, there is still reason to strongly regret the action.

When this presumption is not overridden and the being with FMS is interfered with, then the action is not merely wrong but also the being is wronged.

The reason not to interfere with beings with FMS is stronger than the reason not to interfere with beings that have some, but not full, moral status. For example, the reason not to kill a being with FMS in medical experiments is much stronger than the reason not to kill a similarly situated rabbit, which some consider to have lesser moral status. This means that the set of circumstances in which the reason not to kill a being with FMS can be overridden is much narrower than it is for beings with lower status, other things being equal. And it also means that the reason not to kill a being with FMS silences a broader set of conflicting considerations than the reason not to kill a being with lower moral status, other things being equal.

In addition, FMS is often taken to involve the following further feature, which is more controversial. When two beings both have FMS, the reason not to interfere with them is equally strong, other facts about the action being equal. This idea has been dubbed the "equal wrongness thesis" (McMahan 2002, p. 235). A variety of factors are thought not to affect the wrongness of killing of beings with FMS, in cases when killing is wrong: the being's age, level of intelligence, temperament, social circumstances, etc. For example, for a young and an old person who both have FMS, the reasons not to kill them are claimed to be equally strong despite the fact that the young person stands to lose much more in dying than the old. Note that irrespective of the equal wrongness thesis, one can grant that factors unrelated to the level of harm to the being, such as the mode of agency, defeaters, the number of people affected, and special relationships, do make a difference to the degree to which killing is wrong. Also, when killing is not wrong, as well as in the context of saving, one can grant that factors related to harm, such as age, etc., make a difference to one's decision (McMahan 2002, pp. 236–7). One might accept the equal wrongness thesis but disagree about which factors do or don't affect the wrongness of killing beings with FMS. On the other hand, one might reject the equal wrongness thesis altogether and so also not see FMS as entailing it (see McMahan 2008, and also Arneson 1999, to which we return in 4.1).

2.2 Strong Reason to Aid

While this is less commonly associated with FMS, some philosophers believe that there is a reason to provide aid to beings with FMS and it is stronger than the reason to aid beings who have only some or no moral status (e.g., Jaworska 2007 and Quinn 1984, in contrast to McMahan's interpretation of ordinary moral intuitions in McMahan 2002, pp. 223–224). Imagine a context in which one is saving individuals from a certain level of harm, such as pain, discomfort, or death. When faced with a choice of saving either a being with FMS or one without FMS, barring further reasons that may complicate the moral picture (e.g., indirect consequences of saving the being without FMS for other beings with FMS), there is a stronger reason to pick the being with FMS. Further, even in cases where aiding is not in fact possible, it is a graver moral misfortune, ceteris paribus, to leave a being with FMS unaided, as compared to a being without FMS. Of course, what aid is appropriate for a being depends on the context and on the being's stage of development. FMS is about the strength of the reason to aid and not about what type of aid to give.

Note that even if FMS entails strong reasons to aid, the reverse is not necessarily the case. Stronger reason to aid one being rather than another does not necessarily entail that the aided being has a higher moral status. See more general methodological cautions along these lines in section 2.4.

2.3 Strong Reason to Treat Fairly

While this is even less commonly explicitly associated with FMS, some views emphasize that comparable interests of beings with FMS matter equally in moral decisions, giving rise to strong reasons to treat such beings fairly (Broome 1990–1991 and Jaworska 2007). For example, when distrib-uting goods among such beings, in circumstances when they can all benefit similarly, barring special purposes, relationships, or independent claims on the goods, we have strong reason to distribute the goods equally (or in another way that's fair, depending on the account of fairness). In some cases one will be distributing goods that meet needs and in other cases the goods being distributed are not needed, but will nevertheless be appreciated. In either case, there is a strong reason to distribute the goods fairly among beings with FMS. This reason does not necessarily apply to beings that lack FMS; for example, a farmer need not worry about being fair in distributing food to his cows and chickens.

2.4 Distinguishing Reasons Constitutive of Moral Status from Other Reasons

It is helpful to bring out two points about FMS, the second of which is not discussed in the literature, but both of which, once made explicit, would likely be accepted by those who work on FMS.

First, the reasons mentioned in sections 2.1–2.3 ought to be understood as independent of special relationships and contracts. And thus they are impartial reasons, that is, every moral agent (human, intelligent Martian, etc.) has reason to act or forebear acting in the ways thus far discussed (McMahan 2005). Moreover, these reasons are independent of other facts about the action, for example, the action's possible bad long-term effects. Instead, they are reasons to treat the being this way for the being's own sake. So, for instance, a parent has at least two reasons not to kill his own child: a reason in virtue of the child's FMS, and a reason in virtue of the parental relationship, which generates a special obligation for this particular agent not to kill this particular child.

Second, it is important, methodologically speaking, not to infer moral status (full or otherwise) simply from the degree of wrongness or badness of an act, from the existence of rights, or from the strength of reasons in favor of the act (including omissions). For example, it might be worse for a parent to kill his own child than a stranger's child, but that does not mean that the children have different moral status. The child has a right that her parent not kill her, in virtue of the special relationships between parents and their children, but this is in addition to, and separate from, the right not to be killed that the child has in virtue of her moral status. Or, to take another example, there may be a large difference in the strength of reasons to save each of two beings from death, but this difference may have little to do with the moral status of the beings. Both McMahan (2002) and Singer (1993) hold, on quite different grounds, that death is not very bad for most animals, while it is very bad for ordinary adult human beings. Accordingly, on their views, the reason to save an ordinary adult human being from death is much stronger than the reason to save, say, a rabbit from death. But this is not itself evidence of a higher moral status of the human being: the difference in the strength of reasons is fully explained by the vast difference in the benefits of aid in the two cases, and is fully compatible with the claim that the human and the rabbit have the same moral status. (Of course, one can hold, on other grounds, that they in fact have different status, as McMahan himself does.)

Certain views might acknowledge that some humans lack FMS and yet emphasize that we ought, nevertheless, to treat them as though they have FMS due to the bad effects that would otherwise follow. For example, someone might think that, for practical purposes, we need a very straightforward, stable, and difficult to misinterpret criterion of moral status. If we don't treat all human beings as if they have FMS, unclarity and moral confusion would ensue. It would open the floodgates for different people to set the threshold capacity required for FMS differently, and thereby lead to mistaken underinclusion and consequent mistreatment of humans who do in fact have FMS. Another bad consequence that can arise, at least were we to fail to treat neonates as having FMS by permitting infanticide, is depriving would-be adoptive parents of the opportunity to adopt (Warren 1996, Postscript). There are also more self-interested possible bad consequences to consider. Failure to treat unimpaired infants as having FMS might lead to a lack of tenderness toward them, and thereby contribute to their turning into people who will mistreat us when they are older (Feinberg 1980, p. 198). Moreover, a rule of treating cognitively impaired human beings as having FMS would ensure that we will be treated well should we ever suffer from cognitive impairment (considered without endorsement by McMahan 2002, pp. 227–8).

Kant's remarks about the treatment of animals might indicate a yet further argument for treating humans without FMS as if they nevertheless had FMS. He argued that we have reasons to avoid cruelty to animals, and thus to treat animals better than their moral status implies, since otherwise we might develop psychological propensities that could lead us analogously to mistreat humans who have FMS (Kant [LE], pp. 212–13). Similarly, one might reason, if we do not treat those humans without FMS as having FMS, we might develop psychological propensities that could lead us to mistreat humans who have FMS.

Regardless of the details, on all such proposals, the requirement of treating a being as if it had FMS, or some other degree of moral status, to avoid bad consequences is not equivalent to that being's having this moral status: while the reasons adduced might indeed be good reasons to treat the being as if it had the requisite moral status, these reasons are not for the sake of that being, but rather for the sake of other beings.

Other types of reasons for treating beings as if they had a certain degree of moral status have also been offered. Some virtue ethicists claim that we ought to avoid harming animals because harming them is incompatible with displaying the virtuous character traits we ought to display (see the entry on the moral status of animals for details). Several contractualists (see section 5 below and the entry on contractualism) have argued that one may reasonably opt out of any agreement that does not afford sufficient moral status to one's children and others one cares about, including those who are severely cognitively impaired (Morris 2011, pp. 265–267 and Carruthers 2011, pp. 387–394). Critics and proponents disagree whether these considerations can establish reasons that are for these beings' sake (e.g., reasons not to interfere); hence, it is unclear whether they can establish the moral status of the beings in question.

3. Moral Status versus FMS

Those who accept that moral status comes in degrees have not developed fine-grained accounts of what each degree of status would involve. Their emphasis has been on the difference in status between creatures or entities that have some moral status (dogs, rabbits, etc.), and those who deserve the highest degree of moral status (FMS). However, with the above account of FMS made explicit, one can delineate different paradigms for capturing degrees of moral status, which we will list here simply in the spirit of marking out possible positions, and thus without addressing the pros, cons, and implications of each position.

One way to capture degrees of moral status is to vary the strength of the reasons outlined in section 2 (and hence also the degree of wrongness involved in acting against these reasons – see DeGrazia 2008). For example, while there is a very stringent moral presumption against killing an unimpaired adult human being, there might be only strong but non-stringent reasons not to kill a dog, and very weak reasons not to kill a fish. The weaker the reason, the more easily overridden it is. The other categories of reasons would be handled similarly: when the benefit to be received, the cost of providing that benefit, and other similar factors are on a par, there is a strong reason to aid an unimpaired adult human being, but only some reason to aid a dog, and very little reason to aid a fish, and so on. Alternatively, one could treat FMS as involving a stringent reason not to be killed of the type that, in cases of conflict, would override what maximizes the overall good, whereas, for a being with lesser moral status, what maximizes the overall good – with this being's good included in the calculus – does settle how this being should be treated (McMahan 2002, pp. 245–247).

Another way to capture degrees of moral status is to vary not the strength of the reasons but which reasons apply. Instead of the three categories of reasons discussed above, lesser moral status might involve two kinds of reasons (a stringent moral presumption against interference and a strong reason to aid, but no reason to treat fairly) or only one (a stringent moral presumption against interference, but no reason to aid or treat fairly). This, of course, is compatible with other reasons, in a given context, to aid or treat fairly that do not derive from the being's moral status (see section 2.4). Alternatively, lesser moral status might involve fewer presumptions against different types of interference (e.g., only a presumption against causing pain but not against killing).

Of course, one could combine these two approaches. For example, to have the highest degree of moral status is for there to be very strong reasons of all three types, an intermediate level of moral status (e.g., the status of a dog) might involve some reason not to kill the being but no reason to aid it or treat it fairly, while the lowest degree of moral status would involve a very weak reason of just one type. Although having the lowest degree of moral status would not afford much protection, it nevertheless is different from having no moral status at all. A fingernail has no moral status and so no reasons of any kind need be given for cutting it up and discarding it. But sufficient justification must be provided for doing this to a being with even very low moral status.

4. Grounds of Moral Status

Accounts differ on what it is about the individual that grounds or confers moral status and to what degree, with implications for which beings do or do not have moral status and for their comparative status. We begin with the Sophisticated Cognitive Capacities accounts of moral status and their main strengths and shortcomings. We then show that alternative accounts do not fare any better and so the challenge remains to provide a plausible unified account of the grounds of FMS, especially for those who wish to defend the "commonsense view" discussed in section 1. The order of presentation is, roughly, dialectical, not historical.

For each account discussed, one could hold either a threshold or scalar conception of moral status, though the former is more commonly found in the literature (see the end of section 4.1 for an exception).

According to the threshold conception, as it is usually discussed, if capacity C grounds FMS, then any being that has C, regardless of how well it can exercise this capacity, has as much moral status as any other being that has C and this status is full. If C is not only sufficient but necessary for FMS, then all beings lacking C would not have FMS, though the threshold conception would nevertheless leave it open whether having some other feature (e.g., parts of C or something lesser but akin to C) might ground lesser degrees of moral status. In contrast, a scalar conception of moral status would hold that if capacity C grounds moral status, then any being who has C has some status; the better it can exercise this capacity, the higher its degree of moral status (Arneson 1999).

There is an alternative way to draw the threshold versus scalar distinction of moral status. Instead of focusing on how well capacity C is exercised, the views could instead focus on the number of relevant capacities a being has. A threshold view might specify some number n of the relevant capacities as both necessary and sufficient for FMS. A scalar conception would hold, on the other hand, that a being with n+1 capacities would have a higher moral status than one with merely n capacities.

While both threshold and scalar conceptions of moral status allow for degrees of moral status, each faces its own set of difficulties. For example, the threshold conception allows for the possibility of discontinuities in degrees of moral status that might seem arbitrary. The difference, for example, between a being with C, but who can only exercise it very poorly, and a being without C might not seem to be very great, and yet if C grounds FMS, then the former being will have FMS while the latter might have no moral status. However, advocates of the threshold view could respond that if C is a valuable capacity, then a being with a capacity to do it poorly has achieved something important compared to a being without this capacity. In addition, if there are multiple grounds for lesser degrees of moral status, which threshold views could allow, then this might remove a large gap in status between beings with C and those lacking C but who have other status conferring capacities. Scalar conceptions, on the other hand, can easily account for lesser degrees of moral status, but may defy commonsense intuitions. For example, if intelligence were to play the role of C, then the scalar conception would claim that those who are more intelligent have a stronger right not to be killed than those who are not quite as intelligent, which would be contrary to commonsense intuition (see Wikler 2009 for a discussion of whether degrees of intelligence are relevant to civil rights).

4.1 Sophisticated Cognitive Capacities

According to this type of account, a being has FMS if and only if the being has very sophisticated cognitive capacities. These capacities might be intellectual or emotional. Historically, the most famous sophisticated intellectual capacities account was given by Kant, according to whom autonomy, the capacity to set ends via practical reasoning, must be respected (see the entry on respect) and grounds the dignity of all rational beings ([GMM], pp. 434, 436, Prussian Academy pagination). Beings without reason may be treated as a mere means (p. 428). For a contemporary version, put in terms of the capacity to will as sufficient for rights of respect, see Quinn 1984, pp. 49–52. Other intellectual capacities that have been suggested, even if not always embraced, as grounding FMS, or at least the associated rights and the distinctive value of a person, include self-awareness (McMahan 2002, pp. 45 and 242) or awareness of oneself as a continuing subject of mental states (Tooley 1972, p. 44); being future-oriented in one's desires and plans (Singer 1993, pp. 95 and 100; see, however, section 4.3 for Singer's and Tooley's equal consideration view); capacity to value, to bargain, and to assume duties and responsibilities (all part of a longer list in Feinberg 1980, p. 197). On the emotional side, one sophisticated capacity that has been proposed is the capacity to care, as distinguished from the mere capacity to desire. (Jaworska (2007) posits this as sufficient but perhaps not necessary for FMS.) There are also combination views that appeal to both intellectual and emotional sophisticated cognitive capacities as necessary and sufficient for FMS (Feinberg 1980, p. 197).

According to Sophisticated Cognitive Capacities accounts, the feature grounding FMS is not relational: the source of moral status is neither a relation the individual stands in (e.g., membership in a species) nor a capacity whose exercise requires active participation of another (e.g., the capacity to relate to others in certain mutually responsive ways). In some versions, the exercise of the relevant capacities does not even require the existence of anyone else, while in others it, at most, involves the presence of another being (as in the case of caring about someone) but not necessarily that being's active participation. Individuals have FMS solely because they can engage in certain cognitively sophisticated acts or responses on their own. Moreover, any being that has these sophisticated cognitive capacities has FMS, and so the accounts avoid anthropocentrism. However, since most (but not necessarily all) animals lack sophisticated cognitive capacities, they are not accorded the same moral status as an unimpaired adult human. Similarly, in the case of a living organism such as a redwood tree or a fetus, as well as non-individual entities, such as species and ecosystems, they would not have FMS on these views.

Some of these views (e.g., Kant's) do not allow for any moral status other than FMS, and so would hold that beings who don't meet the threshold for FMS have no moral status at all. Other views are silent on this question and compatible with lower degrees of moral status for beings or entities that are not cognitively sophisticated. Yet others (e.g., McMahan 2002) explicitly insist that all sentient beings have some degree of moral status.

A stock objection to Sophisticated Cognitive Capacities accounts is their underinclusiveness. Not only will some environmentalists and animal activists find the view underinclusive, but so too will those who subscribe to the "commonsense view" articulated in section 1. For example, infants lack sophisticated cognitive capacities, and so fail to meet this necessary condition for FMS. The versions that offer only a sufficient condition for FMS seem more plausible since they leave open alternative routes to FMS. But such accounts still leave the moral status of infants unaccounted for, and possibly on a par with that of dogs and rabbits. Of course, these views nevertheless allow that there are very strong reasons not to kill human infants: it would be disrespectful and harmful to the infant's parents, it would likely cause psychological harm to the killers, etc. But these reasons have nothing to do with the moral status of infants, since they are not reasons for the infants' own sake (Feinberg 1980, p.198 and McMahan 2002, p. 232).

Threshold conceptions of Sophisticated Cognitive Capacities views have been thought by some to entail a claim that is incompatible with the equal wrongness thesis or with any other interpretation of the equal moral status of all beings with FMS (see the entry on egalitarianism). According to the threshold conception of a Sophisticated Cognitive Capacities view, any being that meets the threshold has full moral status. Since the status is full, there is no higher status that a being can achieve. Nevertheless, one might think that if the possession of some threshold level of a sophisticated cognitive capacity (e.g., the capacity to set ends) makes such a difference to moral status, then the possession of the capacity to do this well (e.g., the capacity to set ends well) should lead to an even higher status. Or, as Arneson (1999) would put it, a higher degree of the capacity entails a higher status. And so two beings who meet the threshold would not, after all, have equal moral status. Compare, for example, an ordinary human adult's capacity to set ends to the capacity of a cognitively impoverished being who, in its lifetime, "can set just a few ends and make just a few choices based on considering two or three simple alternatives" (Arneson 1999, pp. 119–120). It is not enough to stipulate that differences in capacity to do an activity well do not affect one's status. The account needs to provide an explanation for why such differences do not matter. And so, if one accepts the claim that the capacity to do an activity well leads to even higher moral status, then one must reject the equal wrongness thesis and the threshold conception of 4.1.

A related way to put the issue is this. According to the "commonsense view," a virtue of the threshold conception of the Sophisticated Cognitive Capacity account is that it distinguishes and elevates the moral status of cognitively unimpaired adult humans compared to other animals. However, once the importance of sophisticated cognitive capacities is highlighted, it seems that not only the possession of the capacity but also how well one exercises it is morally relevant to one's status. Since not all cognitively unimpaired adult humans exercise this capacity equally well, then it would seem that not all cognitively unimpaired adult humans have equal moral status. And so, combining this interpretation of the threshold conception with a Sophisticated Cognitive Capacity account results in not according all cognitively unimpaired adult humans equal moral status – a problem from the commonsense viewpoint.

4.2 Capacity to Develop Sophisticated Cognitive Capacities

The problem, at least from the standpoint of the commonsense view, of underincluding infants can be avoided while still retaining a shared source of FMS. The above accounts can be modified as follows: sophisticated cognitive capacities or the capacity to develop these sophisticated capacities (without losing one's identity) are necessary and sufficient for FMS. This is usually labeled the "potential" account in the literature (e.g., Stone 1987), although some authors do not use this terminology, but rather speak, for example, of the wrongness of killing due to the loss of a "future like ours" (Marquis 1989 and 1995). One can also treat potentiality as a ground for some, but not full, moral status (Harman 1999, notwithstanding the revisions in Harman 2003) or as only an enhancer of moral status (Steinbock 1992, p. 68). Views differ in their interpretation of potentiality. For example, some deny that a fetus that will die as a fetus has the relevant potential (Harman 1999, p. 311).

These potentiality accounts, like the accounts in 4.1, avoid anthropocentrism without according most animals the same elevation in moral status. But, unlike the accounts in 4.1, they also include very underdeveloped human beings: not only infants and one-year-olds, but even early fetuses have the capacity to develop sophisticated cognitive capacities (barring unusual cases). However, these potentiality accounts make no advance with respect to the problem of accounting for the equal status of all beings with FMS, since sophisticated capacities, which can be exercised well to varying degrees, are still treated as the source of moral status. Moreover, these accounts are of no help to those interested in according moral status to non-human animals, trees, species, and ecosystems.

Although Boonin (2003) denies that his view is a potentiality account (p. 62), his view does implicitly appeal to potentiality, albeit with somewhat different implications than those above. He defends having the conjunction of "a future-like-ours" (a kind of potentiality) and "actual conscious desires that can be satisfied only if [one's] personal future is preserved" as sufficient for FMS (p. 84). Barring early death, most two-year-olds and older children meet both conditions: they have a future like ours while also having conscious desires, e.g., for avocado tomorrow, which can only be satisfied if the child lives until the next day. Early fetuses also typically have a future like ours, but they lack mental states such as desires, and thus are excluded from FMS. Boonin is explicitly neutral on the question whether animals have a future-like-ours, so his proposal is compatible with several different views about the moral status of animals (p. 84, note 36).

Any attempt to ground moral status in potentiality introduces its own challenges. One could argue that mere potential cognitive capacity is insufficient for FMS or even a weaker moral status. A potential US president has neither rights nor even a claim to command the military; likewise in the case of potentially cognitively sophisticated beings and the rights associated with moral status (Feinberg 1980, p.193). While this particular analogy has been contested (Wilkins 1993, pp. 126–127 and Boonin 2003, pp. 46–49), one can appeal to other analogies: a small child, a potential adult, doesn't have the rights of adults to own property or to watch any television program it wants (Boonin 2003, p. 48).

Still, there is room to press back on this objection. We do, after all, often treat people with potential differently from those without it. We provide extra music instruction, music scholarships, and create music camps for those with the potential to become great musicians, whereas we do not do so for those lacking such potentiality. While being a potential adult human does not give one a right to vote, perhaps it gives us reason to act as trustees with regard to childrens' future status and interests and thus to educate and prepare them to become voters by the time they are adults; it does seem that children would be wronged if we neglected to so prepare them. In this way, we treat children differently from dogs who lack the potential to become adult humans, even though neither is now an adult human. And perhaps this difference in treatment would extend even to not taking certain actions (e.g., killing) that would result in the loss of the relevant potentiality. This line of response might only go so far when it comes to fetuses. With respect to a future-like-ours, some argue that the loss of this potentiality is morally problematic only if the being is sufficiently psychologically connected to that future person, and a fetus arguably lacks this sufficient connection (McInerney 1990).

Even though the potentiality accounts come closer to capturing the commonsense view than the Sophisticated Cognitive Capacities accounts, they still are, on this view, underinclusive. Many conscious human beings whose cognitive impairment is both severe and permanent cannot meet these accounts' conditions for an elevated moral status. It might be that humans who currently suffer from severe, permanent cognitive impairment, but once had sophisticated cognitive capacities, have FMS in virtue of the past possession of these capacities. But it is unclear how to defend such a claim. Moreover, the moral status of permanently severely cognitively impaired humans who never had sophisticated cognitive capacities remains unaccounted for (see the entry on cognitive disability and moral status). Even the versions of the accounts that offer only a sufficient condition for FMS still leave their moral status open and possibly on a par with animals who similarly lack both the sophisticated cognitive capacities and the capacity to develop them. In Boonin's case, since he is agnostic about animals and so, presumably, about cognitively impaired human beings with similar prospects, his view will either overinclude the former or underinclude the latter, as both types of beings will be treated on a par.

4.3 Rudimentary Cognitive Capacities

In response to the criticisms just discussed, one could lower the standards for the kind of cognitive capacities that are necessary and sufficient for FMS. If the relevant cognitive capacities were rudimentary enough, even severely cognitively impaired human beings would qualify. Such an account might appeal to the capacity to experience pleasure or pain (sentience), to have interests or basic emotions, or the capacity for consciousness. Whether fetuses at various stages of development will thereby have FMS depends on which rudimentary capacity is appealed to. For example, an early fetus has interests but not consciousness.

This accommodation does not fit well with the commonsense view, which would see it as overinclusive. Most (but not all) animals meet these lowered standards for FMS – they have the capacity for pleasure, pain, interests, and consciousness – and so their moral status would be on a par with most human beings (namely all those who possess these rudimentary capacities). For example, some authors claim that respecting rational nature entails respecting beings that have only parts of rational nature or necessary conditions of it (Wood 1998, p. 197). Such a view seems to treat animals, infants, and severely cognitively impaired humans, all of whom exhibit only parts of rational nature, as morally on a par. (See O'Neill 1998 for additional critiques of this kind of Kantian approach.) Many advocates of such views explicitly and gladly embrace this inclusiveness and reject the commonsense view of the status of animals (Regan 2004).

Some philosophers eschew the language of moral status and, in any case, would not allow that it comes in degrees; they claim that all beings who have the relevant rudimentary cognitive capacities deserve "equal moral consideration." For example, the fact that one's act would cause a certain degree of suffering is a reason to avoid the act regardless of what kind of being experiences this suffering. Singer (1993) is famously associated with this "equal consideration" view, though he also seems to implicitly allow a higher moral status and so greater moral consideration (e.g., "right to life") to self-conscious beings, which is more akin to the account in 4.1.

While the equal moral consideration approach may seem to imply treating human beings and most animals alike, many of its defenders deny this counterintuitive implication by showing that two beings can deserve equal consideration and yet require differential treatment due to differences in the interests impacted. What an unimpaired adult human stands to lose in being killed, for example, is much weightier than what a bird would lose. The capacity of foresight, for example, can make for weightier interests, and so human beings with this or other forms of cognitive sophistication are harmed more by death (Rachels 1990, pp.186–194; Regan 2004, pp. 304 and 324; and DeGrazia 1996). Potentiality can also explain differential treatment of two beings based on interests impacted, while maintaining the beings' equal moral status. For example, there is a stronger reason not to harm a baby as opposed to a cat, given the potential of the baby and not the cat for a cognitively sophisticated future (Harman 2003, p. 187, although this is not explicitly an equal consideration view). Even those who do not eschew the language of moral status can appeal to differences in the interests impacted to justify unequal treatment of moral equals. Admittedly, in some cases comparative judgments of whose interests are morally weightier, and hence judgments about differential treatment, can be difficult, in part due to the difficulties in knowing the capabilities of minds very different from ours and of comparing well-being across species (DeGrazia 1996).

In spite of allowing for differential treatment of morally equal beings, the above accounts remain unable to capture the commonsense view: they are unable to account for the differential treatment of both conscious humans with severe irreversible cognitive impairments and infants who will die due to disease before acquiring cognitive sophistication, as compared with many animals (such as a dog), since here the affected interests are similar. Thus, while one may grant that rudimentary capacities ground some moral status, one must look beyond such capacities to explain the difference in moral status between humans and most animals.

Also, despite the name "equal moral consideration," these views seem to be incompatible with the equal wrongness thesis. Admittedly, the views are explicitly concerned with what should be done rather than with how to evaluate an action's degree of wrongness when one fails to do what one should. Nonetheless, in allowing or even requiring differential treatment based on differences in the interests impacted, such views seem to also imply that an action (such as killing) is more wrong if it impacts the victim's interests more severely, directly contradicting the equal wrongness thesis.

Notice that an even more rudimentary feature, which is not cognitive, would have to be considered if one were to accord any moral status to all living beings. For example, one can appeal to having a good or well-being of one's own that can be enhanced or damaged as a ground of moral status (Taylor 1986, p. 75, and Naess 1986, p. 14). If "interests" are understood broadly enough, then nonconscious entities, such as plants, species, and ecosystems have interests (e.g., an interest in fulfilling their nature) and thus some moral standing (Johnson 1993, pp. 146, 148, 184, 287). Of course, the challenge for such views is to explain how and why inevitable conflicts among all those with a well-being or interests should be settled. It is not enough to provide principles adjudicating these conflicts (as does Taylor 1986, p. 261); one must justify these principles in a way that is not grounded in the moral status of the beings under consideration (since their status is taken to be equal). For additional discussion and critique of these and other views, see the entry on environmental ethics.

4.4 Member of Cognitively Sophisticated Species

One way to avoid the key problems of the previous accounts is to posit membership in the human species as a sufficient condition for FMS. This is not the view that the human species itself has FMS, but rather that membership in the species gives an individual FMS. Feinberg (1980) discusses this view, whereas Dworkin (1993, ch. 3) actually posits it, although without distinguishing between this version and the modified version discussed below. Benn (1967, pp. 69–71) considers membership in the human species necessary and sufficient for FMS. Note that belonging to the human species is a relational feature (the relation of being a member of a kind), unlike the features invoked by the accounts considered thus far.

If there are non-human cognitively sophisticated individuals, such as higher animals or alien species, they would seem to deserve a high moral status equal to that of human beings. Thus, this account should not make human species membership a necessary condition for FMS, but rather be disjunctive: having sophisticated cognitive capacities or belonging to the human species is necessary and sufficient for FMS.

By introducing the latter condition (human species membership), such a view can establish FMS not only for infants and severely cognitively impaired human beings but even for fetuses and permanently unconscious human beings. Moreover, any non-human individual who lacks cognitively sophisticated capacities, which includes most (but not all) animals, lacks FMS. Thus this view accounts rather nicely for much of the commonsense view described in section 1. However, it is of no help grounding the claim that non-human animals, trees, species, or ecosystems have any moral status.

One possible cost of this approach is the loss of a unified account of FMS. That is, there are now two routes to FMS: having sophisticated cognitive capacities or belonging to the human species. Whether one is cognitively sophisticated is determined purely by psychology, while whether one belongs to the human species is determined purely by biology. Of course, it is true that the human species (as opposed to its membership criteria) is characterized both psychologically and biologically, and so in this sense the second route is related to the first route to FMS.

A second problem is an arbitrary distinction between severely cognitively impaired humans and members of other similarly cognitively sophisticated species, were they to exist, who have analogous severe cognitive impairments. Imagine, for example, a cognitively sophisticated biological species of "Martians," which has some severely cognitively impaired members. Even if an impaired Martian and an impaired human have similarly limited cognitive capacities, and even though they bear the same metaphysical relation to members of their species (they are both tokens of a biological type whose unimpaired members are cognitively sophisticated), this account nevertheless treats them as having a different moral status. This is unacceptably arbitrary.

One could modify this account by substituting membership in a cognitively sophisticated species for membership in the human species as the second sufficient condition for FMS (Cohen 1986; possibly Scanlon 1998, pp.185–86; and Finnis 1995). This approach is often implicit rather than explicitly stated and defended. For example, Korsgaard (2004) regards infants and severely cognitive impaired human beings as rational agents – presumably in the sense of being members of the kind "rational agents" – and hence deserving of respect.

This version of the account is now more unified and avoids the above charge of arbitrariness, while retaining the alignment with the commonsense view. Both sufficient conditions of FMS now ultimately appeal to the value of cognitively sophisticated capacities, and cognitively impaired members of all cognitively sophisticated species have the same moral status. Moreover, most animals still lack FMS since neither they nor their species are cognitively sophisticated. Also, the account makes considerable inroads in explaining the equal status of those with FMS, since the main route to FMS it proposes, membership in a cognitively sophisticated species, is an all-or-nothing feature and not a matter of degree.

However, even this modified version has problems. First, whether one belongs to a given species depends on biological criteria, such as whom one can mate with, whom one is born of, or having the relevant DNA. But it is unclear why these biological criteria are relevant for moral status. The point can be sharpened this way. The human species, for example, is a morally relevant category because the species is characterized, in part, by morally relevant properties such as sophisticated intellectual and emotional capacities, and not merely by biological criteria (e.g., mating abilities). But it is unclear why a token member of a species, a token lacking any of these morally relevant capacities, should get the moral status from the type it belongs to (the species). If membership in the type does not require any of the morally relevant features, how can the membership be morally relevant? Consequently, this modified account has its own problem of arbitrariness (Feinberg 1980, p. 193; Sumner

1981, pp. 97–101; and McMahan 2002, pp. 212–214, 216). McMahan provides an especially interesting imaginary example involving cognitively enhanced Superchimps, which, on the account under consideration, generates counterintuitive consequences for the moral status of the unenhanced chimps. For example, if the Superchimps came to outnumber ordinary unenhanced chimps, the norm for the chimp species would have changed and for this reason alone the unenhanced chimps would have gained higher moral status. A related counterintuitive consequence, not mentioned by McMahan, is the following: if the Superchimps become their own species (via gene therapy and interbreeding), a cognitively impaired member of this newly created Superchimp species with the same cognitive capacities as a non-impaired ordinary chimp (assumed here not to be sufficiently cognitively sophisticated to have FMS) would have a very different moral status from the ordinary chimp. And yet the two chimps would be alike in every respect other than their species classification.

Notice also that, on this account, an anencephalic human baby (born without the higher brain) is a member of the human species and so would have FMS. But some might find this inclusion counterintuitive.

The possibly problematic inclusion of anencephalic infants does not seem to apply to the view underlying Little's (2008) claim that FMS is achieved late in pregnancy (pp. 332 and 348), when the fetus, which was a human organism, becomes a human being (pp. 339–341). She does not state what the criteria are for being a human being, but she may be partially following Quinn 1984 and conceiving of a human being as one who belongs to the human species and has the capacity to learn (see her page 340), where the latter feature would exclude the anencephalics. While on this view being a human being is not a merely biological matter, the view is still open to the problem of arbitrariness insofar as it holds that the morally irrelevant, merely biological feature of membership in the human species does make a difference to moral status.

One may think that the above objections can be overcome if the relevant criterion for FMS is not conceived of at all in terms of membership in a cognitively sophisticated biological species, but rather in terms of membership in a cognitively sophisticated kind. However, this approach faces a dilemma: either (a) a cognitively sophisticated kind does not include members who can never be cognitively sophisticated and thus leaves out many severely cognitively impaired human beings or (b) cognitive sophistication is not a requirement of membership in a cognitively sophisticated kind, but then this membership does not seem to require any morally relevant features, and its moral relevance becomes dubious.

4.5 Special Relationships

Some views attempt to ground strong reasons not to interfere, and perhaps also to aid and treat fairly, not only by appeal to sophisticated cognitive capacities but also by appeal to special relationships (these are therefore disjunctive accounts). On such accounts, specific agents must not interfere with an individual or must respect that individual's rights in virtue of being in a relationship with that individual. On one popular version, the relevant relationship is being a fellow member of a community, where the community is composed of all those of the same biological species (Nozick 1997 and possibly Scanlon 1998, p.185).

The motivation for this version of the Special Relationship account comes from thinking about the species relationship as analogous to other relationships (biological, social, etc.) that generate special duties and rights. For example, the relationship between a parent and his child creates an especially strong reason for the parent not to kill and to aid his child. Also, some people believe that even a gamete donor has special reason to aid the resulting child.

Other authors focus on non-species relationships not as a sufficient ground for moral status but as an enhancer of moral status. Suppose, for example, that having a well being, sentience, or consciousness (all of which both animals and humans have) is sufficient for some moral status (e.g., weak rights not to be harmed and to be aided). The status is full (e.g., the rights are at full strength) when, for example, the individual is in a specific relationship with a moral agent, where the relationship is that of co-belonging to a community. The community's membership requirements need not be strictly biological, but could be both biological and cognitive or merely social (for the former see Quinn's 1984 appeal to the capacity to learn, pp. 32–33 and 50–54, and for the latter see Warren 1997, pp. 164–166, 174, 176). Being someone's child is also a special relationship that some take to enhance moral status (Steinbock 1992, pp. 9, 13 and 69–

70). This is not to be confused with claims that the biosocial relation of being someone's child is itself sufficient for FMS rather than merely an enhancer of moral status (Kittay 2005).

Anderson (2004) too discusses multiple sufficient grounds for rights to non-interference and aid, though perhaps not as strong as those associated with FMS: the interests of the being itself or the interests of other beings relating to it (pp. 281–3 and 285–6); being a member of human society, where this does not require being a human being (p. 284); and the capacity for reciprocal relations or mutual accommodation (pp. 287–9). The last sufficient condition is a Special Relationship type of view, though some of the other conditions might also be seen as such.

All of these Special Relationship accounts escape one drawback of the Member of a Cognitively Sophisticated Species account. The reason not to interfere (or aid, etc.) is not based on being a token of a type with morally irrelevant criteria for membership. Merely belonging to a species or other type of group is not the source of the reason not to interfere. Instead, by being a member of a species or another group, a token individual is thereby in a relationship with another token member of the group and this relationship is taken to be the source of the reason not to interfere. Also, typically, standing in a special relationship, such as a species relationship, is an all-or-nothing feature and not a matter of degree (for an exception, see Quinn 1984). If so, Special Relationship accounts can explain the equal status of those who have FMS on this basis.

A central problem with these approaches is that they do not truly offer an account of moral status, but only of particular agents' reasons vis-à-vis the individual at issue. A being's moral status should give every moral agent, whether human or not, reasons to protect that being (see section 2.4). But on these accounts, by contrast, only those moral agents who are members of the same species, or are in some other special relationship with the being, have a reason, let us say, not to kill the being (McMahan 2005, p. 355). For example, a human being, in virtue of being in a special relationship (via species community) with a human infant, has a reason not to kill the infant, but a Martian, if there were one, would not have this reason, since he would lack this special relationship with the human infant. Similarly, a human being does not have a reason not to kill an ape infant, even if adult apes are cognitively sophisticated, because the two are not in a special species-based relationship. Reasons of this sort, constitutive of special obligations, are different in kind from, and contrasted with, reasons constitutive of moral status, which are impartial. Notice the contrast between two reasons a parent has not to kill his child: the reason constitutive of his parental obligation versus the impartial reason constitutive of the child's moral status.

Some Special Relationship accounts (Quinn's) do not take themselves to be offering an account of FMS but rather only to be capturing the key components of the notion (e.g., a strong right against others to not be killed). They leave behind both the term "moral status" and the concept of impartiality. Other special relationship accounts (Steinbock's and Kittay's) do use the term "moral status" leaving it unclear whether they think that special relationships could somehow generate impartial reasons.

Another concern with those Special Relationship accounts that attempt to ground rights and requirements analogous to those of FMS is that they are overinclusive (although see exceptions below). If the relevant relationship is with a being in one's social community then, depending on how this is interpreted, any animal incorporated into human social communities (e.g., dogs) would gain strong rights, contrary to the commonsense view. If the relevant relationship is instead with a being in one's species community, then all humans are in a special species relationship with an anencephalic human baby and so, according to such an account, owe it a high level of moral protection. But, as noted earlier, some would find this counterintuitive. A related problem emerges once we notice that humans might have more of a relationship with other "embodied minds" (i.e., any being with both a body and mind, such as an animal) than with human organisms that lack minds (such as an anencephalic baby). The Special Relationship approach would then be committed to claiming that animals have stronger rights than some cognitively impaired humans (McMahan 2002, pp. 225–226). But the account would not welcome these implications of its own approach and, if it did so, it would then suffer the problem of overinclusiveness with respect to animals.

Quinn's view (1984), although quite similar to the species community view, may not be overinclusive with respect to anencephalics or animals.

Though Quinn does not consider this case, he would likely conclude that anencephalic infants are mere human organisms, not human beings (because they lack the capacity to learn), or are at most partially, rather than fully, existent human beings. Thus, they do not stand in a special relationship with other human beings in the way that unimpaired infants or cognitively impaired human beings with the capacity to learn do. Moreover, it is plausible to assume that we have more of a relationship with human beings in Quinn's sense, which are human embodied minds, than with non-human embodied minds, such as animals. Steinbock's view also would not be overinclusive with respect to anencephalics or animals, since the full strength of rights she discusses requires both consciousness and being someone's child.

Insofar as Special Relationship accounts intend to ground the notion of FMS, they will also suffer from another problem encountered earlier: they are not unified since they offer two unconnected routes to FMS (sophisticated cognitive capacities or special relationships).

4.6 Other Grounds

In addition to some of the features noted in section 4.3 (e.g., having interests, having a good, etc.), some philosophers have attempted to ground the moral status of an entity on features that do not connect with interests in any way. One such feature is not being designed by anyone to fulfill any purpose, which some philosophers hold as a ground for being treated as an end and not a mere means, and thus having at least some degree of moral status (Brennan 1984, pp. 44 and 56 and Katz 1997, pp. 129–131). Naturalness, that is, being unaltered by humans, has also been proposed as itself a ground of intrinsic value, and so as grounding at least some degree of moral status (Elliot 1997, p. 80). Perhaps harmony and beauty might be yet other features one could appeal to as grounds of the moral status of ecosystems (Leopold 1949 and Callicott 1980). These views do not discuss whether moral status comes in degrees and provide no guidance for how to adjudicate the numerous conflicts that would arise among entities with moral status. Insofar as these two issues are addressed by supplementing these views with one (or more) of the accounts discussed in sections 4.1–4.5, the views will inherit the problems of those accounts. For elaboration of these and other such views as they arise in environmental ethics, along with critiques, see the entry on environmental ethics.

5. Justifying the Grounds of Moral Status

The survey in section 4 of the various proposed grounds of moral status largely sidestepped the question of why the proposed grounds can play their purported role in grounding moral status. What is so special about these grounds that they can confer special status on their possessors? For most of the proposed grounds this issue is not addressed in the literature. However, this issue is addressed extensively by some views that take sophisticated cognitive capacities, especially the capacity for autonomy, to ground FMS, and also by some views that take rudimentary cognitive capacities, such as sentience, to ground some moral status. So these are the views we will briefly summarize here.

Authors working within the Kantian tradition have elaborated and defended various versions of the claim that autonomy, or the capacity to set ends according to reason, is unconditionally valuable and the ultimate condition of value of everything else (see the entry on autonomy in moral and political philosophy, sections 2 and 2.1). Numerous variants of the argument for this claim can be found in the literature, and the most prominent ones take the transcendental form (see the entry on transcendental arguments, section 5). On one version, in rationally choosing or valuing anything at all one must presuppose the supreme value of one's own rational capacities, and, by extension, the supreme value of rational capacities in general (Korsgaard 1996a and 1996b). On this picture, rational agents must recognize the supreme value of rational capacities as a condition of valuing anything else, and this recognition takes the form of affording FMS to beings with rational capacities. This argument has spawned numerous responses from both critics and proponents. For example, Regan (2002) accepts that rational nature has supreme value but extensively criticizes the Kantian interpretation of rational nature as inadequate for that role. For a response on the Kantians' behalf, see Sussman 2003.

On contractualist conceptions of morality, which see morality as originating – under conditions specified variously by different versions of the view – from a hypothetical reciprocal agreement among rational agents (see the entry on contractualism), it is easy to see why those with sufficient cognitive capacity to participate in the requisite agreement would have FMS, since they are the parties to whom the terms of the moral agreement apply. These views also work well to explain why the capacity to reciprocate morally, that is, the capacity to both demand moral status for oneself and to respect the moral status of others by assuming duties and responsibilities, would confer FMS on an individual, since this capacity goes hand-in-hand with the capacity to make reciprocal agreements.

More generally, on views that conceive of morality as at least partly originating from rational agents actively binding, obligating, or imposing authority on one another, it is easy to see why those with sufficient cognitive capacity to impose authority on others would have FMS that others are bound to respect. For example, Quinn (1984) speaks of a "picture of morality as a nexus of independent spheres of authority to permit, forbid, and require" (49) and, because he sees the capacity to will as sufficient for such authority, it is also sufficient for FMS.

Utilitarians and those sympathetic to utilitarian approaches often see the protection and promotion of interests, where this is understood to presuppose consciousness, as the central subject matter of morality (e.g., DeGrazia 1996, p. 39). On such views it is easy to see why the capacity to have interests is crucial to having any moral status at all. On some views, the capacity to experience pleasure or pain (sentience) is a prerequisite of having interests and this explains why sentience is a ground of moral status (Singer 1993, p. 57). Environmentalists, unlike Utilitarians, do not assume consciousness is a necessary condition for having interests and hence use the term in a broader fashion. However, they do not explain why interests, broadly construed in this way, give rise to moral status.

GROUNDS OF MORAL STATUS

4. PATERNALISM

Paternalism is the interference of a state or an individual with another person, against their will, and defended or motivated by a claim that the person interfered with will be better off or protected from harm. The issue of paternalism arises with respect to restrictions by the law such as anti-drug legislation, the compulsory wearing of seatbelts, and in medical contexts by the withholding of relevant information concerning a patient's condition by physicians. At the theoretical level it raises questions of how persons should be treated when they are less than fully rational.

1. Introduction
2. Conceptual Issues
3. Normative Issues

1. Introduction

The government requires people to contribute to a pension system (Social Security). It requires motorcyclists to wear helmets. It forbids people from swimming at a public beach when lifeguards are not present. It forbids the sale of various drugs deemed to be ineffective. It forbids the sale of various drugs believed to be harmful. It does not allow consent to certain forms of assault to be a defense against prosecution for that assault.

The civil law does not allow the enforcement of certain kinds of contracts, e.g. for gambling debts. It requires minors to have blood transfusions even if their religious beliefs forbid it. Persons may be civilly committed if they are a danger to themselves.

Doctors do not tell their patients the truth about their medical condition. A physician may tell the wife of a man whose car went off a bridge into the water and drowned that he died instantly when in fact he died a rather ghastly death.

A husband may hide the sleeping pills from a depressed wife. A philosophy department may require a student to take logic courses.

A teacher may be less than honest about telling a student that he has little philosophical ability.

All of these rules, policies, and actions may be done for various reasons; may be justified by various considerations. When they are justified solely on the grounds that the person affected would be better off, or would be less harmed, as a result of the rule, policy, etc., and the person in question would prefer not to be treated this way, we have an instance of paternalism.

As the examples indicate the question of paternalism is one that arises in many different areas of our personal and public life. As such, it is an important realm of applied ethics. But it also raises certain theoretical issues. Perhaps the most important is: what powers it is legitimate for a state, operating both coercively and in terms of incentives, to possess? It also raises questions about the proper ways in which individuals, either in an institutional or purely personal setting, should relate to one another. How should we think about individual autonomy and its limits? What is it to respect the personhood of others? What is the trade-off, if any, between regard for the welfare of another and respect for their right to make their own decisions?

This entry examines some of the conceptual issues involved in analyzing paternalism, and then discusses the normative issues concerning the legitimacy of paternalism by the state and various civil institutions.

2. Conceptual Issues

The analysis of paternalism involves at least the following elements. It involves some kind of limitation on the freedom or autonomy of some agent and it does so for a particular class of reasons. As with many other concepts used in normative debate determining the exact boundaries of the concept is a contested issue.

And as often is the case the first question is whether the concept itself is normative or descriptive. Is application of the concept a matter for empirical determination, so that if two people disagree about the application to a particular case they are disagreeing about some matter of fact or of definition? Or does their disagreement reflect different views about the legitimacy of the application in question?

While it is clear that for some to characterize a policy as paternalistic is to condemn or criticize it, that does not establish that the term itself is an evaluative one. As a matter of methodology it is preferable to see if some concept can be defined in non-normative terms and only if that fails to capture the relevant phenomena to accept a normative definition.

I suggest the following conditions as an analysis of X acts paternalistically towards Y by doing (omitting) Z:

Z (or its omission) interferes with the liberty or autonomy of Y.
X does so without the consent of Y.
X does so only because X believes Z will improve the welfare of Y (where this includes preventing his welfare from diminishing), or in some way promote the interests, values, or good of Y.
Condition one is the trickiest to capture. Clear cases include threatening bodily compulsion, lying, withholding information that the person has a right to have, or imposing requirements or conditions. But what about the following case? A father, skeptical about the financial acumen of a child, instead of bequeathing the money directly, gives it to another child with instructions to use it in the best interests of the first child. The first child has no legal claim on the inheritance. There does not seem to be an interference with the child's liberty nor on most conceptions the child's autonomy.

Or consider the case of a wife who hides her sleeping pills so that her potentially suicidal husband cannot use them. Her act may satisfy the second and third conditions but what about the first? Does her action limit the liberty or autonomy of her husband?

The second condition is supposed to be read as distinct from acting against the consent of an agent. The agent may neither consent nor not consent. He may, for example, be unaware of what is being done to him. There is also the distinct issue of whether one acts not knowing about the consent of the person in question. Perhaps the person in fact consents but this is not known to the paternaliser.

The third condition also can be complicated. There may be more than one reason for interfering with Y. In addition to concern for the welfare of Y there may be concern for how Y's actions may affect third-parties. Is the "just for" condition too strong? Or what about the case where a legislature passes a legal rule for paternalistic reasons but there are sufficient non-paternalistic reasons to justify passage of the rule?

If, in order to decide on any of the above issues, one must decide a normative issue, e.g. does someone have a right to some information, then the concept is not purely descriptive. Ultimately the question of how to refine the conditions, and what conditions to use, is a matter for philosophical judgment. The term "paternalism" as used in ordinary contexts may be too amorphous for thinking about particular normative issues. One should decide upon an analysis based on a hypothesis of what will be most useful for thinking about a particular range of problems. One might adopt one analysis in the context of doctors and patients and another in the context of whether the state should ban unhealthy foods.

Given some particular analysis of paternalism there will be various normative views about when paternalism is justified. The following terminology is useful.

Hard vs. soft paternalism
Soft paternalism is the view that the only conditions under which state paternalism is justified is when it is necessary to determine whether the person being interfered with is acting voluntarily and knowledgeably. To use Mill's famous example of the person about to walk across a damaged bridge, if we could not communicate the danger (he speaks only Japanese) a soft paternalist would justify forcibly preventing him from

crossing the bridge in order to determine whether he knows about its condition. If he knows, and wants to, say, commit suicide he must be allowed to proceed. A hard paternalist says that, at least sometimes, it may be permissible to prevent him from crossing the bridge even if he knows of its condition. We are entitled to prevent voluntary suicide.

Broad vs. narrow paternalism

A narrow paternalist is only concerned with the question of state coercion, i.e. the use of legal coercion. A broad paternalist is concerned with any paternalistic action: state, institutional (hospital policy), or individual.

Weak vs. strong paternalism

A weak paternalist believes that it is legitimate to interfere with the means that agents choose to achieve their ends, if those means are likely to defeat those ends. So if a person really prefers safety to convenience then it is legitimate to force them to wear seatbelts. A strong paternalist believes that people may have mistaken, confused or irrational ends and it is legitimate to interfere to prevent them from achieving those ends. If a person really prefers the wind rustling through their hair to increased safety it is legitimate to make them wear helmets while motorcycling because their ends are irrational or mistaken. Another way of putting this: we may interfere with mistakes about the facts but not mistakes about values. So if a person tries to jump out of a window believing he will float gently to the ground we may restrain him. If he jumps because he believes that it is important to be spontaneous we may not.

Pure vs. impure paternalism

Suppose we prevent persons from manufacturing cigarettes because we believe they are harmful to consumers. The group we are trying to protect is the group of consumers not manufacturers (who may not be smokers at all). Our reason for interfering with the manufacturer is that he is causing harm to others. Nevertheless the basic justification is paternalist because the consumer consents (assuming the relevant information is available to him) to the harm. It is not like the case where we prevent manufacturers from polluting the air. In pure paternalism the class being protected is identical with the class being interfered with, e.g. preventing swimmers from swimming when lifeguards are not present. In the case of impure paternalism the class of persons interfered with is larger than the class being protected.

Moral vs. welfare paternalism

The usual justification for paternalism refers to the interests of the person being interfered with. These interests are defined in terms of the things that make a person's life go better; in particular their physical and psychological condition. It is things like death or misery or painful emotional states which are in question. Sometimes, however, advocates of state intervention seek to protect the moral welfare of the person. So, for example, it may be argued that prostitutes are better off being prevented from plying their trade even if they make a decent living and their health is protected against disease. They are better off because it is morally corrupting to sell one's sexual services. The interference is justified, therefore, to promote the moral well-being of the person. This then can be called moral paternalism. Still another distinction within moral paternalism is between interferences to improve a person's moral character, and hence her well-being, and interferences to make someone a better person—even if her life does not go better for her as a result.

Finally, it is important to distinguish paternalism, whether welfare or moral, from other ideas used to justify interference with persons; even cases where the interference is not justified in terms of protecting or promoting the interests of others. In particular moral paternalism should be distinguished from legal moralism, i.e. the idea that certain ways of acting are morally wrong or degrading and may be prohibited. So, for example, the barroom "sport" of dwarf tossing (where dwarfs who are paid, and are protected with helmets, etc. participate in contests to see who can throw them furthest) might be thought to be legitimately prohibited. Not because the dwarf is injured in any way, not because the dwarf corrupts himself by agreeing to participate in such activities, but simply because the activity is wrong.

To be sure it is not always easy to distinguish between legal moralism and moral paternalism. If one believes, as Plato does, that acting wrongly damages the soul of the agent, then it will be possible to invoke moral paternalism rather than legal moralism. What is important is that there are two distinct justifications that are possible; one appealing to the mere immorality of the conduct interfered with, the other to the harm done to the agent's character.

3. Normative Issues

Is there a burden of proof attached to paternalism? Does the paternalist or anti-paternalist have to give a reason for their action? As we have seen the analysis of paternalism seems to cut both ways. It is an interference with liberty which might be thought to place the burden of proof on the paternalist. It is an act intended to produce good for the agent which might be thought to place the burden of proof on those who object to paternalism. It might be thought, as Mill did, that the burden of proof is different depending on who is being treated paternalistically. If it is a child then the assumption is that, other things being equal, the burden of proof is on those who resist paternalism. If it is an adult of sound mind the presumption is reversed.

Suppose we start from the presumption that paternalism is wrong. The question becomes under what, if any, circumstances, can the presumption be overcome? The possible answers are "under no circumstances", "under some circumstances", and "under any circumstances"

The last seems very implausible. Essentially it is the view that the fact that an act is (intended to be) beneficial for a person, and does not affect or violate the interests of others, settles the question of whether it may be done. Only a view which ignores the means by which good is promoted, and the ethical status of such means, can hold this. Any sensible view has to distinguish between good done to agents at their request or with their consent, and good thrust upon them against their will.

So the normative options seem to be just two. Either we are never permitted to aim at doing good for others against their wishes, and in ways which limit their liberty, or we are permitted to do so.

Why might one think that at least the state may never do so? One might think so because of various beliefs about the impossibility of in fact doing good for people against their will or because one thinks that although possible to do good it is in fact inconsistent with some normative standard which ought to prevail.

With respect to the impossibility question one might believe either that it is not possible to do any good by acting paternalistically or that although it is possible to do some good the process will (almost) always produce bads which outweigh the good.

If one thought that (almost) always more harm than good is done by the state when it acts paternalistically this raises the question of whether we can distinguish the conditions in which (rarely) more good than harm is done and build that into our guidelines. If this is possible, and allowing paternalism in these exceptional cases does not create further harms which outweigh the good produced, then we should sometimes be paternalists. If it is impossible to distinguish the "good" from the "bad" cases then, at least if we are rule consequentialists, we ought not to have such a rule; and we ought not to try and make the distinctions on a case by case basis.

But one might believe that the question of whether more good than harm is produced is not simply an empirical one. It depends on our understanding of the good of persons. If the good simply included items such as longer life, greater health, more income, or less depression, then it makes it look like an empirical issue. But if we conceive of the good of individuals as including items such as being respected as an independent agent, having a right to make decisions for oneself, or having one's autonomy not infringed, then the issue of whether the agent is better off after being paternalised is partly a normative matter. One might believe that one cannot make people better off by infringing their autonomy in the same way that some people believe one cannot make a person better off by putting them in a Nozickian experience machine (one in which they are floating in a tank but seem to be having all kinds of wonderful experiences). Compare Mill's statement that "...a man's mode of laying out his own existence is best not because it is the best in itself, but because it is his own mode..." (1859, Chapter III).

Kantian views are frequently absolutistic in their objections to paternalism. On these views we must always respect the rational agency of other persons. To deny an adult the right to make their own decisions, however mistaken from some standpoint they are, is to treat them as simply means to their own good, rather than as ends in themselves. In a way anti-paternalism is already incorporated into Kantian theories by their prohibition against lying and force—the main instruments of paternalistic interference. Since these instrumentalities are already denied even to prevent individuals from harming others, they will certainly be forbidden to prevent them from harming themselves. Of course, one may object to the former absolutism while accepting the latter.

If one believes that sometimes paternalism is justifiable one may do so for various kinds of theoretical reasons. The broadest is simply consequentialist, i.e. more good than harm is produced. A narrower justification is that sometimes the individual's (long-run) autonomy is advanced by restricting his autonomy (short-run). So one might prevent people from taking mind-destroying drugs on the grounds that allowing them to do so destroys their autonomy and preventing them from doing so preserves it. This is essentially Mill's argument against allowing people to contract into slavery. Note that if the theory of the good associated with a particular consequentialism is broad enough, i.e., includes autonomy as one of the goods, it can be equivalent to the autonomy theory (assuming that the structure of the autonomy view is a maximizing one).

A different theoretical basis is (moral) contractualism. On this view if there are cases of justified paternalism they are justified on the basis that we (all of us) would agree to such interference, given suitable knowledge and suitable motivation. So, for instance, it might be argued that since we know we are subject to depression we all would agree, at least, to short-term anti-suicide interventions, to determine whether we are suffering from such a condition, and to attempt to cure it. More generally, we might accept what Feinberg called "soft paternalism." This is the view that when we are not acting fully voluntarily it is permissible to intervene to provide information, or to point out defects in our rationality, but that if we then do make a voluntary choice it must be respected. Or we might agree to being forced to wear seat-belts knowing our disposition to discount future benefits for present ones. The justification here is neither consequentialist nor based simply on the preservation of autonomy. Rather either kind of consideration may be taken into account, as well as others, in determining what we would reasonably agree to.

In recent years there has been a new strand of thought about paternalistic interferences. It has been referred to as New Paternalism or Libertarian Paternalism. It is influenced by research in the behavioral sciences on the many ways in which our cognitive and affective capacities are flawed and limited.

The first theorists to emphasize these findings were the Nudgers – Cass Sunstein and Richard Thaler (2003). They argued that since people were such bad decision makers we should nudge them in the direction of their own desired goals by orchestrating their choices so that they were more likely to do what achieves their ends. By making employment retirement plans opt-out rather than opt-in employees would be more likely to enroll in such programs. By putting the healthy food at eye level, and the bad stuff at a lower level, kids in the school cafeteria would be more likely to choose the healthy stuff. Each year when employees have to choose how much to contribute to their supplementary retirement plan instead of making the default option zero, make it the same amount as the previous year.

The claim is that unlike traditional paternalism which rules out choices by compulsion or adds costs to the choices by coercion nudges simply change the presentation of the choices in such a way that people were more likely to choose options that are best for them. In addition they argue that any arrangement of choices will make some choices more or less likely so that some decision about the choice architecture is inevitable.

A number of issues arise with respect to this new movement. The first is a matter of nomenclature, Why should the recommended actions be thought of as paternalistic at all? The fact they are motivated by a belief that agents are not choosing wisely, and that by acting in certain ways we can can improve the quality of their choices is not sufficient on traditional conceptions of paternalism to fall under that term. One can improve people's choices by providing them with information, by giving them good arguments, by providing them with additional incentives. Normally these are the contrast class to paternalistic acts. Why should re-arranging the location of food be regarded any differently?

Of course the crucial issues are normative not what word we use. Does nudging raise similar moral objections to those raised to coercion and deception when used to promote welfare? Defenders of nudging are aware that certain methods of influence raise questions of legitimacy, e.g. subliminal messaging. They agree that such methods should be avoided on the grounds that they are not transparent and would be self-defeating if publicly advocated. The critical issues are (1) whether nudges are manipulative, and (2) whether that feature makes them normatively objectionable.

The intuitive idea of manipulation is that rather than interfering with the choices of an agent one interferes with the decision-making capacities of the agent. Manipulation involves distorting the way that agents reach decisions, form preferences, and select goals. But only certain ways of doing this count as manipulative. Coercion, for example, is not usually counted as manipulative. But deception does. And so do playing on people's emotions, or weakness of character. Whether nudges fall into the manipulative category has to be argued. If nudges are manipulative then they may be infringements of autonomy which is the main objection that has been directed at the "old" paternalism.

PARTENALISM

5. AUTONOMY IN MORAL AND POLITICAL PHILOSOPHY

Individual autonomy is an idea that is generally understood to refer to the capacity to be one's own person, to live one's life according to reasons and motives that are taken as one's own and not the product of manipulative or distorting external forces. It is a central value in the Kantian tradition of moral philosophy but it is also given fundamental status in John Stuart Mill's version of utilitarian liberalism (Kant 1785/1983, Mill 1859/1975, ch. III). Examination of the concept of autonomy also figures centrally in debates over education policy, biomedical ethics, various legal freedoms and rights (such as freedom of speech and the right to privacy), as well as moral and political theory more broadly. In the realm of moral theory, seeing autonomy as a central value can be contrasted with alternative frameworks such an ethic of care, utilitarianism of some kinds, and an ethic of virtue. Autonomy has traditionally been thought to connote independence and hence to reflect assumptions of individualism in both moral thinking and political designations of political status. In recent decades, however, theorists have increasingly tried to structure the concept so as to sever its ties to this brand of individualism. In all such discussions the concept of autonomy is the focus of much controversy and debate, disputes which focus attention on the fundamentals of moral and political philosophy and the Enlightenment conception of the person more generally.

1. The Concept of Autonomy

AUTONOMY

1. The Concept of Autonomy

In the western tradition, the view that individual autonomy is a basic moral and political value is very much a modern development. Putting moral weight on an individual's ability to govern herself, independent of her place in a metaphysical order or her role in social structures and political institutions is very much the product of the modernist humanism of which much contemporary moral and political philosophy is an offshoot. (For historical discussions of autonomy, see Schneewind 1988, Lindley 1986, Part I). As such, it bears the weight of the controversies that this legacy has attracted. The idea that moral principles and obligations, as well as the legitimacy of political authority, should be grounded in the self-governing individual, considered apart from various contingencies of place, culture, and social relations, invites skeptics from several quarters. Autonomy, then, is very much at the vortex of the complex (re)consideration of modernity.

Put most simply, to be autonomous is to be one's own person, to be directed by considerations, desires, conditions, and characteristics that are not simply imposed externally upon one, but are part of what can somehow be considered one's authentic self. Autonomy in this sense seems an irrefutable value, especially since its opposite — being guided by forces external to the self and which one cannot authentically embrace — seems to mark the height of oppression. But specifying more precisely the conditions of autonomy inevitably sparks controversy and invites skepticism about the claim that autonomy is an unqualified value for all individuals.

Autonomy plays various roles in theoretical accounts of persons, conceptions of moral obligation and responsibility, the justification of social policies and in numerous aspects of political theory. It forms the core of the Kantian conception of practical reason (see, e.g, Korsgaard 1996, Hill 1989) and, relatedly, connects to questions of moral responsibility (see Wolff 1970, 12–19). It is also seen as the aspect of persons that prevents or ought to prevent paternalistic interventions in their lives (Dworkin 1988, 121–29). It plays a role in education theory and policy, on some views specifying the core goal of liberal education generally (Gutmann 1987, Cuypers and Ishtiyaque 2008; for discussion, see Brighouse 2000, 65–111). Also, despite many feminists' reservations concerning the ideal of autonomy, it is sometimes seen as a valuable conceptual element in some feminist ideals, such as the identification and elimination of social conditions that victimize women and other (potentially) vulnerable people (Friedman 1997, Meyers 1987, Christman 1995).

1.1 Basic Distinctions
Several distinctions must be made to zero in on the kind of autonomy that is of greatest interest to moral and political theory. "Moral autonomy" refers to the capacity to impose the (putatively objective) moral law on oneself, and, following Kant, it is claimed as a fundamental organizing principle of all morality (Hill 1989). On the other hand, what can be called "personal autonomy" is meant as a trait that individuals can exhibit relative to any aspects of their lives, not limited to questions of moral obligation (Dworkin 1988, 34–47).

Personal (or individual) autonomy should also be distinguished from freedom, although again, there are many renderings of these concepts, and certainly some conceptions of positive freedom will be equivalent to what is often meant by autonomy (Berlin 1969, 131–34). Generally, one can distinguish autonomy from freedom in that the latter concerns the ability to act, without external or internal constraints and also (on some conceptions) with sufficient resources and power to make one's desires effective (Berlin 1969, Crocker 1980, MacCallum 1967). Autonomy concerns the independence and authenticity of the desires (values, emotions, etc.) that move one to act in the first place. Some distinguish autonomy from freedom by insisting that freedom concerns particular acts while autonomy is a more global notion, referring to states of a person (Dworkin 1988, 13–15, 19–20). But autonomy can be used to refer both to the global condition (autonomous personhood) and as a more local notion (autonomous relative to a particular trait, motive, value, or social condition). Addicted smokers for example are autonomous persons in a general sense but (for some) helplessly unable to control their behavior regarding this one activity (Christman 1989, 13–14).

In addition, we must keep separate the idea of basic autonomy, the minimal status of being responsible, independent and able to speak for oneself, from ideal autonomy, an achievement that serves as a goal to which we might aspire and according to which a person is maximally authentic and free of manipulative, self-distorting influences. Any plausible conceptualization of basic autonomy must, among other things, imply that most adults who are not suffering from debilitating pathologies or are under oppressive and constricting conditions count as autonomous. Autonomy as an ideal, on the other hand, may well be enjoyed by very few if any individuals, for it functions as a goal to be attained.

The reason to construe basic autonomy broadly enough to include most adults is that autonomy connects with other status designators which apply (or, it is claimed, should apply) in this sweeping manner. Autonomy is connected, for example, to moral and legal responsibility, on some views (e.g., Ripstein 1999); it is considered a criterion of political status, in that autonomous agency is seen as necessary (and for some sufficient) for the condition of equal political standing; moreover, being autonomous stands as a barrier to unchecked paternalism, both in the personal, informal spheres and in legal arenas (Feinberg 1986). Lacking autonomy, as young children do, is a condition which allows or invites sympathy, care, paternalism and possibly pity. Therefore, a guiding consideration in evaluating particular conceptions of autonomy (though hardly a hard and fast test) will be whether it connects properly to these ancillary judgments (for discussion of "formal conditions" of a concept of autonomy, see Dworkin 1988, 7–10).

1.2 Conceptual Variations

The variety of contexts in which the concept of autonomy functions has suggested to many that there are simply a number of different conceptions, and that the word simply refers to different elements in each of those contexts (Arpaly 2004). Feinberg has claimed that there are at least four different meanings of "autonomy" in moral and political philosophy: the capacity to govern oneself, the actual condition of self-government, a personal ideal, and a set of rights expressive of one's sovereignty over oneself (Feinberg 1989). One might argue that central to all of these uses is a conception of the person able to act, reflect, and choose on the basis of factors that are somehow her own (authentic in some sense). Nevertheless, it is clear that formulating a "theory" of the concept will involve more than merely uncovering the obscure details of the idea's essence, for autonomy, like many concepts central to contentious moral or political debate is itself essentially contested. So a theory of autonomy is simply a construction of a concept aimed at capturing the general sense of "self-rule" or "self-government" (ideas which obviously admit of their own vagaries) and which can be used to support principles or policies the theory attempts to justify.

The idea of self-rule contains two components: the independence of one's deliberation and choice from manipulation by others, and the capacity to rule oneself (see Dworkin 1989, 61f and Arneson 1991). However, the ability to rule oneself will lie at the core of the concept, since a full account of that capability will surely entail the freedom from external manipulation characteristic of independence. Indeed, it could be claimed that independence per se has no fixed meaning or necessary connection with self-government unless we know what kinds of independence is required for self-rule (cf., however Raz 1986, 373-78).

Focusing, then, on the requirements of self rule, it can be claimed that to govern oneself one must be in a position to act competently based on desires (values, conditions, etc.) that are in some sense one's own. This picks out the two families of conditions often proffered in conceptions of autonomy: competency conditions and authenticity conditions. Competency includes various capacities for rational thought, self-control, and freedom from debilitating pathologies, systematic self-deception, and so on. (Different accounts include different conditions: see, for example, Berofsky 1995, R. Young 1991, Haworth 1986, Meyers 1989.)

Authenticity conditions often include the capacity to reflect upon and endorse (or identify with) one's desires, values, and so on. The most influential models of authenticity in this vein claim that autonomy requires second-order identification with first order desires. For Frankfurt, for instance, such second-order desires must actually have the structure of a volition: wanting that the first order desires issue in action, that they comprise one's will. Moreover, such identification, on his view, must be "wholehearted" for the resulting action to count as free (autonomous).[1]

This overall approach to autonomy has been very influential, and several writers have developed variations of it and defended it against objections. The most prominent objections concern, on the one hand, the fatal ambiguities of the concept of "identification" and, on the other, the threat of an infinite regress of conditions. The first problem surrounds the different ways that one can be said to "identify" with a desire, each of which render the view conceptually suspect. Either one identifies with an aspect of oneself in the sense of simply acknowledging it (without judgment) or one identifies with a desire in an aspirational, approving sense of that term. In the first case, however, identification would clearly not be a consistent mark of autonomy, for one could easily identify as part of oneself any manner of addictive, constricting, or imposed aspects of one's make-up. But approving of a trait is also problematic as a requirement of autonomy, for there are many perfectly authentic aspects of myself (ones for which I can and should be held fully responsible for example) which I do not fully approve of. I'm not perfect, but does that mean that I am thereby not autonomous? (Cf. Watson 1989, Berofsky 1995, 99–102).[2]

This model stresses internal self-reflection and procedural independence. However, the view includes no stipulations about the content of the desires, values, and so on, in virtue of which one is considered autonomous, specifically there is no requirement that one act from desires independently of others. Were there to be such a requirement, it would involve what is called "substantive independence". Some writers have insisted that the autonomous person must enjoy substantive independence as well as procedural independence (e.g., Stoljar 2000, Benson 1987, 2005, Oshana 2006). The motivation for such a position is that autonomy should not be understood as consistent with certain constrained life situations no matter how the person came to choose such a situation (cf. Meyers 2000). This claim, however, threatens to rob the attribution of autonomy of any claim to value neutrality it may otherwise carry, for if, conceptually, one is not autonomous when one (freely, rationally, without manipulation) chooses to enter conditions of severely limited choice, then the concept is reserved to only those lifestyles and value pursuits that are seen as acceptable from a particular political or theoretical point of view. I will return to this line of thought in a moment.

One variation on the internal self-reflection model focuses on the importance of the personal history of the agent as an element of her autonomy (Christman 1991, Mele 1993; cf. Fisher & Ravizza 1998; cf. also Raz 1986, 371). On these views, the question of whether a person is autonomous at a time depends on the processes by which she came to be the way she is. It is not clear that such a focus will be able to avoid the problems raised about internal reflection models (see Mele 1991, Mackenzie & Stoljar 2000b, 16–17), but such a move attempts to embrace a conception of the self of self-government which is not only social but diachronically structured (see, e.g., Atkins 2008, Cuypers 2001).

For those who are wary of the postulate of reflective self endorsement, an alternative approach is to equate autonomy with simply a set of competences, such as the capacity to choose deliberatively, rationally, and, as Berofsky claims, "objectively" (see Berofsky 1995, Meyers 1989). This locates autonomy in the general capacity to respond to reasons, and not, for example, in acts of internal self-identification. However, even in these accounts, the capacity to think critically and reflectively is necessary for autonomy as one of the competences in question, even though the reflective thought required need not refer to external values or ideals (Berofsky 1995, ch. 5).

Further difficulties have been raised with the requirement of second order self-appraisal for autonomy. For it is unclear that such higher level judgments have any greater claim to authenticity than their first order cousins. Clearly if a person is manipulated or oppressed (and hence non-autonomous), it could well be that the reflective judgments she makes about herself are just as tainted by that oppression as are her ground-level decisions (Thalberg 1989, Friedman 1986, Meyers 1989, 25–41, Noggle 2005), and often our second order reflective voices are merely rationalizations and acts of self-deception rather than true and settled aspects of our character (for general discussion see the essays in Veltman and Piper 2014). This has led to the charge that models of autonomy which demand second-order endorsement merely introduce an infinite regress: for second-level judgments must be tested for their authenticity in the same way as first order desires are, but if that is so, then ever higher levels of endorsement would be called for. Various responses to this problem have been made, for the most part involving the addition of conditions concerning the manner in which such reflection must be made, for example that it must be free of certain distorting factors itself, it must reflect an adequate causal history, and the like (Christman 1991, Mele 1995).

Other aspects of the inner reflection model should be noted. As just mentioned, this view of autonomy is often stated as requiring critical self reflection (see, e.g., Haworth 1986). This has been understood as involving a rational appraisal of one's desires, testing them for internal consistency, their relation to reliable beliefs, and the like. But an overly narrow concentration on rational assessment exposes such conceptions to charges of hyper intellectualism, painting a picture of the autonomous person as a cold, detached calculator (see Meyers 2004, 111–37). Connections to values, desires, and personal traits are often grounded in emotional and affective responses, ones connected with care, commitment, and relations to others (see Friedman 1998, MacKenzie & Stoljar 2000b, Meyers 1989). For parallel reasons, some theorists have noted that concentration on only desires as the focal point of autonomy is overly narrow, as people can (fail to) exhibit self-government relative to a wide range of personal characteristics, such as values, physical traits, relations to others, and so on (see Double 1992, 66).

2. Autonomy in Moral Philosophy
Autonomy is central in certain moral frameworks, both as a model of the moral person — the feature of the person by virtue of which she is morally obligated — and as the aspect of persons which ground others' obligations to her or him. For Kant, the self-imposition of universal moral law is the ground of both moral obligation generally and the respect others owe to us (and we owe ourselves). In short, practical reason — our ability to use reasons to choose our own actions — presupposes that we understand ourselves as free. Freedom means lacking barriers to our action that are in any way external to our will, though it also requires that we utilize a law to guide our decisions, a law that can come to us only by an act of our own will (for further discussion see Hill 1989). This self-imposition of the moral law is autonomy. And since this law must have no content provided by sense or desire, or any other contingent aspect of our situation, it must be universal. Hence we have the (first formulation of the)

Categorical Imperative, that by virtue of our being autonomous we must act only on those maxims that we can consistently will as a universal law.

The story continues, however: for the claim is that this capacity (to impose upon ourselves the moral law) is the ultimate source of all moral value — for to value anything (instrumentally or intrinsically) implies the ability to make value judgments generally, the most fundamental of which is the determination of what is morally valuable. Some theorists who are not (self-described) Kantians have made this inference central to their views of autonomy. Paul Benson, for example, has argued that being autonomous implies a measure of self-worth in that we must be in a position to trust our decision-making capacities to put ourselves in a position of responsibility (Benson 1994; cf. also Grovier 1993, Lehrer 1997, and Westlund 2014). But the Kantian position is that such self-regard is not a contingent psychological fact about us, but an unavoidable implication of the exercise of practical reason (cf. Taylor 2005).

So we owe to ourselves moral respect in virtue of our autonomy. But insofar as this capacity depends in no way on anything particular or contingent about ourselves, we owe similar respect to all other persons in virtue of their capacity. Hence (via the second formulation of the Categorical Imperative), we are obliged to act out of fundamental respect for other persons in virtue of their autonomy. In this way, autonomy serves as both a model of practical reason in the determination of moral obligation and as the feature of other persons deserving moral respect from us. (For further discussion, see Immanual Kant and moral philosophy.)

Recent discussions of Kantian autonomy have downplayed the transcendental nature of practical reason in this account (see, for example, Herman 1993 and Hill 1991). For example, Christine Korsgaard follows Kant in seeing our capacity for self-reflection as both the object of respect and the seat of normativity generally. On her view, we are all guided by what she calls a "practical identity", a point of view which orients reflection on values and manifests an aspect of our self concept. But unlike Kant, Korsgaard argues that we have different practical identities that are the source of our normative commitments, and not all of them are of fundamental moral worth. But the most general of such identities — that which makes us members of a kingdom of ends — is our moral identity, which yields universal duties and obligations independent of contingent factors. Autonomy is the source of all obligations, whether moral or non-moral, since it is the capacity to impose upon ourselves, by virtue of our practical identities, obligations to act (Korsgaard 1996).

Traditional critiques of autonomy-based moral views, and Kant's in particular, have been mounted along various lines. I mention two here, as they connect with issues concerning autonomy in social and political theory. The first concerns the way in which autonomy-based moral theory grounds obligation in our cognitive abilities rather than in our emotions and affective connections (see, e.g., Williams 1985, Stocker 1976). The claim is that Kantian morality leaves too little room for the kinds of emotional reactions that are constitutive of moral response in many situations: the obligations of parents for example concern not only what they do but the passions and care they bring forth in doing it. To view obligation as arising from autonomy but understanding autonomy in a purely cognitive manner makes such an account vulnerable to this kind of charge.

The difficulty this criticism points to resides in the ambiguities of the self-description that we might utilize in valuing our "humanity" — our capacity to obligate ourselves. For we can reflect upon our decision-making capacities and value this positively (and fundamentally) but regard that "self" engaging the capacity in different ways. The Kantian model of such a self is of a pure cognizer — a reflective agent engaged in practical reason. But also involved in decision-making are our passions — emotions, desires, felt commitments, senses of attraction and aversion, alienation and comfort. These are both the objects of our judgement and partly constitutive of them — to passionately embrace an option is different from cooly determining it to be best. Judgment is involved with all such passions when decisions are made. And it (judgment) need not be understood apart from them, but as an ability to engage in those actions whose passionate and reasoned support we muster up. So when the optimal decision for me is an impassioned one, I must value my ability to engage in the right passions, not merely in the ability to cold-heartedly reflect and choose. Putting the passions outside the scope of reasoned reflection, as merely an ancillary quality of the action — to consider how to do something not merely what we are doing — is to make one kind of decision. Putting passions inside that scope — saying that what it is right to do now is to act with a certain affect or passion — is another. When we generalize from our ability to make the latter sort of decisions, we must value not only the ability to weigh options and universalize them but also the ability to engage the right affect, emotion, etc. Therefore, we value ourselves and others as passionate reasoners not merely reasoners per se.

The implications of this observation is that in generalizing our judgments in the manner Korsgaard (following Kant) says we must, we need not commit ourselves to valuing only the cognitive capacities of humanity but also its (relatively) subjective elements. This directly relates to the nature of autonomy, for the question of whether moral obligation rests upon and contains affective elements depends on the conception of autonomy at work and whether affective elements are included in the types of reflective judgments that form its core.

A second question is this: since the reflection that is involved in autonomy (and which, according to this view, is the source of normativity) need only be hypothetical reflection upon one's desires and mental capacities, then the question arises: under what conditions is this hypothetical reflection meant to take place? If the capacity for reflection is the seat of obligation, then we must ask if the conditions under which such hypothetical reflection takes place are idealized in any sense — if they are assumed to be reasonable for example. Are we considering merely the reflections the (actual) person would make were she to turn her attention to the question, no matter how unreasonable such reflections might be? If so, why should we think this grounds obligations? If we assume they are reasonable, then under some conditions moral obligations are not imposed by the actual self but rather by an idealized, more rational self. This implies that morality is not literally self-imposed if by "self" one means the actual set of judgments made by the agent in question. Indeed, a Platonist/realist about moral value could claim that the objective values which (according to the theory) apply to all agents independent of choice are in fact "self-imposed" in this idealized sense: they would be imposed were the person to reflect on the matter, acting as a perfectly reasonable agent. This shows the complex and potentially problematic implications of this ambiguity.

This points to the question of whether autonomy can be the seat of moral obligation and respect if autonomy is conceived in a purely procedural manner. If no substantive commitments or value orientations are included in the conceptual specification of autonomy, then it is unclear how this capacity grounds any particular substantive value commitments. On the other hand, if autonomy includes a specification of particular values in its conditions — that the autonomous person must value her own freedom for example — then it turns out that moral obligation (and respect) attaches only to those already committed in this way, and not more generally to all rational agents as such (as traditionally advertised by the view). This echoes, of course, Hegel's critique of Kant.

These difficulties point to ambiguities in autonomy-based moral views, ones which may well be clarified in further developments of those theories. They also pick up on traditional problems with Kantian ethics (though there are many other such difficulties not mentioned here). Before leaving moral philosophy, we should consider ethical views which focus on autonomy but which do not depend directly on a Kantian framework.

2.1 Autonomy as an Object of Value
Autonomy can play a role in moral theory without that theory being fully Kantian in structure. For example, it is possible to argue that personal autonomy has intrinsic value independent of

a fully worked out view of practical reason. Following John Stuart Mill, for example, one can claim that autonomy is "one of the elements of well-being" (Mill 1859/1975, ch. III). Viewing autonomy as an intrinsic value or as a constitutive element in personal well-being in this way opens the door to a generally consequentialist moral framework while paying heed to the importance of self-government to a fulfilling life (for discussion see Sumner 1996).

It may also be unclear why autonomy — viewed here as the capacity to reflect on and endorse one's values, character and commitments — should have value independent of the results of exercising that capacity. Why is one person's autonomy intrinsically valuable when she uses it to, say, harm herself or make rash or morally skewed choices? More generally, how can we take account of the systematic biases and distortions that plague typical human reasoning in valuing people's capacity to make decisions for themselves (see, e.g., Conly 2013)? This question becomes more acute as we consider ways that autonomy can obtain in degrees, for then it is unclear why personal autonomy should be seen as equally valuable in persons who display different levels of it (or different levels of those abilities that are its conditions, such as rationality).

Indeed, autonomy is often cited as the ground of treating all individuals equally from a moral point of view. But if autonomy is not an all-or-nothing characteristic, this commitment to moral equality becomes problematic (Arneson 1999). It can be argued that insofar as the abilities required for autonomy, such as rational reflectiveness, competences in carrying out one's decisions, and the like, vary across individuals (within or between species as well), then it is difficult to maintain that all autonomous beings have equal moral status or that their interests deserve the same weight in considering decisions that affect them.

The move that must be made here, I think, picks up on Korsgaard's gloss on Kantianism and the argument that our reflective capacities ultimately ground our obligations to others and, in turn, others' obligations to regard us as moral equals. Arneson argues, however, that people surely vary in this capacity as well — the ability to reflectively consider options and choose sensibly from among them. Recall what we said above concerning the ambiguities of Korsgaard's account concerning the degree to which the self-reflection that grounds obligation is idealized at all. If it is, then it is not the everyday capacity to look within ourselves and make a choice that gives us moral status but the more rarified ability to do so rationally, in some full sense. But we surely vary in our ability to reach that ideal, so why should our autonomy be regarded as equally worthy?

The answer may be that our normative commitments do not arise from our actual capacities to reflect and to choose (though we must have such capacities to some minimal degree), but rather from the way in which we must view ourselves as having these capacities. We give special weight to our own present and past decisions, so that we continue on with projects and plans we make because (all other things being equal) we made them, they are ours, at least when we do them after some reflective deliberation. The pull that our own decisions have on our ongoing projects and actions can only be explained by the assumption that we confer status and value on decisions simply because we reflectively made them (perhaps, though, in light of external, objective considerations). This is an all-or-nothing capacity and hence may be enough to ground our equal status even if perhaps, in real life, we exercise this capacity to varying degrees.[3] Much has been written about conceptions of well being that rehearse these worries (see Sumner 1996, Griffin 1988). Such a view might be buttressed with the idea that the attribution of autonomous agency, and the respect that purportedly goes with it, is itself a normative stance, not a mere observation of how a person actually thinks and acts (for discussion of this position see Christman 2005 and Korsgaard 2014)

2.2 Autonomy and Paternalism
Autonomy is the aspect of persons that undue paternalism offends against. Paternalistic interventions can be both

interpersonal (governed by social and moral norms) and a matter of policy (mediated by formal or legal rules). Such interventions are identified not by the kind of acts they involve but by the justification given for them, so that paternalism involves interference with a person's actions or knowledge against that person's will for the purpose of advancing that person's good. Respect for autonomy is meant to prohibit such interventions because they involve a judgment that the person is not able to decide for herself how best to pursue her own good. Autonomy is the ability to so decide, so for the autonomous subject of such interventions paternalism involves a lack of respect for autonomy. See also Paternalism.

But as our discussion of the nature of autonomy indicated, it is often unclear exactly what that characteristic involves. Important in this context is whether autonomy can be manifested in degrees — whether the abilities and capacities that constitute autonomy obtain all at once or progressively. If the latter is the case, then it is unclear that a blanket prohibition against paternalism is warranted. Some people will be less able to judge for themselves what their own good is and hence be more susceptible to (justified) paternalistic intervention (Conly 2013).

Often such an obligation toward another person requires us to treat her as autonomous, independent of the extent to which she is so concerning the choice in question. At least this is the case when a person is autonomous above a certain threshold: she is an adult, not under the influence of debilitating factors, and so on. I might know that a person is to some degree under the sway of external pressures that are severely limiting her ability to govern her life and make independent choices. But as long as she has not lost the basic ability to reflectively consider her options and make choices, if I intervene against her will (for her own good), I show less respect for her as a person than if I allow her to make her own mistakes. (Which is not to say, of course, that intervention in such cases might not, in the end, be justified; only that something is lost when it is engaged in, and what is lost is a degree of interpersonal respect we owe each other.)

However, as we saw in the last section, this move depends on the determination of basic autonomy and an argument that such a threshold is non-arbitrary. Also relevant here is the question of procedural versus substantive autonomy as the ground of the prohibition of paternalism. For if by "autonomy" we mean the ability to govern oneself no matter how depraved or morally worthless are the options being exercised, it is unclear that the bar to paternalism (and respect for persons generally) retains its normative force. As I mentioned above, the response to this challenge must be that the decision making capacity itself is of non-derivative value, independent of the content of those decisions, at least if one wishes to avoid the difficulties of positing a substantive (and hence non-neutral) conception of autonomy as the basis for interpersonal respect.

This is merely a sampling of some of the central ways that the idea of autonomy figures in moral philosophy. Not discussed here are areas of applied ethics, for example in medical ethics, where respect for autonomy grounds such principles as that of informed consent. Such contexts illustrate the fundamental value that autonomy generally is thought to represent as expressive of one of the fundamentals of moral personhood.

3. Autonomy in Social and Political Philosophy
3.1 Autonomy and the Foundations of Liberalism
The conception of the autonomous person plays a variety of roles in various constructions of liberal political theory (for recent discussion, see, e.g., Coburn 2010 and the essays in Christman and Anderson, eds. 2005). Principally, it serves as the model of the person whose perspective is used to formulate and justify political principles, as in social contract models of principles of justice (Rawls 1971). Also (and correspondingly) it serves as the model of the citizen whose basic interests are reflected in those principles, such as in the claim that basic liberties, opportunities, and other primary goods are fundamental to flourishing lives no matter what moral commitments, life plans, or other particulars of the person might obtain (Kymlicka 1989, 10–19, Waldron 1993: 155–6).[4] Moreover, autonomy is ascribed to persons (or projected as an ideal) in order to delineate and critique

oppressive social conditions, liberation from which is considered a fundamental goal of justice (whether or not those critiques are described as within the liberal tradition or as a specific alternative to it) (cf. Keornahan 1999, Cornell 1998, Young 1990, Gould 1988; cf. also Hirschmann 2002, 1–29).

For our purposes here, liberalism refers generally to that approach to political power and social justice that determines principles of right (justice) prior to, and largely independent of, determination of conceptions of the good (though see Liberalism; see also Christman 2002, ch. 4). This implies that the liberal conception of justice, and the legitimation of political power more generally, can be specified and justified without crucial reference to controversial conceptions of value and moral principles (what Rawls calls "comprehensive moral conceptions" (Rawls 1993, 13–15). The fact of permanent pluralism of such moral conceptions is therefore central to liberalism.[5]

One manner in which debates concerning autonomy directly connect to controversies within and about liberalism concerns the role that state neutrality is to play in the justification and application of principles of justice. Neutrality is a controversial standard, of course, and the precise way in which liberal theory is committed to a requirement of neutrality is complex and controversial (see Raz 1986, 110–64, Waldron 1993, 143–67). The question to be asked here is whether the conception of autonomy utilized in liberal theories must itself attempt to be neutral concerning various conceptions of morality and value, or, alternatively, does the reliance on autonomy in the justification and specification of liberal theories of justice render them non-neutral simply because of this reliance (no matter how "neutral" the conception of autonomy utilized turns out to be).

Let us consider this first question and in so doing revisit the issue of whether the independence implicit in autonomy should best be conceived in a purely "procedural" manner or more substantively. Recall that some theorists view autonomy as requiring minimal competence (or rationality) along with authenticity, where the latter condition is fleshed out in terms of the capacity to reflectively endorse (or not be alienated from) aspects of oneself. This view can be called "proceduralist" because it demands that the procedure by which a person comes to identify a desire (or trait) as her own is what is crucial in the determination of its authenticity and hence autonomy. This conception of autonomy is adopted, according to its defenders, because doing so is the only way to ensure that autonomy is neutral toward all conceptions of value and the good that reasonable adults may come to internalize (Dworkin 1989).

Critics of this view have pointed to cases where it is imagined that persons adopt what we all would call oppressive and overly restrictive life situations but in a way that meets the minimal conditions of autonomy on proceduralist accounts, so that on such accounts they count as autonomous because of the self-governing processes by which they entered such oppressive conditions. These critics argue that any conception of autonomy that ascribes that trait to such people is wrongly conceived (Benson 1987, MacKenzie & Stoljar 2001b, Waller 1993, Oshana 1998, Stoljar 2000). On the basis of such a judgment, they argue that normatively substantive conditions should be added to the requirements of autonomy, conditions such as the ability to recognize and follow certain moral or political norms (See Benson 1987, Wolf 1980; for criticism, see Berofsky 1995, ch. 7). This criticism suggests that considerations concerning the autonomous self cannot avoid questions of identity and hence whether the self of self-government can be understood independently of the (perhaps socially defined) values in terms of which people conceive of themselves; this is a subject to which we now turn.

3.2 Identity and Conceptions of the Self

Autonomy, as we have been describing it, certainly attaches paradigmatically to individual persons; it is not (in this usage) a property of groups or peoples. So the autonomy that grounds basic rights and which connects to moral responsibility, as this concept is thought to do, is assigned to persons without essential reference to other people, institutions, or traditions within which they may live and act. Critics claim, however, that such a view runs counter to the manner in which most of us (or all of us in some ways) define ourselves, and hence diverges problematically from the aspects of identity that motivate action, ground moral commitments, and by which people formulate life plans. Autonomy, it is argued, implies the ability to reflect wholly on oneself, to accept or reject one's values, connections, and self-defining features, and change such elements of one's life at will. But we are all not only deeply enmeshed in social relations and cultural patterns, we are also defined by such relations, some claim(Sandel 1982, 15–65). For example, we use language to engage in reflection but language is itself a social product and deeply tied to various cultural forms. In any number of ways we are constituted by factors that lie beyond our reflective control but which nonetheless structure our values, thoughts, and motivations (Taylor 1991, 33f; for discussion see Bell 1993, 24–54). To say that we are autonomous (and hence morally responsible, bear moral rights, etc.) only when we can step back from all such connections and critically appraise and possibly alter them flies in the face of these psychological and metaphysical realities.[6]

In a different manner, critics have claimed that the liberal conception of the person, reflected in standard models of autonomy, under-emphasizes the deep identity-constituting connections we have with gender, race, culture, and religion, among other things. Such "thick" identities are not central to the understanding of the self-governing person who, according to standard liberal models, is fully able to abstract from such elements of her self-concept and to either identify with or to reject such them. But such an ideal too narrowly valorizes the life of the cosmopolitan "man" — the world traveler who freely chooses whether to settle into this or that community, identify with this or that group, and so on (see Young 1991, Alcoff 2006 and Appiah 2010; for discussion, see Meyers, 2000b).

These challenges have also focused on the relation of the self to its culture (Margalit and Raz, 1990, Tamir 1993). What is at issue from a policy perspective is that emphasis on the individual's self-government, with the cosmopolitan perspective that this entails, makes it difficult if not impossible to ground rights to the protection and internal self- government of traditional cultures themselves (Kymlicka, 1995). This is problematic in that it excludes from the direct protection of liberal policies those individuals and groups whose self-conceptions and value commitments are deeply constituted by cultural factors. Or, conversely, the assumption that the autonomous person is able to separate himself from all cultural commitments forestalls moves to provide state protection for cultural forms themselves, insofar as such state policies rest on the value of autonomy.

There have been many responses to these charges on behalf of a liberal outlook (e.g., Kymlicka, 1989, Gutman, 1985, Appiah 2005; for a general response to question of cultural identities see Kymlicka 1997). The most powerful response is that autonomy need not require that people be in a position to step away from all of their connections and values and to critically appraise them. Mere piecemeal reflection is all that is required. As Kymlicka puts it: "No particular task is set for us by society, and no particular cultural practice has authority that is beyond individual judgement and possible rejection" (Kymlicka, 1989:, 50).

There is a clarification that is needed in this exchange, however. For insofar as defenders of liberal principles (based on the value of autonomy) claim that all aspects of a person's self-concept be subject to alteration in order to manifest autonomy, they needlessly exaggerate the commitments of the liberal position. For such a view is open to the charge that liberal conceptions fail to take seriously the permanent and unalterable aspects of the self and its social position (Young, 1990, 46). Our embodiment, for example, is often not something which we can alter other than marginally, and numerous other self-defining factors such as sexual orientation (for some), native language, culture and race, are not readily subject to our manipulation and transformation, even in a piecemeal manner. To say that we are heteronomous because of this is therefore deeply problematic. What must be claimed by the defender of autonomy-based liberalism is that the ability in question is to change those aspects of oneself from which one is deeply alienated (or with which one does not identify, etc.). For in those cases where, upon reflection, one experiences one's body, culture, race, or sexuality as an external burden constricting one's more settled and authentic nature, and still one cannot alter that factor, then one lacks autonomy relative to it (see Christman, 2001, 2009 ch. 6). But if one feels fully at home within those unalterable parameters one does not lack autonomy because of that unalterability

3.3 Relational Autonomy

Several writers have claimed that proceduralist accounts of autonomy would wrongly attribute autonomy to those whose restricted socialization and stultifying life conditions pressure them into internalizing opressive values and norms, for example women who have internalized the belief in the social authority of husbands, or that only by having and raising children are their lives truly complete, and the like. If such women reflect on these values they may well endorse them, even if doing so is free of any specific reflection-inhibiting conditions. But such women surely lack autonomy, it is claimed; so only if autonomy includes a requirement that one be able to recognize basic value claims (such as the person's own equal moral standing) will that concept be useful in describing the oppressive conditions of a patriarchal society (see, e.g., Oshana, 1998, Stoljar, 2000; for discussion see Christman 1995, Benson, 1990, Friedman, 2000, Meyers, 1987, 1989).[7]

These and related considerations have sparked some to develop an alternative conception of autonomy meant to replace allegedly overly individualistic notions. This replacement has been called "relational autonomy" (MacKenzie and Stoljar, 2000a). Spurred by feminist critiques of traditional conceptions of autonomy and rights (Nedelsky, 1989, Code, 1991), relational conceptions of autonomy stress the ineliminable role that relatedness plays in both persons' self- conceptions, relative to which autonomy must be defined, and the dynamics of deliberation and reasoning. These views offer a provocative alternative to traditional models of the autonomous individual, but it must be made clear what position is being taken on the issue: on the one hand, relational accounts can be taken as resting on a non-individualist conception of the person and then claim that insofar as autonomy is self-government and the self is constituted by relations with others, then autonomy is relational; or these accounts may be understood as claiming that whatever selves turn out to be, autonomy fundamentally involves social relations rather than individual traits (Oshana, 2006). Some such views also waiver between claiming that social and personal relations play a crucial causal role in the development and enjoyment of autonomy and claiming that such relations constitute autonomy (for discussion see Mackenzie and Stoljar, 2000b, 21–26; for a recent overview, see Mackenzie 2014).

Another relational element to autonomy that has been developed connects social support and recognition of the person's status to her capacities for self-trust, self-esteem, and self-respect. The core argument in these approaches is that autonomy requires the ability to act effectively on one's own values (either as an individual or member of a social group), but that oppressive social conditions of various kinds threaten those abilities by removing one's sense of self-confidence required for effective agency. Social recognition and/or support for this self-trusting status is required for the full enjoyment of these abilities (see Anderson and Honneth 2005, Grovier 1993, Benson 2005, McCleod and Sherwin 2005, and Westlund 2014).

These claims often are accompanied with a rejection of purportedly value-neutral, proceduralist accounts of autonomy, even those that attempt to accommodate a fully social conception of the self. One question that arises with relational views connected to self-trust in this way, is why, exactly such relations are seen as conceptually constitutive of autonomy rather than contributory to it (and its development), where the self-confidence or self-trust in question is the core element to which these sorts of social relations are an important (albeit contingent) contributor. Another question to be considered arises from those cases where self-trust is established despite lack of social recognition, as when runaway slaves manage to heroically push on with their quest for freedom while facing violent denials from surrounding others (and surrounding social structures) that they enjoy the status of a full human being capable of authentic decision making. Finally, self-trust is not always merited: consider the brash teenager who insists on exercising social independence based on her unwarranted confidence in her abilities to make good judgments (see Mackenzie 2008, n. 36).

Nevertheless, these approaches have all importantly shifted philosophical attention concerning autonomy to the social and interpersonal dynamics that shape its enjoyment, connecting ideas about autonomy with broader issues of social justice, recognition, and social practices. This brings us back, then, to considerations of the liberal project and its potential limitations, where autonomy remains central.

3.4 Autonomy, Liberalism, and Perfectionism
As noted earlier, there are various versions of liberal political philosophy. All of them, however, are committed to a conception of political legitimacy in which political power and authority is justified only if such authority is acceptable to all citizens bound by it (see Rawls 1993, 144–50). This connects to a broader view of the foundations of value that at least some liberal theorists present as central to that tradition. That is the claim that values are valid for a person only if those values are or can be reasonably endorsed by the person in question. By extension, principles guiding the operation of institutions of social and political power — what Rawls calls the institutions of the basic structure (Rawls 1993, 258) — are legitimate only if they can be endorsed in this way by those subject to them. In this way, liberalism (in most of its forms) is committed to what some have called the "endorsement constraint" (Kymlicka 1989, 12f, R. Dworkin 2000, 216–18).

Models of autonomy considered above include a condition that mirrors this constraint, in that a person is autonomous relative to some action-guiding norm or value only if, upon critical reflection of that value, she identifies with it, approves of it, or does not feel deeply alienated from it. Combining this view with the endorsement constraint, liberalism carries the implication that autonomy is respected only when guiding values or principles in a society can be embraced in some way by those governed by them. This will connect directly to the liberal theory of legitimacy to be discussed below.

Perfectionists reject this set of claims. Perfectionism is the view that there are values valid for an individual or a population even when, from the subjective point of view of those agents or groups, that value is not endorsed or accepted (Wall 1998, Sumner 1996, 45–80, Hurka 1993, Sher 1997; see also Perfectionism). In short, it is the view that there are entirely objective values. While there are perfectionist liberals, this view generally resists the liberal claim that the autonomous acceptance of the central components of political principles is a necessary condition for the legitimacy of those principles. Moreover, perfectionists question the liberal commitment to neutrality in the formulation and application of political principles (Hurka 1993, 158–60).

Perfectionists specifically target the liberal connection between respect for autonomy and neutrality of political principles (Wall 1998, 125–204). For many, liberalism rests on the value of individual autonomy, but this reliance either assumes that respect for autonomy is merely one value among others in the liberal view, or autonomy has overriding value. In either case, however, neutrality is not supported. If autonomy is merely one value among others, for example, then there will clearly be times when state support of those other values will override respect for autonomy (paternalistic restrictions imposed to promote citizen safety, for example) (Sher 1997, 45–105, Hurka 1993, 158–60). On the other hand, autonomy could be seen as an absolute constraint on the promotion of values, or, more plausibly, as a constitutive condition of the validity of all values for a person, as the endorsement constraint implies. Perfectionists reply, however, that this is itself a controversial value position, one that may not find unqualified general support (Hurka 1993, 148–52, Sher 1997, 58–60, Sumner 1996, 174–83; cf. Griffin 1986, 135–36). To answer these objections, one must turn to consideration of the liberal principle of legitimacy. For the claim that liberals make concerning the limits of state promotion of the good — a limit set by respect for autonomy — depends heavily on their view about the ultimate ground of political power.

3.5 Autonomy and Political Liberalism
Liberalism is generally understood to arise historically out of the social contract tradition of political philosophy and hence rests on the idea of popular sovereignty. The concept of autonomy, then, figures centrally in at least one dominant strand in this tradition, the strand the runs through the work of Kant. The major alternative version of the liberal tradition sees popular sovereignty as basically a collective expression of rational choice and that the principles of the basic institutions of political power are merely instrumental in the maximization of aggregate citizen welfare (or, as with Mill, a constitutive element of welfare broadly considered).

But it is the Kantian brand of liberalism that places autonomy of persons at center stage. Rawls's Theory of Justice was seen as the contemporary manifestation of this Kantian approach to justice, where justice was conceived as those principles that would be chosen under conditions of unbiased rational decision-making (from behind the veil of ignorance). The original position where such principles would be chosen was said by Rawls to mirror Kant's Categorical Imperative. That is, it is a device in which persons can choose principles to impose upon themselves in a way which is independent of contingencies of social position, race, sex, or conception of the good (Rawls 1971, 221–27). But as is well known, the Kantian foundations of Rawls's theory of justice rendered it vulnerable to the charge that it was inapplicable to those populations (all modern populations in fact) where deep moral pluralism abounds. For under such conditions, no theory of justice which rests on a metaphysically grounded conception of the person could claim full allegiance from members of a population whose deep diversity causes them to disagree about metaphysics itself, as well as about moral frameworks and conceptions of value related to it. For this reason, Rawls developed a new (or further developed) understanding of the foundations of his version of liberalism, a political conception (Rawls 1993).

Under political liberalism, autonomy of persons is postulated, not as a metaphysically grounded "fact" about moral personality or practical reason as such, but rather as one of several "device[s] of representation" under which diverse citizens can focus on the methods of derivation (such as the original position) for substantive principles of justice (Rawls 1999, 303–58). Justice is achieved only when an overlapping consensus among people moved by deeply divergent but reasonable comprehensive moral views can be attained, a consensus in which such citizens can affirm principles of justice from within those comprehensive views.

Political Liberalism shifts the focus from a philosophical conception of justice, formulated abstractly and meant to apply universally, to a practical conception of legitimacy where consensus is reached without pretension of deep metaphysical roots for the principles in question. More than merely a "modus vivendi" for the participating parties, justice must be affirmed in a way that finds a moral basis for all participating citizens, albeit from different frameworks of value and moral obligation. The operation of public reason and deliberation, then, serves as the means by which such a consensus might be established, and hence public discussion and democratic institutions must be seen as a constitutive part of the justification of principles of justice rather than merely a mechanism for collective determination of the social good.

But the role of autonomy in the specification of this picture should not be under- emphasized (or the controversies it invites ignored). For such a consensus counts as legitimate only when achieved under conditions of free and authentic affirmation of shared principles. Only if the citizens see themselves as fully able to reflectively endorse or reject such shared principles, and to do so competently and with adequate information and range of options, can the overlapping political consensus step beyond the purely strategic dynamics of a modus vivendi and ground legitimate institutions of political power.

Therefore, social conditions that hamper the equal enjoyment of capacities to reflectively consider and (if necessary) reject principles of social justice, due, say, to extreme poverty, disability, ongoing injustice and inequality, or the like, restrict the establishment of just principles. Autonomy, then, insofar as that concept picks out the free reflective choice operating in the establishment of legitimacy, is basic to, and presupposed by, even such non-foundational (political) conceptions of justice.

Critics of political liberalism arise from several quarters. However, among the objections to it that focus on autonomy are those that question whether a political conception of legitimacy that rests on shared values can be sustained without the validity of those values being seen as somehow objective or fundamental, a position that clashes with the purported pluralism of political liberalism. Otherwise, citizens with deeply conflicting worldviews could not be expected to affirm the value of autonomy except as a mere modus vivendi (see, e.g., Wall 2009; cf. also Larmore 2008, 146–6). A line of response to this worry that could be pursued would be one that claimed that values that amount to autonomy (in some conceptualization of that idea) are already functional in the social structures and cultural practices of otherwise defensible democratic practices (as well as some critical projects that emphasize oppression and domination, as we saw above). This point raises the issue, to which we now turn, of the connection between autonomy, political liberalism, and democracy.

3.6 Autonomy, Justice and Democracy
In closing, we should add a word about the implications of political liberalism for the traditional division between liberal justice and democratic theory. I say "division" here, but different views of justice and democracy will convey very different conceptions of the relation between the two (see Christiano 1996, Lakoff 1996). But traditionally, liberal conceptions of justice have viewed democratic mechanisms of collective choice as

essential but highly circumscribed by the constitutional provisions that principles of justice support. Individual rights and freedoms, equality before the law, and various privileges and protections associated with citizen autonomy are protected by principles of justice and hence not subject to democratic review, on this approach (Gutman 1993).

However, liberal conceptions of justice have themselves evolved (in some strains at least) to include reference to collective discussion and debate (public reason) among the constitutive conditions of legitimacy. It could be claimed, then, that basic assumptions about citizens' capacities for reflective deliberation and choice — autonomy — must be part of the background conditions against which an overlapping consensus or other sort of political agreement concerning principles of justice is to operate.

Some thinkers have made the connection between individual or "private" autonomy and collective or "public" legitimacy — prominent, most notably Habermas (Habermas 1994). On this view, legitimacy and justice cannot be established in advance through philosophical construction and argument, as was thought to be the case in natural law traditions in which classical social contract theory flourished and which is inherited (in different form) in contemporary perfectionist liberal views. Rather, justice amounts to that set of principles that are established in practice and rendered legitimate by the actual support of affected citizens (and their representatives) in a process of collective discourse and deliberation (see e.g., Fraser 1997, 11–40 and Young 2000). Systems of rights and protections (private, individual autonomy) will necessarily be protected in order to institutionalize frameworks of public deliberation (and, more specifically, legislation and constitutional interpretation) that render principles of social justice acceptable to all affected (in consultation with others) (Habermas 1994, 111).

This view of justice, if at all acceptable, provides an indirect defense of the protection of autonomy and, in particular, conceptualizing autonomy in a way that assumes reflective self-evaluation. For only if citizen participants in the public discourse that underlies justice are assumed to have (and provided the basic resources for having) capacities for competent self-reflection, can the public defense and discussion of competing conceptions of justice take place (cf. Gaus 1996, Parts II and III, Gaus 2011). Insofar as autonomy is necessary for a functioning democracy (considered very broadly), and the latter is a constitutive element of just political institutions, then autonomy must be seen as reflective self-appraisal (and, I would add, non-alienation from central aspects of one's person) (see Cohen 2002, Richardson 2003).

This approach to justice and autonomy, spelled out here in rough and general form, has certainly faced criticism. In particular, those theorists concerned with the multi-dimensional nature of social and cultural "difference" have stressed how the conception of the autonomous person assumed in such principles (as well as criteria for rational discourse and public deliberation) is a contestable ideal not internalized by all participants in contemporary political life (see, e.g., Brown 1995, Benhabib 1992). Others motivated by post-modern considerations concerning the nature of the self, rationality, language, and identity, are also suspicious of the manner in which the basic concepts operative in liberal theories of justice ("autonomy" for example) are understood as fixed, transparent, and without their own political presuppositions (see, e.g., Butler 1990; for general discussion see White 1990).

These charges are stated here much too generally to give an adequate response in this context. But the challenge remains for any theory of justice which rests on a presumption of the normative centrality of autonomy. To be plausible in a variously pluralistic social setting, such a view must avoid the twin evils of forcibly imposing a (reasonably) contested value on resistant citizens, on the one hand, and simply abandoning all normative conceptions of social order in favor of open ended struggle for power on the other. The view that individuals ought to be treated as, and given the resources to become, autonomous in one of the minimal senses outlined here will, I submit, be a central element in any political view that steers between the Scylla of oppressive forms of perfectionism and the Charybdis of interest-group power politics.

AUTONOMY

6 DEONTOLOGICAL ETHICS

The word deontology derives from the Greek words for duty (deon) and science (or study) of (logos). In contemporary moral philosophy, deontology is one of those kinds of normative theories regarding which choices are morally required, forbidden, or permitted. In other words, deontology falls within the domain of moral theories that guide and assess our choices of what we ought to do (deontic theories), in contrast to (aretaic [virtue] theories) that—fundamentally, at least—guide and assess what kind of person (in terms of character traits) we are and should be. And within that domain, deontologists—those who subscribe to deontological theories of morality—stand in opposition to consequentialists.

deontological rationality?

5.2 Making no concessions to deontology: a purely consequentialist rationality?

6. Deontological Theories and Metaethics

1. Deontology's Foil: Consequentialism

Because deontological theories are best understood in contrast to consequentialist ones, a brief look at consequentialism and a survey of the problems with it that motivate its deontological opponents, provides a helpful prelude to taking up deontological theories themselves. Consequentialists hold that choices—acts and/or intentions—are to be morally assessed solely by the states of affairs they bring about. Consequentialists thus must specify initially the states of affairs that are intrinsically valuable—often called, collectively, "the Good." They then are in a position to assert that whatever choices increase the Good, that is, bring about more of it, are the choices that it is morally right to make and to execute. (The Good in that sense is said to be prior to "the Right.")

Consequentialists can and do differ widely in terms of specifying the Good. Some consequentialists are monists about the Good. Utilitarians, for example, identify the Good with pleasure, happiness, desire satisfaction, or "welfare" in some other sense. Other consequentialists are pluralists regarding the Good. Some of such pluralists believe that how the Good is distributed among persons (or all sentient beings) is itself partly constitutive of the Good, whereas conventional utilitarians merely add or average each person's share of the Good to achieve the Good's maximization.

Moreover, there are some consequentialists who hold that the doing or refraining from doing, of certain kinds of acts are themselves intrinsically valuable states of affairs constitutive of the Good. An example of this is the positing of rights not being violated, or duties being kept, as part of the Good to be maximized—the so-called "utilitarianism of rights" (Nozick 1974).

None of these pluralist positions erase the difference between consequentialism and deontology. For the essence of consequentialism is still present in such positions: an action would be right only insofar as it maximizes these Good-making states of affairs being caused to exist.

However much consequentialists differ about what the Good consists in, they all agree that the morally right choices are those that increase (either directly or indirectly) the Good. Moreover, consequentialists generally agree that the Good is "agent-neutral" (Parfit 1984; Nagel 1986). That is, valuable states of affairs are states of affairs that all agents have reason to achieve without regard to whether such states of affairs are achieved through the exercise of one's own agency or not.

Consequentialism is frequently criticized on a number of grounds. Two of these are particularly apt for revealing the temptations motivating the alternative approach to deontic ethics that is deontology. The two criticisms pertinent here are that consequentialism is, on the one hand, overly demanding, and, on the other hand, that it is not demanding enough. The criticism regarding extreme demandingness runs like this: for consequentialists, there is no realm of moral permissions, no realm of going beyond one's moral duty (supererogation), no realm of moral indifference. All acts are seemingly either required or forbidden. And there also seems to be no space for the consequentialist in which to show partiality to one's own projects or to one's family, friends, and countrymen, leading some critics of consequentialism to deem it a profoundly alienating and perhaps self-effacing moral theory (Williams 1973).

On the other hand, consequentialism is also criticized for what it seemingly permits. It seemingly demands (and thus, of course, permits) that in certain circumstances innocents be killed, beaten, lied to, or deprived of material goods to produce greater benefits for others. Consequences—and only consequences—can conceivably justify any kind of act, for it does not matter how harmful it is to some so long as it is more beneficial to others.

A well-worn example of this over-permissiveness of consequentialism is that of a case standardly called, Transplant. A surgeon has five patients dying of organ failure and one healthy patient whose organs can save the five. In the right circumstances, surgeon will be permitted (and indeed required) by consequentialism to kill the healthy patient to obtain his organs, assuming there are no relevant consequences other than the saving of the five and the death of the one. Likewise, consequentialism will permit (in a case that we shall call, Fat Man) that a fat man be pushed in front of a runaway trolley if his being crushed by the trolley will halt its advance towards five workers trapped on the track. We shall return to these examples later on.

Consequentialists are of course not bereft of replies to these two criticisms. Some retreat from maximizing the Good to "satisficing"—that is, making the achievement of only a certain level of the Good mandatory (Slote 1984). This move opens up some space for personal projects and relationships, as well as a realm of the morally permissible. It is not clear, however, that satisficing is adequately motivated, except to avoid the problems of maximizing. Nor is it clear that the level of mandatory satisficing can be nonarbitrarily specified, or that satisficing will not require deontological constraints to protect satisficers from maximizers.

Another move is to introduce a positive/negative duty distinction within consequentialism. On this view, our (negative) duty is not to make the world worse by actions having bad consequences; lacking is a corresponding (positive) duty to make the world better by actions having good consequences (Bentham 1789 (1948); Quinton 2007). We thus have a consequentialist duty not to kill the one in Transplant or in Fat Man; and there is no counterbalancing duty to save five that overrides this. Yet as with the satisficing move, it is unclear how a consistent consequentialist can motivate this restriction on all-out optimization of the Good.

Yet another idea popular with consequentialists is to move from consequentialism as a theory that directly assesses acts to consequentialism as a theory that directly assesses rules—or character-trait inculcation—and assesses acts only indirectly by reference to such rules (or character-traits) (Alexander 1985). Its proponents contend that indirect consequentialism can avoid the criticisms of direct (act) consequentialism because it will not legitimate egregious violations of ordinary moral standards—e.g., the killing of the innocent to bring about some better state of affairs—nor will it be overly demanding and thus alienating each of us from our own projects.

The relevance here of these defensive maneuvers by consequentialists is their common attempt to mimic the intuitively plausible aspects of a non-consequentialist, deontological approach to ethics. For as we shall now explore, the strengths of deontological approaches lies:

(1) in their categorical prohibition of actions like the killing of innocents, even when good consequences are in the offing; and (2) in their permission to each of us to pursue our own projects free of any constant demand that we shape those projects so as to make everyone else well off.

2. Deontological Theories

Having now briefly taken a look at deontologists' foil, consequentialist theories of right action, we turn now to examine deontological theories. In contrast to consequentialist theories, deontological theories judge the morality of choices by criteria different from the states of affairs those choices bring about. The most familiar forms of deontology, and also the forms presenting the greatest contrast to consequentialism, hold that some choices cannot be justified by their effects—that no matter how morally good their consequences, some choices are morally forbidden. On such familiar deontological accounts of morality, agents cannot make certain wrongful choices even if by doing so the number of those exact kinds of wrongful choices will be minimized (because other agents will be prevented from engaging in similar wrongful choices). For such deontologists, what makes a choice right is its conformity with a moral norm. Such norms are to be simply obeyed by each moral agent; such norm-keepings are not to be maximized by each agent. In this sense, for such deontologists, the Right is said to have priority over the Good. If an act is not in accord with the Right, it may not be undertaken, no matter the Good that it might produce (including even a Good consisting of acts in accordance with the Right).

Analogously, deontologists typically supplement non-consequentialist obligations with non-consequentialist permissions (Scheffler 1982). That is, certain actions can be right even though not maximizing of good consequences, for the rightness of such actions consists in their instantiating certain norms (here, of permission and not of obligation). Such actions are permitted, not just in the weak sense that there is no obligation not to do them, but also in the strong sense that one is permitted to do them even though they are productive of less good consequences than their alternatives (Moore 2008). Such strongly permitted actions include actions one is obligated to do, but (importantly) also included are actions one is not obligated to do. It is this last feature of such actions that warrants their separate mention for deontologists.

2.1 Agent-Centered Deontological Theories

The most traditional mode of taxonomizing deontological theories is to divide them between agent-centered versus victim-centered (or "patient-centered") theories (Scheffler 1988; Kamm 2007). Consider first agent-centered deontological theories. According to agent-centered theories, we each have both permissions and obligations that give us agent-relative reasons for action. An agent-relative reason is an objective reason, just as are agent neutral reasons; neither is to be confused with the subjective reasons that form the nerve of psychological explanations of human action (Nagel 1986). An agent-relative reason is so-called because it is a reason relative to the agent whose reason it is; it need not (although it may) constitute a reason for anyone else. Thus, an agent-relative obligation is an obligation for a particular agent to take or refrain from taking some action; and because it is agent-relative, the obligation does not necessarily give anyone else a reason to support that action. Each parent, for example, is commonly thought to have such special obligations to his/her child, obligations not shared by anyone else. Likewise, an agent-relative permission is a permission for some agent to do some act even though others may not be permitted to aid that agent in the doing of his permitted action. Each parent, to revert to the same example, is commonly thought to be permitted (at the least) to save his own child even at the cost of not saving two other children to whom he has no special relation. Agent-centered theories and the agent-relative reasons on which they are based not only enjoin each of us to do or not to do certain things; they also instruct me to treat my friends, my family, my promisees in certain ways because they are mine, even if by neglecting them I could do more for others' friends, families, and promisees.

At the heart of agent-centered theories (with their agent-relative reasons) is the idea of agency. The moral plausibility of agent-centered theories is rooted here. The idea is that morality is intensely personal, in the sense that we are each enjoined to keep our own moral house in order. Our categorical obligations are not to focus on how our actions cause or enable other agents to do evil; the focus of our categorical obligations is to keep our own agency free of moral taint.

Each agent's distinctive moral concern with his/her own agency puts some pressure on agent-centered theories to clarify how and when our agency is or is not involved in various situations. Agent-centered theories famously divide between those that emphasize the role of intention or other mental states in constituting the morally important kind of agency, and those that emphasize the actions of agents as playing such a role. There are also agent-centered theories that emphasize both intentions and actions equally in constituting the morally relevant agency of persons.

On the first of these three agent-relative views, it is most commonly asserted that it is our intended ends and intended means that most crucially define our agency. Such intentions mark out what it is we set out to achieve through our actions. If we intend something bad as an end, or even as a means to some more beneficent end, we are said to have "set ourselves at evil," something we are categorically forbidden to do (Aquinas Summa Theologica).

Three items usefully contrasted with such intentions are belief, risk, and cause. If we predict that an act of ours will result in evil, such prediction is a cognitive state (of belief); it is not a conative state of intention to bring about such a result, either as an end in itself or as a means to some other end. In this case, our agency is involved only to the extent that we have shown ourselves as being willing to tolerate evil results flowing from our acts; but we have not set out to achieve such evil by our acts. Likewise, a risking and/or causing of some evil result is distinct from any intention to achieve it. We can intend such a result, and we can even execute such an intention so that it becomes a trying, without in fact either causing or even risking it. (It is, however, true that we must believe we are risking the result to some extent, however minimal, for the result to be what we intend to bring about by our act.) Also, we can cause or risk such results without intending them. For example, we can intend to kill and even try to kill someone without killing him; and we can kill him without intending or trying to kill him, as when we kill accidentally. Intending thus does not collapse into risking, causing, or predicting; and on the version of agent-centered deontology here considered, it is intending (or perhaps trying) alone that marks the involvement of our agency in a way so as to bring agent-centered obligations and permissions into play.

Deontologists of this stripe are committed to something like the doctrine of double effect, a long-established doctrine of Catholic theology

(Woodward 2001). The Doctrine in its most familiar form asserts that we are categorically forbidden to intend evils such as killing the innocent or torturing others, even though doing such acts would minimize the doing of like acts by others (or even ourselves) in the future. By contrast, if we only risk, cause, or predict that our acts will have consequences making them acts of killing or of torture, then we might be able to justify the doing of such acts by the killing/torture-minimizing consequences of such actions. Whether such distinctions are plausible is standardly taken to measure the plausibility of an intention-focused version of the agent-centered version of deontology.

There are other versions of mental-state focused agent relativity that do not focus on intentions (Hurd 1994). Some of these versions focus on predictive belief as much as on intention (at least when the belief is of a high degree of certainty). Other versions focus on intended ends ("motives") alone. Still others focus on the deliberative processes that precede the formation of intentions, so that even to contemplate the doing of an evil act impermissibly invokes our agency (Anscombe 1958; Geach 1969; Nagel 1979). But intention-focused versions are the most familiar versions of so-called "inner wickedness" versions of agent-centered deontology.

The second kind of agent-centered deontology is one focused on actions, not mental states. Such a view can concede that all human actions must originate with some kind of mental state, often styled a volition or a willing; such a view can even concede that volitions or willings are an intention of a certain kind (Moore 1993, Ch. 6). Indeed, such source of human actions in willing is what plausibly connects actions to the agency that is of moral concern on the agent-centered version of deontology. Yet to will the movement of a finger on a trigger is distinct from an intention to kill a person by that finger movement. The act view of agency is thus distinct from the intentions (or other mental state) view of agency.

On this view, our agent-relative obligations and permissions have as their content certain kinds of actions: we are obligated not to kill innocents for example. The killing of an innocent of course requires that there be a death of such innocent, but there is no agency involved in mere events such as deaths. Needed for there to be a killing are two other items. One we remarked on before: the action of the putative agent must have its source in a willing. But the other maker of agency here is more interesting for present purposes: the willing must cause the death of the innocent for an act to be a killing of such innocent. Much (on this view) is loaded into the requirement of causation.

First, causings of evils like deaths of innocents are commonly distinguished from omissions to prevent such deaths. Holding a baby's head under water until it drowns is a killing; seeing a baby lying face down in a puddle and doing nothing to save it when one could do so easily is a failure to prevent its death. Our categorical obligations are usually negative in content: we are not to kill the baby. We may have an obligation to save it, but this will not be an agent-relative obligation, on the view here considered, unless we have some special relationship to the baby.

Second, causings are distinguished from allowings. In a narrow sense of the word we will here stipulate, one allows a death to occur when: (1) one's action merely removes a defense the victim otherwise would have had against death; and (2) such removal returns the victim to some morally appropriate baseline (Moore 1993; Kamm 1994, 1996; Moore 2008; MacMahan 2003). Thus, mercy-killings, or euthanasia, are outside of our deontological obligations (and thus eligible for justification by good consequences) so long as one's act: (1) only removes a defense against death that the agent herself had earlier provided, such as disconnecting medical equipment that is keeping the patient alive when that disconnecting is done by the medical personnel that attached the patient to the equipment originally; and (2) the equipment could justifiably have been hooked up to another patient, where it could do some good, had the doctors known at the time of connection what they know at the time of disconnection.

Third, one is said not to cause an evil such as a death when one's acts merely enable (or aid) some other agent to cause such evil (Hart and Honore 1985). Thus, one is not categorically forbidden to drive the terrorists to where they can kill the policeman (if the alternative is death of one's family), even though one would be categorically forbidden to kill the policeman oneself (even where the alternative is death of one's family) (Moore 2008). Nor is one categorically forbidden to select which of a group of villagers shall be unjustly executed by another who is pursuing his own purposes (Williams 1973).

Fourth, one is said not to cause an evil such as a death when one merely redirects a presently existing threat to many so that it now threatens only one (or a few) (Thomson 1985). In the time-honored example of the run-away trolley (Trolley), one may turn a trolley so that it runs over one trapped workman so as to save five workmen trapped on the other track, even though it is not permissible for an agent to have initiated the movement of the trolley towards the one to save five (Foot 1967; Thomson 1985).

Fifth, our agency is said not to be involved in mere accelerations of evils about to happen anyway, as opposed to causing such evils by doing acts necessary for such evils to occur (G. Williams 1961; Brody 1996). Thus, when a victim is about to fall to his death anyway, dragging a rescuer with him too, the rescuer may cut the rope connecting them. Rescuer is accelerating, but not causing, the death that was about to occur anyway.

All of these last five distinctions have been suggested to be part and parcel of another centuries-old Catholic doctrine, that of the doctrine of doing and allowing (see the entry on doing vs. allowing harm) (Moore 2008; Kamm 1994; Foot 1967; Quinn 1989). According to this doctrine, one may not cause death, for that would be a killing, a "doing;" but one may fail to prevent death, allow (in the narrow sense) death to occur, enable another to cause death, redirect a life-threatening item from many to one, or accelerate a death about to happen anyway, if good enough consequences are in the offing. As with the Doctrine of Double Effect, how plausible one finds these applications of the doctrine of doing and allowing will determine how plausible one finds this cause-based view of human agency.

A third kind of agent-centered deontology can be obtained by simply conjoining the other two agent-centered views (Hurd 1994). This view would be that agency in the relevant sense requires both intending and causing (i.e., acting) (Moore 2008). On this view, our agent-relative obligations do not focus on causings or intentions separately; rather, the content of such obligations is focused on intended causings. For example, our deontological obligation with respect to human life is neither an obligation not to kill nor an obligation not to intend to kill; rather, it is an obligation not to murder, that is, to kill in execution of an intention to kill.

By requiring both intention and causings to constitute human agency, this third view avoids the seeming overbreadth of our obligations if either intention or action alone marked such agency. Suppose our agent-relative obligation were not to do some action such as kill an innocent –is that obligation breached by a merely negligent killing, so that we deserve the serious blame of having breached such a categorical norm (Hurd 1994)? (Of course, one might be somewhat blameworthy on consequentialist grounds (Hurd 1995), or perhaps not blameworthy at all (Alexander 1990; Moore and Hurd 2011).) Alternatively, suppose our agent-relative obligation were not to intend to kill—does that mean we could not justify forming such an intention when good consequences would be the result, and when we are sure we cannot act so as to fulfill such intention (Hurd 1994)? If our agent-relative obligation is neither of these alone, but is rather, that we are not to kill in execution of an intention to kill, both such instances of seeming overbreadth in the reach of our obligations, are avoided.

Whichever of these three agent-centered theories one finds most plausible, they each suffer from some common problems. A fundamental worry is the moral unattractiveness of the focus on self that is the nerve of any agent-centered deontology. The importance of each person's agency to himself/herself has a narcissistic flavor to it that seems unattractive to many. It seemingly justifies each of us keeping our own moral house in order even at the expense of the world becoming much worse. The worry is not that agent-centered deontology is just another form of egoism, according to which the content of one's duties exclusively concern oneself; even so, the character of agent-relative duties is such that they betoken an emphasis on self that is unattractive in the same way that such emphasis makes egoism unattractive. Secondly, many find the distinctions invited by the Doctrine of Double Effect and the (five versions of the) Doctrine of Doing and Allowing to be either morally unattractive or conceptually incoherent. Such critics find the differences between intending/foreseeing, causing/omitting, causing/allowing, causing/enabling, causing/redirecting, causing/accelerating to be morally insignificant. (On act/omission (Rachels 1975); on doing/allowing (Kagan 1989); on intending/foreseeing (Bennett 1981; Davis 1984).) They urge, for example, that failing to prevent a death one could easily prevent is as blameworthy as causing a death, so that a morality that radically distinguishes the two is implausible. Alternatively, such critics urge on conceptual grounds that no clear distinctions can be drawn in these matters, that foreseeing with certainty is indistinguishable from intending (Bennett 1981), that omitting is one kind of causing (Schaffer 2012), and so forth.

Thirdly, there is the worry about "avoision." By casting our categorical obligations in such agent-centered terms, one invites a kind of manipulation that is legalistic and Jesuitical, what Leo Katz dubs "avoision" (Katz 1996). Some think, for example, that one can transform a prohibited intention into a permissible predictive belief (and thus escape intention-focused forms of agent-relative duty) by the simple expedient of finding some other end with which to motivate the action in question.

Such criticisms of the agent-centered view of deontology drive most who accept their force away from deontology entirely and to some form of consequentialism. Alternatively, some of such critics are driven to patient-centered deontology, which we discuss immediately below. Yet still other of such critics attempt to articulate yet a fourth form of agent-centered deontology. This might be called the "control theory of agency." On this view, our agency is invoked whenever our choices could have made a difference. This cuts across the intention/foresight, act/omission, and doing/allowing distinctions, because in all cases we controlled what happened through our choices (Frey 1995). Yet as an account of deontology, this seems worrisomely broad. It disallows consequentialist justifications whenever: we foresee the death of an innocent; we omit to save, where our saving would have made a difference and we knew it; where we remove a life-saving device, knowing the patient will die. If deontological norms are so broad in content as to cover all these foreseeings, omittings, and allowings, then good consequences (such as a net saving of innocent lives) are ineligible to justify them. This makes for a wildly counterintuitive deontology: surely I can, for example, justify not throwing the rope to one (and thus omit to save him) in order to save two others equally in need. This breadth of obligation also makes for a conflict-ridden deontology: by refusing to cabin our categorical obligations by the distinctions of the Doctrine of Double Effect and the Doctrine of Doing and Allowing, situations of conflict between our stringent obligations proliferate in a troublesome way (Anscombe 1962).

2.2 Patient-Centered Deontological Theories

A second group of deontological moral theories can be classified, as patient-centered, as distinguished from the agent-centered version of deontology just considered. These theories are rights-based rather than duty-based; and some versions purport to be quite agent-neutral in the reasons they give moral agents.

All patient-centered deontological theories are properly characterized as theories premised on people's rights. An illustrative version posits, as its core right, the right against being used only as means for producing good consequences without one's consent. Such a core right is not to be confused with more discrete rights, such as the right against being killed, or being killed intentionally. It is a right against being used by another for the user's or others' benefit. More specifically, this version of patient-centered deontological theories proscribes the using of another's body, labor, and talent without the latter's consent. One finds this notion expressed, albeit in different ways, in the work of the so-called Right Libertarians (e.g., Robert Nozick, Eric Mack), but also in the works of the Left-Libertarians as well (e.g., Michael Otsuka, Hillel Steiner, Peter Vallentyne) (Nozick 1974; Mack 2000; Steiner 1994; Vallentyne and Steiner 2000; Vallentyne, Steiner, and Otsuka 2005). On this view, the scope of strong moral duties—those that are the correlatives of others' rights—is jurisdictionally limited and does not extend to resources for producing the Good that would not exist in the absence of those intruded upon—that is, their bodies, labors, and talents. In addition to the Libertarians, others whose views include this prohibition on using others include Quinn, Kamm, Alexander, Ferzan, and Gauthier (Quinn 1989; Kamm 1996; Alexander 2004; Alexander and Ferzan 2009, 2012; Gauthier 1986).

Just as do agent-centered theories, so too do patient-centered theories (such as that forbidding the using of another) seek to explain common intuitions about such classic hypothetical cases as Trolley and Transplant (or Fat Man) (Thomson 1985). In Trolley, a runaway trolley will kill five workers unless diverted to a siding where it will kill one worker. Most people regard it as permissible and perhaps mandatory to switch the trolley to the siding. By contrast, in Transplant, where a surgeon can kill one healthy patient and transplant his organs to five dying patients, thereby saving their lives, the universal reaction is condemnation. (The same is by-and-large true in Fat Man, where the runaway trolley cannot be switched off the main track but can be stopped before reaching the five workers by pushing a fat man into its path, resulting in his death.)

The injunction against using arguably accounts for these contrasting reactions. After all, in each example, one life is sacrificed to save five. Yet there appears to be a difference in the means through which the net four lives are saved. In Transplant (and Fat Man), the doomed person is used to benefit the others. They could not be saved in the absence of his body. In Trolley, on the other hand, the doomed victim is not used. The workers would be saved whether or not he is present on the second track.

Notice, too, that this patient-centered libertarian version of deontology handles Trolley, Transplant et al. differently from how they are handled by agent-centered versions. The latter focus on the agent's mental state or on whether the agent acted or caused the victim's harm. The patient-centered theory focuses instead on whether the victim's body, labor, or talents were the means by which the justifying results were produced. So one who realizes that by switching the trolley he can save five trapped workers and place only one in mortal danger—and that the danger to the latter is not the means by which the former will be saved—acts permissibly on the patient-centered view if he switches the trolley even if he does so with the intention of killing the one worker. Switching the trolley is causally sufficient to bring about the consequences that justify the act— the saving of net four workers—and it is so even in the absence of the one worker's body, labor, or talents. (The five would be saved if the one escaped, was never on the track, or did not exist.) By contrast, on the intent and intended action versions of agent-centered theories, the one who switches the trolley does not act permissibly if he acts with the intention to harm the one worker. (This could be the case, for example, when the one who switches the trolley does so to kill the one whom he hates, only knowing that he will thereby save the other five workmen.) On the patient-centered version, if an act is otherwise morally justifiable by virtue of its balance of good and bad consequences, and the good consequences are achieved without the necessity of using anyone's body, labor, or talents without that person's consent as the means by which they are achieved, then it is morally immaterial (to the permissibility of the act but not to the culpability of the actor) whether someone undertakes that act with the intention to achieve its bad consequences. (This is true, of course, only so long as the concept of using does not implicitly refer to the intention of the user) (Alexander and Ferzan 2012).

Patient-centered deontologists handle differently other stock examples of the agent-centered deontologist. Take the acceleration cases as an example. When all will die in a lifeboat unless one is killed and eaten; when Siamese twins are conjoined such that both will die unless the organs of one are given to the other via an operation that kills the first; when all of a group of soldiers will die unless the body of one is used to hold down the enemy barbed wire, allowing the rest to save themselves; when a group of villagers will all be shot by a blood-thirsty tyrant unless they select one of their numbers to slake the tyrants lust for death—in all such cases, the causing/accelerating-distinguishing agent-centered deontologists would permit the killing but the usings-focused patient-centered deontologist would not. (For the latter, all killings are merely accelerations of death.)

The restriction of deontological duties to usings of another raises a sticky problem for those patient-centered deontological theories that are based on the core right against using: how can they account for the prima facie wrongs of killing, injuring, and so forth when done not to use others as means, but for some other purpose or for no purpose at all? The answer is that such patient-centered deontological constraints must be supplemented by consequentialist-derived moral norms to give an adequate account of morality. Killing, injuring, and so forth will usually be unjustifiable on a consequentialist calculus, especially if everyone's interests are given equal regard. It is when killing and injuring are otherwise justifiable that the deontological constraint against using has its normative bite over and against what is already prohibited by consequentialism. (This narrowness of patient-centered deontology makes it counterintuitive to agent-centered deontologists, who regard prohibitions on killing of the innocent, etc., as paradigmatically deontological.)

The patient-centered version of deontology is aptly labeled libertarian in that it is not plausible to conceive of not being aided as being used by the one not aiding. Using is an action, not a failure to act. More generally, it is counterintuitive to many to think that any of us have a right to be aided. For if there were a strong (that is, enforceable or coercible) duty to aid others, such that, for example, A had a duty to aid X, Y, and Z; and if A could more effectively aid X, Y, and Z by coercing B and C to aid them (as is their duty), then A would have a duty to "use" B and C in this way. For these reasons, any positive duties will not be rights-based ones on the view here considered; they will be consequentially-justified duties that can be trumped by the right not to be coerced to perform them.

Patient-centered deontological theories are often conceived in agent-neutral reason-giving terms. John has a right to the exclusive use of his body, labor, and talents, and such a right gives everyone equal reason to do actions respecting it. But this aspect of patient-centered deontological theories gives rise to a particularly virulent form of the so-called paradox of deontology (Scheffler 1988)—that if respecting Mary's and Susan's rights is as important morally as is protecting John's rights, then why isn't violating John's rights permissible (or even obligatory) when doing so is necessary to protect Mary's and Susan's rights from being violated by others? Patient-centered deontological theories might arguably do better if they abandoned their pretense of being agent-neutral. They could conceive of rights as giving agent-relative reasons to each actor to refrain from doing actions violative of such rights. Take the core right against being used without one's consent hypothesized earlier. The correlative duty is not to use another without his consent. If such duty is agent-relative, then the rights-based deontologist (no less than the agent-centered deontologist) has the conceptual resources to answer the paradox of deontology. That is, each of us may not use John, even when such using of John would minimize usings of John by others in the future. Such duties are personal to each of us in that we may not justify our violating such a duty now by preventing others' similar violations in the future. Such personal duties are agent-centered in the sense that the agency of each person is central to the duties of each person, so that your using of another now cannot be traded off against other possible usings at other times by other people.

Patient-centered deontologies are thus arguably better construed to be agent-relative in the reasons they give. Even so construed, such deontologies join agent-centered deontologies in facing the moral (rather than the conceptual) versions of the paradox of deontology. For a critic of either form of deontology might respond to the categorical prohibition about using others as follows: If usings are bad, then are not more usings worse than fewer? And if so, then is it not odd to condemn acts that produce better states of affairs than would occur in their absence? Deontologists of either stripe can just deny that wrong acts on their account of wrongness can be translated into bad states of affairs. Two wrongings are not "worse" than one. Such wrongs cannot be summed into anything of normative significance. After all, the victim of a rights-violating using may suffer less harm than others might have suffered had his rights not been violated; yet one cannot, without begging the question against deontological constraints, argue that therefore no constraint should block minimizing harm. That is, the deontologist might reject the comparability of states of affairs that involve violations and those that do not. Similarly, the deontologist may reject the comparability of states of affairs that involve more or fewer rights-violations (Brook 2007). The deontologist might attempt to back this assertion by relying upon the separateness of persons. Wrongs are only wrongs to persons. A wrong to Y and a wrong to Z cannot be added to make some greater wrong because there is no person who suffers this greater wrong (cf. Taurek 1977).

This solution to the paradox of deontology, may seem attractive, but it comes at a high cost. In Trolley, for example, where there is neither agency nor using in the relevant senses and thus no bar to switching, one cannot claim that it is better to switch and save the five. For if the deaths of the five cannot be summed, their deaths are not worse than the death of the one worker on the siding. Although there is no deontological bar to switching, neither is the saving of a net four lives a reason to switch. Worse yet, were the trolley heading for the one worker rather than the five, there would be no reason not to switch the trolley, so a net loss of four lives is no reason not to switch the trolley. If the numbers don't count, they seemingly don't count either way.

The problem of how to account for the significance of numbers without giving up deontology and adopting consequentialism, and without resurrecting the paradox of deontology, is one that a number of deontologists are now working to solve (e.g., Kamm 1996; Scanlon 2003; Otsuka 2006, Hsieh et al. 2006). Until it is solved, it will remain a huge thorn in the deontologist's side.

2.3 Contractarian Deontological Theories

Somewhat orthogonal to the distinction between agent-centered versus patient-centered deontological theories are contractualist deontological theories. Morally wrong acts are, on such accounts, those acts that would be forbidden by principles that people in a suitably described social contract would accept (e.g., Rawls 1971; Gauthier 1986), or that would be forbidden only by principles that such people could not "reasonably reject" (e.g., Scanlon 2003).

In deontology, as elsewhere in ethics, is not entirely clear whether a contractualist account is really normative as opposed to metaethical. If such account is a first order normative account, it is probably best construed as a patient-centered deontology; for the central obligation would be to do onto others only that to which they have consented. But so construed, modern contractualist accounts would share the problems that have long bedeviled historical social contract theories: how plausible is it that the "moral magic" of consent is the first principle of morality? And how much of what is commonly regarded as permissible to do to people can (in any realistic sense of the word) be said to be actually consented to by them, expressly or even implicitly?

In fact modern contractualisms look meta-ethical, and not normative. Thomas Scanlon's contractualism, for example, which posits at its core those norms of action that we can justify to each other, is best construed as an ontological and epistemological account of moral notions. The same may be said of David Gauthier's contractualism. Yet so construed, metaethical contractualism as a method for deriving moral norms does not necessarily lead to deontology as a first order ethics. John Harsanyi, for example, argues that parties to the social contract would choose utilitarianism over the principles John Rawls argues would be chosen (Harsanyi 1973). Nor is it clear that meta-ethical contractualism, when it does generate a deontological ethic, favors either an agent centered or a patient centered version of such an ethic.

2.4 Deontological Theories and Kant

If any philosopher is regarded as central to deontological moral theories, it is surely Immanuel Kant. Indeed, each of the branches of deontological ethics—the agent-centered, the patient-centered, and the contractualist—can lay claim to being Kantian.

The agent-centered deontologist can cite Kant's locating the moral quality of acts in the principles or maxims on which the agent acts and not primarily in those acts' effects on others. For Kant, the only thing unqualifiedly good is a good will (Kant 1785). The patient-centered deontologist can, of course, cite Kant's injunction against using others as mere means to one's end (Kant 1785). And the contractualist can cite, as Kant's contractualist element, Kant's insistence that the maxims on which one acts be capable of being willed as a universal law—willed by all rational agents (Kant 1785). (See generally the entry on Kant.)

3. The Advantages of Deontological Theories

Having canvassed the two main types of deontological theories (together with a contractualist variation of each), it is time to assess deontological morality more generally. On the one hand, deontological morality, in contrast to consequentialism, leaves space for agents to give special concern to their families, friends, and projects. At least that is so if the deontological morality contains no strong duty of general beneficence, or, if it does, it places a cap on that duty's demands. Deontological morality, therefore, avoids the overly demanding and alienating aspects of consequentialism and accords more with conventional notions of our moral duties.

Likewise, deontological moralities, unlike most views of consequentialism, leave space for the supererogatory. A deontologist can do more that is morally praiseworthy than morality demands. A consequentialist cannot, assuming none of the consequentialists' defensive maneuvers earlier referenced work. For such a pure or simple consequentialist, if one's act is not morally demanded, it is morally wrong and forbidden. Whereas for the deontologist, there are acts that are neither morally wrong nor demanded, some—but only some—of which are morally praiseworthy.

As we have seen, deontological theories all possess the strong advantage of being able to account for strong, widely shared moral intuitions about our duties better than can consequentialism. The contrasting reactions to Trolley, Fat Man, Transplant, and other examples earlier given, are illustrative of this.

Finally, deontological theories, unlike consequentialist ones, have the potential for explaining why certain people have moral standing to complain about and hold to account those who breach moral duties. For the moral duties typically thought to be deontological in character—unlike, say, duties regarding the environment—are duties to particular people, not duties to bring about states of affairs that no particular person has an individual right to have realized.

4. The Weaknesses of Deontological Theories

On the other hand, deontological theories have their own weak spots. The most glaring one is the seeming irrationality of our having duties or permissions to make the world morally worse. Deontologists need their own, non-consequentialist model of rationality, one that is a viable alternative to the intuitively plausible, "act-to-produce-the-best-consequences" model of rationality that motivates consequentialist theories. Until this is done, deontology will always be paradoxical. Patient-centered versions of deontology cannot easily escape this problem, as we have shown. It is not even clear that they have the conceptual resources to make agency important enough to escape this moral paradox. Yet even agent-centered versions face this paradox; having the conceptual resources (of agency and agent-relative reasons) is not the same as making it plausible just how a secular, objective morality can allow each person's agency to be so uniquely crucial to that person.

Second, it is crucial for deontologists to deal with the conflicts that seem to exist between certain duties, and between certain rights. For more information, please see the entry on moral dilemmas. Kant's bold proclamation that "a conflict of duties is inconceivable" (Kant 1780, p. 25) is the conclusion wanted, but reasons for believing it are difficult to produce. The intending/foreseeing, doing/allowing, causing/aiding, and related distinctions certainly reduce potential conflicts for the agent-centered versions of deontology; whether they can totally eliminate such conflicts is a yet unresolved question.

One well known approach to deal with the possibility of conflict between deontological duties is to reduce the categorical force of such duties to that of only "prima facie" duties (Ross 1930, 1939). This idea is that conflict between merely prima facie duties is unproblematic so long as it does not infect what one is categorically obligated to do, which is what overall, concrete duties mandate. Like other softenings of the categorical force of deontological obligation we mention briefly below (threshold deontology, mixed views), the prima facie duty view is in some danger of collapsing into a kind of consequentialism. This depends on whether "prima facie" is read epistemically or not, and on (1) whether any good consequences are eligible to justify breach of prima facie duties; (2) whether only such consequences over some threshold can do so; or (3) whether only threatened breach of other deontological duties can do so.

Thirdly, there is the manipulability worry mentioned before with respect to agent-centered versions of deontology. To the extent potential conflict is eliminated by resort to the Doctrine of Double Effect, the Doctrine of Doing and Allowing, and so forth (and it is not clear to what extent patient-centered versions rely on these doctrines and distinctions to mitigate potential conflict), then a potential for "avoision" is opened up. Such avoision is the manipulation of means (using omissions, foresight, risk, allowings, aidings, acceleratings, redirectings, etc.) to achieve permissibly what otherwise deontological morality would forbid (see Katz 1996). Avoision is an undesirable feature of any ethical system that allows such strategic manipulation of its doctrines.

Fourth, there is what might be called the paradox of relative stringency. There is an aura of paradox in asserting that all deontological duties are categorical—to be done no matter the consequences—and yet asserting that some of such duties are more stringent than others. A common thought is that "there cannot be degrees of wrongness with intrinsically wrong acts... (Frey 1995, p. 78 n. 3). Yet relative stringency—"degrees of wrongness"—seems forced upon the deontologist by two considerations. First, duties of differential stringency can be weighed against one another if there is conflict between them, so that a conflict-resolving, overall duty becomes possible if duties can be more or less stringent. Second, when we punish for the wrongs consisting in our violation of deontological duties, we (rightly) do not punish all violations equally. The greater the wrong, the greater the punishment deserved; and relative stringency of duty violated (or importance of rights) seems the best way of making sense of greater versus lesser wrongs.

Fifth, there are situations—unfortunately not all of them thought experiments—where compliance with deontological norms will bring about disastrous consequences. To take a stock example of much current discussion, suppose that unless A violates the deontological duty not to torture an innocent person (B), ten, or a thousand, or a million other innocent people will die because of a hidden nuclear device. If A is forbidden by deontological morality from torturing B, many would regard that as a reductio ad absurdum of deontology.

Deontologists have six possible ways of dealing with such "moral catastrophes" (although only two of these are very plausible). First, they can just bite the bullet and declare that sometimes doing what is morally right will have tragic results but that allowing such tragic results to occur is still the right thing to do. Complying with moral norms will surely be difficult on those occasions, but the moral norms apply nonetheless with full force, overriding all other considerations. We might call this the Kantian response, after Kant's famous hyperbole: "Better the whole people should perish," than that injustice be done (Kant 1780, p. 100). One might also call this the absolutist conception of deontology, because such a view maintains that conformity to norms has absolute force and not merely great weight.

This first response to "moral catastrophes," which is to ignore them, might be further justified by denying that moral catastrophes, such as a million deaths, are really a million times more catastrophic than one death. This is the so-called "aggregation" problem, which we alluded to in section 2.2 in discussing the paradox of deontological constraints. John Taurek famously argued that it is a mistake to assume harms to two persons are twice as bad as a comparable harm to one person. For each of the two suffers only his own harm and not the harm of the other (Taurek 1977). Taurek's argument can be employed to deny the existence of moral catastrophes and thus the worry about them that deontologists would otherwise have. Robert Nozick also stresses the separateness of persons and therefore urges that there is no entity that suffers double the harm when each of two persons is harmed (Nozick 1974). (Of course, Nozick, perhaps inconsistently, also acknowledges the existence of moral catastrophes.) Most deontologists reject Taurek's radical conclusion that we need not be morally more obligated to avert harm to the many than to avert harm to the few; but they do accept the notion that harms should not be aggregated. Deontologists' approaches to the nonaggregation problem when the choice is between saving the many and saving the few are: (1)

save the many so as to acknowledge the importance of each of the extra persons; (2) conduct a weighted coin flip; (3) flip a coin; or (4) save anyone you want (a denial of moral catastrophes) (Broome 1998; Hirose 2007; Hsieh et al. 2006; Huseby 2011; Kamm 1993; Saunders 2009; Scanlon 2003; Suikkanen 2004; Timmerman 2004; Wasserman and Strudler 2003).

The second plausible response is for the deontologist to abandon Kantian absolutism for what is usually called "threshold deontology." A threshold deontologist holds that deontological norms govern up to a point despite adverse consequences; but when the consequences become so dire that they cross the stipulated threshold, consequentialism takes over (Moore 1997, ch. 17). A may not torture B to save the lives of two others, but he may do so to save a thousand lives if the "threshold" is higher than two lives but lower than a thousand.

There are two varieties of threshold deontology that are worth distinguishing. On the simple version, there is some fixed threshold of awfulness beyond which morality's categorical norms no longer have their overriding force. Such a threshold is fixed in the sense that it does not vary with the stringency of the categorical duty being violated. The alternative is what might be called "sliding scale threshold deontology." On this version, the threshold varies in proportion to the degree of wrong being done—the wrongness of stepping on a snail has a lower threshold (over which the wrong can be justified) than does the wrong of stepping on a baby.

Threshold deontology (of either stripe) is an attempt to save deontological morality from the charge of fanaticism. It is similar to the "prima facie duty" version of deontology developed to deal with the problem of conflicting duties, yet threshold deontology is usually interpreted with such a high threshold that it more closely mimics the outcomes reached by a "pure," absolutist kind of deontology. Threshold deontology faces several theoretical difficulties. Foremost among them is giving a theoretically tenable account of the location of such a threshold, either absolutely or on a sliding scale (Alexander 2000; Ellis 1992). Why is the threshold for torture of the innocent at one thousand lives, say, as opposed to nine hundred or two thousand? Another problem is that whatever the threshold, as the dire consequences approach it, counterintuitive results appear to follow. For example, it may be permissible, if we are one-life-at-risk short of the threshold, to pull one more person into danger who will then be saved, along with the others at risk, by killing an innocent person (Alexander 2000). Thirdly, there is some uncertainty about how one is to reason after the threshold has been reached: are we to calculate at the margin on straight consequentialist grounds, use an agent-weighted mode of summing, or do something else? A fourth problem is that threshold deontology threatens to collapse into a kind of consequentialism. Indeed, it can be shown that the sliding scale version of threshold deontology is extensionally equivalent to an agency-weighted form of consequentialism (Sen 1982).

The remaining four strategies for dealing with the problem of dire consequence cases all have the flavor of evasion by the deontologist. Consider first the famous view of Elizabeth Anscombe: such cases (real or imagined) can never present themselves to the consciousness of a truly moral agent because such agent will realize it is immoral to even think about violating moral norms in order to avert disaster (Anscombe 1958; Geach 1969; Nagel 1979). Such rhetorical excesses should be seen for what they are, a peculiar way of stating Kantian absolutism motivated by an impatience with the question.

Another response by deontologists, this one most famously associated with Bernard Williams, shares some of the "don't think about it" features of the Anscombean response. According to Williams (1973), situations of moral horror are simply "beyond morality," and even beyond reason. (This view is reminiscent of the ancient view of natural necessity, revived by Sir Francis Bacon, that such cases are beyond human law and can only be judged by the natural law of instinct.) Williams tells us that in such cases we just act. Interestingly, Williams contemplates that such "existentialist" decision-making will result in our doing what we have to do in such cases—for example, we torture the innocent to prevent nuclear holocaust.

Surely this is an unhappy view of the power and reach of human law, morality, or reason. Indeed, Williams (like Bacon and Cicero before him) thinks there is an answer to what should be done, albeit an answer very different than Anscombe's. But both views share the weakness of thinking that morality and even reason runs out on us when the going gets tough.

Yet another strategy is to divorce completely the moral appraisals of acts from the blameworthiness or praiseworthiness of the agents who undertake them, even when those agents are fully cognizant of the moral appraisals. So, for example, if A tortures innocent B to save a thousand others, one can hold that A's act is morally wrong but also that A is morally praiseworthy for having done it.

Deontology does have to grapple with how to mesh deontic judgments of wrongness with "hypological" (Zimmerman 2002) judgments of blameworthiness (Alexander 2004). Yet it would be an oddly cohering morality that condemned an act as wrong yet praised the doer of it. Deontic and hypological judgments ought to have more to do with each other than that. Moreover, it is unclear what action-guiding potential such an oddly cohered morality would have: should an agent facing such a choice avoid doing wrong, or should he go for the praise?

The last possible strategy for the deontologist in order to deal with dire consequences, other than by denying their existence, as per Taurek, is to distinguish moral reasons from all-things-considered reasons and to argue that whereas moral reasons dictate obedience to deontological norms even at the cost of catastrophic consequences, all-things-considered reasons dictate otherwise. (This is one reading of Bernard William's famous discussion of moral luck, where non-moral reasons seemingly can trump moral reasons (Williams 1975, 1981); this is also a strategy some consequentialists (e.g., Portmore 2003) seize as well in order to handle the demandingness and alienation problems endemic to consequentialism.) But like the preceding strategy, this one seems desperate. Why should one even care that moral reasons align with deontology if the important reasons, the all-things-considered reasons that actually govern decisions, align with consequentialism?

5. Deontology's Relation(s) to Consequentialism Reconsidered

The perceived weaknesses of deontological theories have led some to consider how to eliminate or at least reduce those weaknesses while preserving deontology's advantages. One way to do this is to embrace both consequentialism and deontology, combining them into some kind of a mixed theory. Given the differing notions of rationality underlying each kind of theory, this is easier said than done. After all, one cannot simply weigh agent-relative reasons against agent-neutral reasons, without stripping the former sorts of reasons of their distinctive character.

A time-honored way of reconciling opposing theories is to allocate them to different jurisdictions. Tom Nagel's reconciliation of the two theories is a version of this, inasmuch as he allocates the agent-neutral reasons of consequentialism to our "objective" viewpoint, whereas the agent-relative reasons of deontology are seen as part of our inherent subjectivity (Nagel 1986). Yet Nagel's allocations are non-exclusive; the same situation can be seen from either subjective or objective viewpoints, meaning that it is mysterious how we are to combine them into some overall view.

A less mysterious way of combining deontology with consequentialism is to assign to each a jurisdiction that is exclusive of the other. One possibility here is to regard the agent-neutral reasons of consequentialism as a kind of default rationality/morality in the sense that when an agent-relative permission or obligation applies, it governs, but in the considerable logical space where neither applies, consequentialism holds sway (Moore 2008). Remembering that for the threshold deontologist, consequentialist reasons may still determine right action even in areas governed by agent-relative obligations or permissions, once the level of bad consequences crosses the relevant threshold (Moore 2012).

5.1 Making no concessions to consequentialism: a purely deontological rationality?
In contrast to mixed theories, deontologists who seek to keep their deontology pure hope to expand agent-relative reasons to cover all of morality and yet to mimic the advantages of consequentialism. Doing this holds out the promise of denying sense to the otherwise damning question, how could it be moral to make (or allow) the world to be worse (for they deny that there is any states-of-affairs "worseness" in terms of which to frame such a question) (Foot 1985). To make this plausible, one needs to expand the coverage of agent-relative reasons to cover what is now plausibly a matter of consequentialist reasons, such as positive duties to strangers. Moreover, deontologists taking this route need a content to the permissive and obligating norms of deontology that allows them to mimic the outcomes making consequentialism attractive. This requires a picture of morality's norms that is extremely detailed in content, so that what looks like a consequentialist balance can be generated by a

complex series of norms with extremely detailed priority rules and exception clauses (Richardson 1990). Few consequentialists will believe that this is a viable enterprise.

5.2 Making no concessions to deontology: a purely consequentialist rationality?

The mirror image of the pure deontologist just described is the indirect or two-level consequentialist. For this view too seeks to appropriate the strengths of both deontology and consequentialism, not by embracing both, but by showing that an appropriately defined version of one can do for both. The indirect consequentialist, of course, seeks to do this from the side of consequentialism alone.

Yet as many have argued (Lyons 1965; Alexander 1985), indirect consequentialism collapses either into: blind and irrational rule-worship ("why follow the rules when not doing so produces better consequences?"); direct consequentialism ("acts in conformity to the rules rather miraculously produce better consequences in the long run"); or nonpublicisability ("ordinary folks should be instructed to follow the rules but should not be told of the ultimate consequentialist basis for doing so, lest they depart from the rules mistakenly believing better consequences will result"). For more information, please see the entry on rule consequentialism. Nor can the indirect consequentialist adequately explain why those who violate the indirect consequentialist's rules have "wronged" those who might be harmed as a result, that is, why the latter have a personal complaint against the former. (This is true irrespective of whether the rule-violation produces good consequences; but it is especially so when good consequences result from the rule-violation.) The bottom line is that if deontology has intuitive advantages over consequentialism, it is far from obvious whether those advantages can be captured by moving to indirect consequentialism, even if there is a version of indirect consequentialism that could avoid dire consequences problem that bedevils deontological theories.

6. Deontological Theories and Metaethics

Deontological theories are normative theories. They do not presuppose any particular position on moral ontology or on moral epistemology. Presumably, a deontologist can be a moral realist of either the natural (moral properties are identical to natural properties) or nonnatural (moral properties are not themselves natural properties even if they are nonreductively related to natural properties) variety. Or a deontologist can be an expressivist, a constructivist, a transcendentalist, a conventionalist, or a Divine command theorist regarding the nature of morality. Likewise, a deontologist can claim that we know the content of deontological morality by direct intuition, by Kantian reflection on our normative situation, or by reaching reflective equilibrium between our particular moral judgments and the theories we construct to explain them (theories of intuitions).

Nonetheless, although deontological theories can be agnostic regarding metaethics, some metaethical accounts seem less hospitable than others to deontology. For example, the stock furniture of deontological normative ethics—rights, duties, permissions—fits uneasily in the realist-naturalist's corner of the metaethical universe. (Which is why many naturalists, if they are moral realists in their meta-ethics, are consequentialists in their ethics.) Nonnatural realism, conventionalism, transcendentalism, and Divine command seem more hospitable metaethical homes for deontology. (For example, the paradox of deontology above discussed may seem more tractable if morality is a matter of personal directives of a Supreme Commander to each of his human subordinates.) If these rough connections hold, then weaknesses with those metaethical accounts most hospitable to deontology will weaken deontology as a normative theory of action. Some deontologists have thus argued that these connections need not hold and that a naturalist-realist meta-ethics can ground a deontological ethics (Moore 2004).

7. CIVIL DISOBEDIENCE

What makes a breach of law an act of civil disobedience? When is civil disobedience morally justified? How should the law respond to people who engage in civil disobedience? Discussions of civil disobedience have tended to focus on the first two of these questions. On the most widely accepted account of civil disobedience, famously defended by John Rawls (1971), civil disobedience is a public, non-violent and conscientious breach of law undertaken with the aim of bringing about a change in laws or government policies. On this account, people who engage in civil disobedience are willing to accept the legal consequences of their actions, as this shows their fidelity to the rule of law. Civil disobedience, given its place at the boundary of fidelity to law, is said to fall between legal protest, on the one hand, and conscientious refusal, revolutionary action, militant protest and organised forcible resistance, on the other hand.

This picture of civil disobedience raises many questions. Why must civil disobedience be non-violent? Why must it be public, in the sense of forewarning authorities of the intended action, since publicity gives authorities an opportunity to interfere with the action? Why must people who engage in civil disobedience be willing to accept punishment? A general challenge to Rawls's conception of civil disobedience is that it is overly narrow, and as such it predetermines the conclusion that most acts of civil disobedience are morally justifiable. A further challenge is that

Rawls applies his theory of civil disobedience only to the context of a nearly just society, leaving unclear whether a credible conception of either the nature or the justification of civil disobedience could follow the same lines in the context of less just societies. Some broader accounts of civil disobedience offered in response to Rawls's view (Raz, 1979; Greenawalt, 1987) will be examined in the first section of this entry.

This entry has four main sections. The first considers some definitional issues and contrasts civil disobedience with both ordinary offences and other types of dissent. The second analyses two sets of factors relevant to the justification of civil disobedience; one set concerns the disobedient's particular choice of action, the other concerns her motivation for so acting. The third section examines whether people have a right to engage in civil disobedience. The fourth considers what kind of legal response to civil disobedience is appropriate.

1. Definitions
The term 'civil disobedience' was coined by Henry David Thoreau in his 1848 essay to describe his refusal to pay the state poll tax implemented by the American government to prosecute a war in Mexico and to enforce the Fugitive Slave Law. In his essay, Thoreau observes that only a very few people – heroes, martyrs, patriots, reformers in the best sense – serve their society with their consciences, and so necessarily resist society for the most part, and are commonly treated by it as enemies. Thoreau, for his part, spent time in jail for his protest. Many after him have proudly identified their protests as acts of civil disobedience and

have been treated by their societies – sometimes temporarily, sometimes indefinitely – as its enemies.

Throughout history, acts of civil disobedience famously have helped to force a reassessment of society's moral parameters. The Boston Tea Party, the suffragette movement, the resistance to British rule in India led by Gandhi, the US civil rights movement led by Martin Luther King Jr., Rosa Parks and others, the resistance to apartheid in South Africa, student sit-ins against the Vietnam War, the democracy movement in Myanmar/Burma led by Aung San Suu Kyi, to name a few, are all instances where civil disobedience proved to be an important mechanism for social change. The ultimate impact of more recent acts of civil disobedience – anti-abortion trespass demonstrations or acts of disobedience taken as part of the environmental movement and animal rights movement – remains to be seen.

Certain features of civil disobedience seem vital not only to its impact on societies and governments, but also to its status as a potentially justifiable breach of law. Civil disobedience is generally regarded as more morally defensible than both ordinary offences and other forms of protest such as militant action or coercive violence. Before contrasting civil disobedience with both ordinary offences and other types of protest, attention should be given to the features exemplified in the influential cases noted above. These features include, amongst other things, a conscientious or principled outlook and the communication of both condemnation and a desire for change in law or policy. Other features commonly cited – publicity, non-violence, fidelity to law – will also be considered here though they prove to be less central than is sometimes assumed. The second part of this section contrasts civil disobedience with ordinary offences and the third part contrasts it with legal protest, rule departures by officials, conscientious objection, radical protest (often labelled 'terrorism'), and revolutionary action.

1.1 Features of Civil Disobedience
Conscientiousness: This feature, highlighted in almost all accounts of civil disobedience, points to the seriousness, sincerity and moral conviction with which civil disobedients breach the law. For many disobedients, their breach of law is demanded of them not only by self-respect and moral consistency but also by their perception of the interests

of their society. Through their disobedience, they draw attention to laws or policies that they believe require reassessment or rejection. Whether their challenges are well-founded is another matter, which will be taken up in Section 2.

On Rawls's account of civil disobedience, in a nearly just society, civil disobedients address themselves to the majority to show that, in their considered opinion, the principles of justice governing cooperation amongst free and equal persons have not been respected by policymakers. Rawls's restriction of civil disobedience to breaches that defend the principles of justice may be criticised for its narrowness since, presumably, a wide range of legitimate values not wholly reducible to justice, such as transparency, security, stability, privacy, integrity, and autonomy, could motivate people to engage in civil disobedience. However, Rawls does allow that considerations arising from people's comprehensive moral outlooks may be offered in the public sphere provided that, in due course, people present public reasons, given by a reasonable political conception of justice, sufficient to support whatever their comprehensive doctrines were introduced to support (Rawls, 1996). Rawls's proviso grants that people often engage in the public sphere for a variety of reasons; so even when justice figures prominently in a person's decision to use civil disobedience, other considerations could legitimately contribute to her decision to act. The activism of Martin Luther King Jr. is a case in point. King was motivated by his religious convictions and his commitments to democracy, equality, and justice to undertake protests such as the Montgomery bus boycott. Rawls maintains that, while he does not know whether King thought of himself as fulfilling the purpose of the proviso, King could have fulfilled it; and had he accepted public reason he certainly would have fulfilled it. Thus, on Rawls's view, King's activism is civil disobedience.

Since people can undertake political protest for a variety of reasons, civil disobedience sometimes overlaps with other forms of dissent. A US draft-dodger during the Vietnam War might be said to combine civil disobedience and conscientious objection in the same action. And, most famously, Gandhi may be credited with combining civil disobedience with revolutionary action. That said, despite the potential for overlap, some broad distinctions may be drawn between civil disobedience and other forms of protest in terms of the scope of the action and agents' motivations (Section 1.3).

Communication: In civilly disobeying the law, a person typically has both forward-looking and backward-looking aims. She seeks not only to convey her disavowal and condemnation of a certain law or policy, but also to draw public attention to this particular issue and thereby to instigate a change in law or policy. A parallel may be drawn between the communicative aspect of civil disobedience and the communicative aspect of lawful punishment by the state (Brownlee, 2012; 2004). Like civil disobedience, lawful punishment is associated with a backward-looking aim to demonstrate condemnation of certain conduct as well as a forward-looking aim to bring about a lasting change in that conduct. The forward and backward-looking aims of punishment apply not only to the particular offence in question, but also to the kind of conduct of which this offence is an example.

There is some dispute over the kinds of policies that civil disobedients may target through their breach of law. Some exclude from the class of civilly disobedient acts those breaches of law that protest the decisions of private agents such as trade unions, banks, private universities, etc. (Raz, 1979, 264). Others, by contrast, maintain that disobedience in opposition to the decisions of private agents can reflect a larger challenge to the legal system that permits those decisions to be taken, which makes it appropriate to place this disobedience under the umbrella of civil disobedience (Brownlee, 2012; 2007). There is more agreement amongst thinkers that civil disobedience can be either direct or indirect. In other words, civil disobedients can either breach the law they oppose or breach a law which, other things being equal, they do not oppose in order to demonstrate their protest against another law or policy. Trespassing on a military base to spray-paint nuclear missile silos in protest against current military policy would be an example of indirect civil disobedience. It is worth noting that the distinction often drawn between direct civil disobedience and indirect civil disobedience is less clear-cut than generally assumed. For example, refusing to pay taxes that support the military could be seen as either indirect or direct civil disobedience against military policy. Although this act typically would be classified as indirect disobedience, a part of one's taxes, in this case, would have gone directly to support the policy one opposes.

Publicity: The feature of communication may be contrasted with that of publicity. The latter is endorsed by Rawls who argues that civil disobedience is never covert or secretive; it is only ever committed in public, openly, and with fair notice to legal authorities (Rawls, 1971, 366). Hugo A. Bedau adds to this that usually it is essential to the dissenter's purpose that both the government and the public know what she intends to do (Bedau, 1961, 655). However, although sometimes advance warning may be essential to a dissenter's strategy, this is not always the case. As noted at the outset, publicity sometimes detracts from or undermines the attempt to communicate through civil disobedience. If a person publicises her intention to breach the law, then she provides both political opponents and legal authorities with the opportunity to abort her efforts to communicate (Smart, 1991, 206). For this reason, unannounced or (initially) covert disobedience is sometimes preferable to actions undertaken publicly and with fair warning. Examples include releasing animals from research laboratories or vandalising military property; to succeed in carrying out these actions, disobedients would have to avoid publicity of the kind Rawls defends. Such acts of civil disobedience nonetheless may be regarded as 'open' when followed soon after by an acknowledgment of the act and the reasons for acting. Openness and publicity, even at the cost of having one's protest frustrated, offer ways for disobedients to show their willingness to deal fairly with authorities.

Non-violence: A controversial issue in debates on civil disobedience is non-violence. Like publicity, non-violence is said to diminish the negative effects of breaching the law. Some theorists go further and say that civil disobedience is, by definition, non-violent. According to Rawls, violent acts likely to injure are incompatible with civil disobedience as a mode of address. 'Indeed', says Rawls, 'any interference with the civil liberties of others tends to obscure the civilly disobedient quality of one's act.'(Rawls, 1971, 366).

Even though paradigmatic disobedients like Gandhi and Martin Luther King Jr embody Rawls's image of non-violent direct action, opponents of Rawls's view have challenged the centrality of non-violence for civil disobedience on several fronts. First, there is the problem of specifying an appropriate notion of violence. It is unclear, for example, whether violence to self, violence to property, or minor violence against others (such as a vicious pinch) should be included in a conception of the relevant kinds of violence. If the significant criterion for a commonsense notion of a violent act is a likelihood of causing injury, however minor, then these kinds of acts count as acts of violence (See Morreall, 1991). Second, non-violent acts or legal acts sometimes cause more harm to others than do violent acts (Raz, 1979, 267). A legal strike by ambulance workers may well have much more severe consequences than minor acts of vandalism. Third, violence, depending on its form, does not necessarily obscure the communicative quality of a disobedient's action as Rawls and Peter Singer suggests it does (Singer, 1973, 86). Limited violence used to achieve a specific objective might heighten the communicative quality of the act by drawing greater attention to the dissenter's cause and by emphasising her seriousness and frustration.

These observations do not alter the fact that non-violent dissent normally is preferable to violent dissent. As Raz observes, non-violence avoids the direct harm caused by violence, and non-violence does not encourage violence in other situations where violence would be wrong, something which an otherwise warranted use of violence may do. Moreover, as a matter of prudence, non-violence does not carry the same risk of antagonising potential allies or confirming the antipathy of opponents (Raz, 1979, 267). Furthermore, non-violence does not distract the attention of the public, and it probably denies authorities an excuse to use violent countermeasures against disobedients.

Non-violence, publicity and a willingness to accept punishment are often regarded as marks of disobedients' fidelity to the legal system in which they carry out their protest. Those who deny that these features are definitive of civil disobedience endorse a more inclusive conception according to which civil disobedience involves a conscientious and communicative breach of law designed to demonstrate condemnation of a law or policy and to contribute to a change in that law or policy. Such a conception allows that civil disobedience can be violent, partially covert, and revolutionary. This conception also accommodates vagaries in the practice and justifiability of civil disobedience for different political contexts: it grants that the appropriate model of how civil disobedience works in a context such as apartheid South Africa may differ from the model that applies to a well-ordered, liberal, just democracy. An even broader conception of civil disobedience would draw no clear boundaries between civil disobedience and other forms of protest such as conscientious objection, forcible resistance, and revolutionary action. A disadvantage of this last conception is that it blurs the lines between these different types of protest and so might both weaken claims about the defensibility of civil disobedience and invite authorities and opponents of civil disobedience to lump all illegal protest under one umbrella.

1.2 Ordinary Offences

In democratic societies, civil disobedience as such is not a crime. If a disobedient is punished by the law, it is not for civil disobedience, but for the recognised offences she commits, such as blocking a road or disturbing the peace, or trespassing, or damaging property, etc. Therefore, if judges are persuaded, as they sometimes are, either not to punish a disobedient or to punish her differently from other people who breach the same laws, it must be on the basis of some feature or features of her action which distinguish it from the acts of ordinary offenders.

Typically a person who commits an offence has no wish to communicate with her government or society. This is evinced by the fact that usually an offender does not intend to make it known that she has breached the law. Since, in most cases, she wishes to benefit or, at least, not to suffer from her unlawful action, it is in her interests to preserve the secrecy of her conduct. An exception might be where a person's breach is sufficiently minor, such as jaywalking, that concealment is unnecessary since sanction is unlikely to follow. Another exception might be where a person wishes to thumb her nose at authorities by advertising that she has committed a crime. By making an exception of herself and by distancing herself from a legal rule, this ordinary offender communicates a certain disregard for the law. This communication, however, does not normally reflect an aim either to demonstrate conscientiously held objections to that law or to lead society to reform the law. Civil disobedients, by contrast, seek to make their disobedience known to specific members of the community either before or after the fact to demonstrate both the seriousness of their condemnation of that law or policy and their sincere desire for policy change. The difference in communication between the civil disobedient and the ordinary offender reflects a deeper difference in motivation for breaching the law (Brownlee, 2012).

A further difference between civil disobedience and common crimes pertains to the willingness of the offender to accept the legal consequences. The willingness of disobedients to accept punishment is taken not only as a mark of (general) fidelity to the law, but also as an assertion that they differ from ordinary offenders. Accepting punishment also can have great strategic value, as Martin Luther King Jr observes: 'If you confront a man who has been cruelly misusing you, and say "Punish me, if you will; I do not deserve it, but I will accept it, so that the world will know I am right and you are wrong," then you wield a powerful and just weapon.' (Washington, 1991, 348). Moreover, like non-violence, a willingness to accept the legal consequences normally is preferable, and often has a positive impact on the disobedient's cause. This willingness may make the majority realise that what is for them a matter of indifference is for disobedients a matter of great importance (Singer, 1973, 84). Similarly, it may demonstrate the purity or selflessness of the disobedient's motives or serve as a means to mobilise more broad-based support (Raz, 1979, 265). And yet, punishment can also be detrimental to dissenters' efforts by compromising future attempts to assist others through protest (Greenawalt, 1987, 239). Furthermore, the link between a willingness to accept punishment and respect for law can be pulled apart. A revolutionary like Gandhi was happy to go to jail for his offences, but felt no fidelity toward the particular legal system in which he acted.

1.3 Other Types of Dissent
Although civil disobedience often overlaps broadly with other types of dissent, nevertheless some rough distinctions may be drawn between the key features of civil disobedience and the key features of these other practices.

Legal Protest: The obvious difference between legal protest and civil disobedience is that the former lies within the bounds of the law, but the latter does not. Most of the other features exemplified in civil disobedience can be found in legal protest including a conscientious and communicative demonstration of protest, a desire to bring about through moral dialogue some lasting change in policy or principle, an attempt to educate and to raise awareness, and so on. The difference in legality translates into a more significant, moral difference when placed against the backdrop of a general moral obligation to follow the law. If it is morally wrong to breach the law, then special justification is required for civil disobedience which is not required for legal protest. However, the political regime in which obedience is demanded may be relevant here. David Lyons maintains that the Jim Crow laws (racial segregation laws in force in the southern US until 1964), British colonial rule in India, and chattel slavery in antebellum America offer three refutations of the view that civil disobedience requires moral justification in morally objectionable regimes. According to Lyons, there can be no moral presumption in favour of obedience to the law in such regimes, and therefore no moral justification is required for civil disobedience. 'Insofar as civil disobedience theory assumes that political resistance requires moral justification even in settings that are morally comparable to Jim Crow,' says Lyons, 'it is premised on serious moral error.' (Lyons, 1998, 39). If one takes the view that there is no general moral obligation to follow the law (irrespective of regime), then both adherence to the law and breach of law must be judged not on their legality, but on their character and consequences. And this would mean that, even in morally reprehensible regimes, justification may be demanded for civil disobedience that either has significant negative consequences or falls below certain moral standards.

Although questions of justification will be addressed more fully in the next section, it is worth noting here one point in favour of civil disobedience over legal protest. As Bertrand Russell observes, typically it is difficult to make the most salient facts in a dispute known through conventional channels of participation. The controllers of mainstream media tend to give defenders of unpopular views limited space to make their case. Given the sensational news value of illegal methods, however, engaging in civil disobedience often leads to wide dissemination of a position (Russell, 1998, 635). John Stuart Mill observes, with regard to dissent in general, that sometimes the only way to make a view heard is to allow, or even to invite, society to ridicule and sensationalise it as intemperate and irrational (Mill, 1999). Admittedly, the success of this strategy depends partly on the character of the society in which it is employed; but it should not be ruled out as a strategy for communication.

Rule Departures: A practice distinct from, but related to, civil disobedience is rule departure on the part of authorities. Rule departure is essentially the deliberate decision by an official, for conscientious reasons, not to discharge the duties of her office (Feinberg, 1979). It may involve a decision by police not to arrest offenders (cf. Smith, 2012) or a decision by prosecutors not to proceed to trial, or a decision by a jury or by a judge to acquit an obviously guilty person. Whether these conscientious acts actually contravene the general duties of the office is debatable. If an official's breach of a specific duty is more in keeping with the spirit and overall aims of the office than a painstaking respect for its particular duties is, then the former might be said to adhere better than the latter does to the demands of the office (Greenawalt, 1987, 281)

Rule departures resemble civil disobedience in that both involve dissociation from and condemnation of certain policies and practices. Moreover, both are communicative, though their audiences may differ. The official who departs from the rules of her office addresses her action principally to the individuals or groups whom she intends to assist through her breach of a specific duty. Her action demonstrates to these parties both that she disagrees with a policy that would treat them in a certain way and that her actions align with her commitments. Where civil disobedience and rule departure differ is, first, in the identity of their practitioners. Whereas rule departure typically is an action taken by an agent of the state (including juries), civil disobedience typically is an action taken by citizens (including officials acting as ordinary citizens and not in the capacity of their official role). Second these practices differ in their legality. Whether rule departure actually involves a breach of law is unclear. Civil disobedience, by contrast, involves the breach of a law currently on the books. A third difference between rule departure and civil disobedience is that, unlike civil disobedience, rule departure does not usually expose those who employ it to the risks of sanction or punishment (Feinberg, 1979)

Conscientious Objection: This kind of protest may be understood as a violation of the law motivated by the dissenter's belief that she is morally prohibited to follow the law because the law is either bad or wrong, totally or in part. The conscientious objector may believe, for example, that the general character of the law in question is morally wrong (as an absolute pacifist would believe of conscription), or that the law extends to certain cases which it should not cover (an orthodox Christian would regard euthanasia as murder) (Raz, 1979, 263). While commonly taken to refer to pacifist objections to military service, conscientious objection, says Raz, may apply to any law, negative or positive, that a person believes for moral reasons she is compelled to disobey. A narrower conception of conscientious objection, described as conscientious refusal, characterises this kind of disobedience as non-compliance with a more or less direct legal injunction or administrative order (Rawls, 1971, 368). Examples would be the refusal of Jehovah's Witnesses to salute the flag or Thoreau's refusal to pay his taxes (it is interesting that the action of the man who coined the term 'civil disobedience' is regarded by many as lying at the periphery of what counts as civil disobedience). Whereas conscientious refusal is undertaken with the assumption that authorities are aware of the breach of law, conscientious evasion is undertaken with the assumption that the breach of law is wholly covert. The devout person who continues to practice her religion in secret after it has been banned does not protest against the law, but breaches it covertly for moral reasons. The personal nature of this disobedience commands respect, as it suggests modesty and reflection, which more vocal and confident displays of conviction may lack.

The differences between civil disobedience and conscientious evasion are easier to identify than those between civil disobedience and conscientious refusal or conscientious objection. Although conscientious objection typically is not characterised by the aim to communicate to government and society either that a law has been breached or the reasons behind the breach, nevertheless many acts commonly classified as conscientious objection – tax avoidance and resistance to conscription – have a public or communicative component. Moreover, when such actions are taken by many people their collective impact can approximate the kind of communicative protest exemplified in civil disobedience.

A more obvious difference between civil disobedience and conscientious objection is that, whereas the former is invariably illegal, sometimes the latter is legal. In the context of military conscription, some legal systems regard conscientious objection as a legitimate ground for avoiding frontline military service.

Radical Protest: Some forms of dissent such as coercive violence, organised forcible resistance, militant action, intimidation, and terrorisation lie further outside the realm of tolerated (or tolerable) political action than civil disobedience does. There are reasons to avoid labelling such disobedience (or anything else) as 'terrorism'. Not only is the term 'terrorism' inflammatory, but also it is bandied about by governments to capture an overly broad range of actions. Whereas 'civil disobedience' has developed as a positive term which many people apply to their own protests, 'terrorism' is an epithet applied only to the actions of others. Given the highly negative connotations of this term, its (philosophical) usefulness is questionable. Less loaded notions of intimidation, terrorisation, forcible resistance, and severe violence offer greater space for a proper analysis of the justifiability of using such measures in political protest.

While a civil disobedient does not necessarily oppose the regime in which she acts, the militant or radical protester is deeply opposed to that regime (or a core aspect of that regime). This protester uses modes of communication unlikely to persuade others of the merits of her position. Her aims are more urgent and extreme than those of the civil disobedient; she seeks rapid change through brutal strategies of coercion and intimidation, not through strategies of persuasion and moral appeal. And often her action includes force or extreme violence as a key component. Given the nature of her conduct and objectives, she is likely to try to evade the legal consequences of her action. This is less often the case for civil disobedients.

Revolutionary Action: The difference between radical protest and revolutionary action may be as difficult to specify as that between revolutionary action and civil disobedience. One point of difference amongst the three concerns the nature of the objectives. Acts of civil disobedience often have focused and limited objectives. Acts of terrorisation or large-scale coercive violence are typically associated with a general aim of generating fear and insecurity while keeping any specific aims or demands oblique. Revolutionary action is typified by a comprehensive objective to bring about a regime change. Both acts of radical protest and acts of civil disobedience can of course fall within a revolutionary project, and may even coincide with each other (as they perhaps did in the sabotage strategies used by Nelson Mandela and the African National Congress).

As a general practice, revolution, like radical protest, does not seek to persuade the government to change established policies. But, unlike much radical protest, revolutionary action may seek to persuade the society under that government that a change in regime is required. If revolutionaries seek to persuade the government of anything, it is that it should cease to be the government. In India, Gandhi had some success in this project. Once the movement became irresistible, the British left India fairly peacefully. But Gandhi's revolutionary project may be contrasted with other revolutions such as the French revolution, or even the South African revolution, where there were endorsements of revolutionary terror. Large-scale resistance that incorporates terrorisation is quite a different enterprise from the non-violent resistance that distinguished Gandhi's protest. Since, as noted above, people may engage in dissent for numerous reasons, acts of civil disobedience like Gandhi's that are guided by conscientious commitments can also be driven by revolutionary aims.

The various points of contact and overlap amongst different types of political protest suggest that there is no one-dimensional continuum from weak to strong dissent. There is more plausibility in the idea of a multi-dimensional continuum of protest, which recognises the complexities in such critical points of contrast as legality, violence, harm, communication, motivation, and persuasiveness.

2. Justification

On many views, an analysis of the justifiability of civil disobedience must consider not only the dissenter's particular action and its likely consequences, but also her motivation for engaging in this act of civil disobedience. Factors relevant to a disobedient's choice of action include: its illegality, its use as a last resort or first resort, any coordination with other dissenters, the likelihood of success, the directness or indirectness of the action, and the expected harm. Factors relevant to motivation include: the merit or lack thereof in the dissenter's cause, her reasons for defending that cause, and her reasons for engaging in this form of protest. Although they are examined separately below, these two sets of factors inevitably overlap.

2.1 Mode of Action

The task of defending civil disobedience is commonly undertaken with the assumption that in reasonably just, liberal societies people have a general moral obligation to follow the law. In the history of philosophy, many arguments have been given for legal obligation (often called 'political obligation'). Plato's Socrates, in the Crito, offers at least two lines of argument for legal obligation in order to defend his decision not to escape from prison. First, Socrates emphasises the importance of moral consistency; he would prefer to give up his life than to compromise his principles. A basic principle for Socrates is that a person must never do wrong or injury in return for wrong. To escape without persuading the state would be to try to destroy it and its laws. Second, Socrates maintains that he has an obligation to follow the laws of Athens since he has tacitly agreed to do so and since he enjoys the rights and benefits of citizenship. This voluntarist line of argument is also espoused later by John Locke, who argues that we have a duty to follow the law only when we have consented to its rule. This view contrasts with the non-voluntarist position of David Hume, according to which the obligation to follow the law is rooted in the value of government under law. From these two traditions rise the principal contemporary arguments for legal obligation, which concern respectively consent, gratitude, promise-keeping, fairness, necessary institutions, and public good. Many of the contemporary voluntarist and non-voluntarist arguments have been criticised in recent debates, giving rise to the view that, while there are both ordinary reasons to follow the law and strong moral obligations to follow particular laws, there is no general moral obligation to follow the law. One reason to think there is no such obligation is that the legality of an action does not significantly affect its moral status (Smith, 1973). The claim is that jaywalking across an empty street, for example, is hardly reprehensible and its illegality does not make it more reprehensible. Similarly, spitting at someone's feet or refusing without cause to acknowledge that person is reprehensible and its legality does not diminish that.

On the assumption that people have a pro tanto obligation to follow the law (or at least those laws that are not excessively unjust), it follows that people then have a pro tanto obligation to use the proper legal channels of political participation before resorting to illegal methods. On this view, civil disobedience can be justified only when employed as a last resort. But since causes defended by a minority are often those most opposed by persons in power, legal channels may be less than wholly effective. Moreover, it is unclear when a person could claim to have reached the situation of last resort; she could continue to use the same tired legal methods without end. To ward off such challenges, Rawls suggests that, if past actions have shown the majority to be immovable or apathetic, then further attempts may reasonably be thought fruitless and one may be confident one's civil disobedience is a last resort.

Another condition for civil disobedience to be justified, according to

Rawls, is that disobedients coordinate with other minorities. Since minority groups are equally justified in resorting to civil disobedience when they have sufficiently weighty objections, these groups should avoid undermining each others' efforts through simultaneous appeals to the attention of society and government. Some coordination of activities is required, says Rawls, to regulate the overall level of dissent (Rawls, 1971, 374–5). While there is some merit to this condition, civil disobedience that does not meet it might still be justifiable. In some cases, there will be no time or opportunity to coordinate with other minorities. And in other cases, other minority groups may be unable or unwilling to coordinate. It is an open question then whether the refusal or inability of other groups to cooperate should affect the ultimate defensibility of a person's decision to engage in civil disobedience.

A reason for Rawls to defend this coordination requirement is that, in most cases, it serves a more important concern, namely, the achievement of good consequences. It is often argued that civil disobedience can only be justified if there is a high probability of producing positive change through that disobedience. Only this can justify exposing one's society to the risk of harm. The harms usually identified with civil disobedience are as follows. First, civil disobedience can be a divisive force in society. Second, since civil disobedience is normally designed to attract public attention, it can lead people, as a result, to think of resorting to disobedience to achieve whatever changes in law or policy they find justified (Raz, 1979, 262). Third, civil disobedience can encourage more than just other civil disobedience; it can encourage a general disrespect for the law, particularly where the law is perceived as being lenient toward certain kinds of offences.

In response to these challenges, one might question the empirical claims that civil disobedience is divisive and that it has the consequence of leading others to use disobedience to achieve changes in policy. One might also question whether it necessarily would be a bad thing if civil disobedience had these consequences. Concerning likelihood of success, civil disobedience actually can seem most justifiable when the situation appears hopeless and when the government refuses to listen to conventional forms of communication. Additionally, even when general success seems unlikely, civil disobedience might be defended for any reprieve from harm that it brings to victims of a bad law or policy. Tree-hugging, for example, can delay or curtail a clear-cut logging scheme and thereby prolong the protection of an eco-system.

Two final factors concerning a disobedient's choice of action are non-violence and directness. Many theorists regard non-violence as necessary to the justifiability of civil disobedience. But, as noted earlier, there can be good reasons to prefer strategic use of violence in civil disobedience to the harm and injustice of the law. Sometimes the wrong that a dissenter perceives may be so iniquitous that it is right to use violence to root it out. Such violence may be necessary to preserve or to re-establish the rights and civil liberties that coercive practices seek to suspend (Raz, 1979). Concerning directness, some argue that civil disobedience is more justifiable the more direct it is since direct disobedience targets the specific legal wrong that prompted it (Greenawalt, 1987, 235). While directness may ensure that the objective of the dissent is understood, it has disadvantages; and in some contexts direct action cannot be justified. When direct disobedience would fail to treat others with respect or would cause far greater harm than either adherence to the law or indirect disobedience would cause, then indirect disobedience has a greater claim to justification. But, when indirect civil disobedience would be either misconstrued or viewed in isolation from the law opposed, then direct disobedience, assuming it meets certain moral requirements (which are determined by the content of the law opposed), may have greater justification. People who use indirect disobedience have, other things being equal, no objective reasons to breach the law that they breach. This means that the justification for their disobedience must turn solely on the value of that action as the appropriate vehicle through which to communicate their objection.

As a vehicle for communication, civil disobedience has much to be said for it. It was noted in Section 1.3 that civil disobedience can often better contribute to a dialogue with society and the state than legal protest can since controllers of mainstream media tend not to give unpopular views a hearing unless they are advocated through sensational means such as illegal protest. But, as the above points have indicated, the justifiability of an act of civil disobedience depends greatly on its specific features. Civil disobedience sometimes serves primarily to inform and to educate the public about an issue. But other times, it acts by confronting the majority with the higher costs of retaining a given law or policy in the face of continued, concerted opposition. The nature of these strategies and, as discussed below, the motivations for selecting one over another inform an analysis of justifiability.

2.2 Motivation for Acting

On many views, for an act of civil disobedience to be justified, it is insufficient that the dissenter's act meet criteria such as those noted above. It is equally important that she choose that action for the right reasons. The first requirement she must satisfy is that her cause be well-founded. A dissenter may believe that her cause is just and that her disobedience is morally permissible, but she might be mistaken either about the facts or about her principles. Assuming her challenge is well-founded, there are two further issues. The first pertains to her reasons for supporting this cause. The second pertains to her reasons for taking this particular act of disobedience.

Concerning the former, if a person advocates a legitimate cause such as equal rights for black Americans simply for the reason that she seeks re-election or promotion or the admiration of friends while having no real sympathy for this cause, then she acts not for decisive reasons. To be fully justified in her defence of this cause, she must act on the basis of good reasons to support equality amongst peoples; such reasons could include her sense of injustice for the ill-treatment of black Americans or her respect for the dignity of persons or her appreciation that real equality of rights best serves the interests of all American people. It would be appropriate to judge negatively the character of a person who was improperly motivated to take praiseworthy action in defence of others' rights.

Concerning the latter, sometimes reasons apply to a situation but do not favour the particular action that a person takes. When deciding how best to defend a legitimate cause, a person must give thought to the appropriate strategy to adopt. A person may have reasons for engaging in one form of disobedience, but choose to engage in another form that is not supported by these reasons. For example, she may have an undefeated reason to participate in a road block because this action is well suited to her political concerns and is one that her government understands and responds well to or because this action has a public impact that does not greatly harm the interests of others; but, she has no undefeated reason, say, to trespass on government property or to engage in vandalism. In taking the latter actions, she is guilty of a certain error of judgment about which actions are supported by reasons that admittedly apply (See Gardner and Macklem 2002). Given her error, the best she could claim is that her conduct is excused, as she had reason to believe that she had reason to undertake that particular form of civil disobedience. When, by contrast, a person's civilly disobedient action is supported by undefeated reasons that apply to her situation then her choice of action is justified. The justification for her action stems from its appropriateness as the action to take. Its appropriateness is structured in part by the political regime, the tone of the social environment, the actions taken by other political participants, and so on. All of these factors bear on the appropriateness of a given action and the manner in which it is performed, and thus determine to what extent the reasons that support it provide a justification.

The various constraints and requirements discussed above do not amount to a complete defence for civil disobedience. A fuller defence would appeal to the social value of civil disobedience. Justified civil disobedience, says Rawls, can serve to inhibit departures from justice and to correct departures when they occur; thus it can act as a stabilising force in society (Rawls, 1971, 383). Justice aside, civil disobedience and dissent more generally contribute to the democratic exchange of ideas by forcing the champions of dominant opinion to defend their views. Mill maintains in On Liberty that if there are any persons who contest a received opinion, we should thank them for it, open our minds to listen to them, and rejoice that there is someone to do for us what we otherwise ought to do ourselves (Mill, 1999, 90). In fact, one could argue that those who breach the law in justified civil disobedience demonstrate responsible citizenship or civic virtue. Richard Dagger argues that

To be virtuous...is to perform well a socially necessary or important role. This does not mean that the virtuous person must always go along with the prevailing views or attitudes. On the contrary, Socrates and John Stuart Mill have persuaded many people to believe that questioning and challenging the prevailing views are among the highest forms of virtue (Dagger, 1997, 14).

This view of dissent and justified civil disobedience aligns with an increasingly common perception that our responsibilities as citizens go well beyond any obligation to follow the law. Indeed, under certain conditions, our obligations are to resist unjust and unfair schemes, and this can include a duty to disobey the law (Delmas, forthcoming).

3. Rights

An issue associated with, but distinct from, that of justification is whether people have a right to engage in civil disobedience. Most thinkers who have considered civil disobedience defend a limited right to such protest. Rawls, for example, maintains that, even in a nearly just society, a person may be supposed to have a right to engage in civil disobedience when three conditions are met. These are the conditions he sets for justified civil disobedience: it is undertaken 1) in response to an instance of substantial and clear injustice, 2) as a last resort and 3) in coordination with other minority groups. Rawls's approach has been criticised for not clearly distinguishing his account of justified civil disobedience from an account of the disobedience which people have a right to take. There is much disagreement over the kinds of actions that can be captured by rights. Some theorists, such as John Mackie, argue that there can be no right to perform a morally wrong action since wrong actions are acts we are morally required not to perform (Mackie, 1978). Others, such as Raz, argue that to restrict rights to morally right actions is to misunderstand the nature of rights. Rights of conduct protect a certain sphere of autonomy and liberty for the agent with which interference by others is restricted, that is to say, rights of conduct imply that interference with that conduct is unjustified even when the conduct is itself unjustified. One does not require a right, Raz observes, to do the right thing. But one often does require a right to do what one should not do (Cf. Waldron, 1981). On this view, the limits of the right to political participation, for example, are set not by the nature of people's political objectives, but by the form of the actions they employ to realise those objectives.

According to Raz, when one considers the idea of a moral right to civil disobedience, one must appreciate that this right extends to cases in which people should not exercise it. To say that there is a right to civil disobedience is to allow the legitimacy of resorting to this form of political action to one's political opponents. It is to allow that the legitimacy of civil disobedience does not depend on the rightness of one's cause (Raz, 1979, 268).

In his account of a right to civil disobedience, Raz places great emphasis on the kind of regime in which a disobedient acts. Raz argues that only in an illiberal regime do certain individuals have a right to civil disobedience.

Given that the illiberal state violates its members' right to political participation, individuals whose rights are violated are entitled, other things being equal, to disregard the offending laws and exercise their moral right as if it were recognised by law... [M]embers of the illiberal state do have a right to civil disobedience which is roughly that part of their moral right to political participation which is not recognised in law (Raz, 1979, 272–273).

By contrast, in a liberal state, Raz argues, a person's right to political activity is, by hypothesis, adequately protected by law. Therefore, in such a regime, the right to political participation cannot ground a right to civil disobedience.

Against Raz, one could argue, as David Lefkowitz does, that when a person appeals to political participation rights to defend her disobedience she does not necessarily criticise the law for outlawing her action. Lefkowitz maintains that members of minorities can appreciate that democratic discussions often must be cut short so that decisions may be taken. As such, persons who engage in political disobedience may view current policy as the best compromise between the need to act and the need to accommodate continued debate. Nonetheless, they also can observe that, with greater resources or further time for debate, their view might have held sway. Given this possibility, the right to political participation must include a right to continue to contest the result after the votes are counted or the decisions taken. And this right should include suitably constrained civil disobedience because the best conception of political participation rights is one that reduces as much as possible the impact that luck has on the popularity of a view (Lefkowitz, 2007; see also Ceva, forthcoming).

An alternative response to Raz questions whether the right to civil disobedience must be derived from rights to political participation. Briefly, the right to civil disobedience could be grounded on something other than participation rights such as a right to object on the basis of conscience. Whether such a right to conscience would fall under participation rights depends on the expansiveness of the latter rights. When the right to participate is understood to accommodate only legal protest, then the right conscientiously to object, which commonsensically includes civil disobedience, must be viewed as distinct from political participation rights.

A further challenge to Raz might be that real societies do not align with this dichotomy between liberal and illiberal regimes; rather they fall along a spectrum of liberality and illiberality, being both more or less liberal relative to each other and being more or less liberal in some domains than in others. Given the stringency of Raz's notion of a liberal regime, it is unlikely that any society could be wholly liberal. So, although Raz may have grounds to hold that in the truly liberal society a right to civil disobedience would not exist and that, to the extent that our society approximates such a regime, the case for such a right diminishes, nevertheless in the majority of real societies, if not all real societies, a right to civil disobedience does exist. Note that to make legally protected participation fully adequate, the liberal society would have to address Russell's charge that controllers of the media give defenders of unpopular views few opportunities to make their case unless they resort to sensational methods such as disobedience.

Ronald Dworkin rests the right to civil disobedience not just on a person's right to political participation, but on all of the rights that she has against her government. People may be supposed to have a fundamental right against the government, such as freedom of expression, when that right is important to their dignity, to their standing as persons equally entitled to concern and respect, or to some other personal value of consequence. A person has a right to disobey a law, says Dworkin, whenever that law wrongly invades her rights against the government (Dworkin, 1977, 192). Thus, the moral right to breach the law is not a separate right, like a right of conscience, additional to other rights against the government. It is that part of people's rights against the government which the government fails to honour.

Together the three above positions bring out some key points of disagreement amongst philosophers on the issue of a right to civil disobedience. First, philosophers disagree over the grounds of this right. Is it derivative of a right to participate in the political decision-making process? Is it derivative of other rights? Is it founded on a person's equal status as a being worthy of concern and respect? Second, philosophers disagree over the parameters of the right. Does it extend to all acts of civil disobedience or only to those acts that meet certain conditions of justifiability? Third, philosophers differ over the kinds of regimes in which the right arises. Does it exist only in illiberal regimes or does it hold in all regimes including just regimes? A final issue, not brought out in any of the above views, is whether the right to civil disobedience extends to indirect civil disobedience. Presumably, it should, but none of the above positions offer arguments on which one could base such a claim.

4. Punishment

The final issue to consider is how authorities should respond to civil disobedience. The question of appropriate legal response applies, first, to the actions of law-enforcers when deciding whether and how to intervene in a civilly disobedient action, whether to arrest, whether to charge, and so on. It applies, second, to the actions of prosecutors when deciding whether to proceed to trial. Finally, it applies to the actions of judges (and juries) when deciding whether to convict and (for judges) how much to punish. The focus here will be the issue of appropriate punishment.

4.1 Theories of Punishment

To determine when, if ever, punishment of civil disobedience is appropriate, it is necessary first to say a few things about the nature, purposes, and justification of lawful punishment by the state. The three basic issues of punishment are: Why punish?, Whom to punish?, and How much to punish? The justifications for punishment can be forward-looking, backward-looking or some combination of the two. Jeremy Bentham, for one, takes a forward-looking, consequentialist view of punishment. He holds that punishment is an evil that is only ever justified if its employment prevents some greater evil that would arise from not punishing (Bentham, 1789, 158).

A key variant of the consequentialist approach focuses on deterrence. Punishment is justified on deterrence grounds if it prevents and/or discourages both the offender and others from breaching the law. Deterrence theories are criticised for treating people as brutes not rational agents capable of responding to moral reasons because the deterrent element of punishment gives people a prudential reason (relating to the prospect of punishment), not a moral reason, to refrain from breaching the law. Deterrence theories also are criticised for allowing persons who are not proper objects of punishment to be punished when this succeeds in deterring other people from breaching the law. Finally, deterrence theories are criticised for making the parameters for appropriate punishment excessively broad in allowing that whatever punishment is needed to deter people is the justified punishment.

Desert theory, by contrast, takes a backward-looking view of the purpose and justification of punishment, focusing on what the offender deserves for her action. Desert theory is much more concerned than is deterrence theory with punishing only persons who are the proper objects of punishment and with punishing those persons only as much as they deserve. Desert theory aims at a response to the offence that is proportionate to its seriousness as an offence. Seriousness is determined by two factors: an offender's culpability and the harm caused by her action. Desert theories are criticised for insufficiently defending the view that the guilty always should be punished. Although the intuition that the guilty deserve to suffer is widely shared, it is not obvious why they deserve this. Desert theories are also criticised for assuming both that fact-finders can determine what offenders deserve and that the deserved punishment is necessarily the justified punishment: should people always be punished as they deserve?

A variant of desert theory is the communicative theory of punishment, which takes both a forward-looking and a backward-looking view of the purposes of punishment. The purposes of punishment on a communicative account are both to convey the state's condemnation of the action and to lead the offender to repent her action and to reform her conduct. On a communicative conception of punishment, the state aims to engage with the offender in a moral dialogue so that she appreciates the moral reasons she has to follow the law. According to some communicative theories, condemnation itself sufficiently justifies punishment. Punishment may be seen as a secular form of penance that vividly confronts the offender with the effects of her crime (Duff, 1998, 162). According to other, less monistic communicative theories, communication of censure alone is insufficient to justify punishment; added to it must be the aim of deterrence (von Hirsch, 1998, 171). Still other communicative theories add different considerations to the grounds for justification. On one pluralistic view, a distinction is drawn between the punishment that is deserved according to justice and the punishment that is actually justified. When, for example, an offender demonstrates repentance for her offence prior to punishment, the law has reason to be merciful toward her and to impose a less severe punishment than that which she deserves (Tasioulas, 2006). Mercy involves a charitable concern for the well-being of the offender as a potential recipient of deserved punishment. Given this offender's repentance, the justified punishment in this case is less than it would be were there no grounds for mercy.

4.2 Punishing Civil Disobedience

Deterrence systems of punishment recommend a simple approach to civil disobedience. Since the purpose and justification of punishment is to deter people from breaching the law, a deterrence system would impose on civil disobedients whatever punishment was necessary and sufficient to achieve that end. Whether that punishment would be less or more severe than, or equal to, that imposed on ordinary offenders depends on empirical considerations. Sometimes greater punishment than that required for ordinary offenders would be in order since disobedients who are serious in their moral conviction may not be deterred by standard punishments. Other times, however, less punishment than that for ordinary offenders would be in order since disobedients usually are not 'hardened' criminals and thus may need less severe treatment to deter them from offending.

In contrast to deterrence systems, monistic desert systems and communicative systems of punishment would only punish civil disobedients if, and to the extent that, they deserve to be punished. A pluralistic communicative system, which gives weight to considerations of mercy as well as retribution or desert, would only punish to the extent that the punishment was justified (not to the extent that it was deserved) since mercy toward the offender might recommend punishing her less than she deserves according to justice. The pluralistic approach raises the question whether being motivated by civil disobedience might give the law a reason to show mercy towards an offender. One might argue that a disobedient's conviction and commitments, which make it very difficult for her both to adhere to norms that violate those commitments and to desist from using effective means of protest, are facts about her circumstances that give the law reason to show mercy toward her. This would lessen the severity of any justified response from the law.

For desert and communicative theories concerned solely with justice-based desert, the key question is whether disobedients deserve censure, and if so, how much? There are at least three possible replies. One is that disobedients deserve the same punishment as the ordinary offenders who breach the same laws. There are several reasons to take this view. First, as Greenawalt puts it, the demands of proportionality would seem to recommend a uniform application of legal prohibitions. Since trespass is prohibited, persons who breach trespass laws in protest of either those laws or other laws are equally liable to persons who breach trespass laws for private purposes. Second, also from Greenawalt comes the suggestion that any principle that officials may excuse justified illegal acts will result in some failures to punish unjustified acts, for which the purposes of punishment would be more fully served. Even when officials make correct judgments about which acts to excuse, citizens may draw mistaken inferences, and restraints of deterrence and norm acceptance may be weakened for unjustified acts that resemble justified ones (Greenawalt, 1987, 273). Therefore all such violations, justified and unjustified, should be treated the same.

But much of this turns on the assumption that civilly disobedient breaches of law are in fact comparable to ordinary offences and deserve a comparable response from the law. The discussion in Section 1 of the key features of civil disobedience showed that it differs greatly from ordinary offences both in motivation and in mode of action, let alone moral justification. This would suggest that civil disobedience should be regarded in the eyes of the law as a different kind of disobedience from common crimes. This leaves two options: civil disobedience deserves greater censure or it deserves less censure than ordinary crimes do.

There are reasons to believe that civil disobedients should be dealt with more severely than ordinary offenders are. First, there is the fact that disobedients seem to have put themselves above the law in preferring their own moral judgment about a certain issue to that of the democratic decision-making process and the rule of law. (Although some judges have endorsed this caricature, it is worth noting that it clashes with how both dissenters and many theorists characterise their activities (Cf. Rawls,

1971; Greenawalt, 1987; Markovits, 2006).) Second, the communicative aspect of civil disobedience could be said to aggravate such offences since it usually is attended by much greater publicity than most covert violations are. This forces legal authorities to concern themselves with the possibility that law-abiding citizens will feel distressed, insecure and perhaps imposed on if no action is taken. So, notes Greenawalt, while authorities may quietly let minor breaches pass, failure to respond to violations performed, in some respect, in the presence of authority, may undercut claims that the rules and the persons who administered them deserve respect (Greenawalt, 1987, 351–2). Third, any use of violence would seem to aggravate civil disobedience particularly when it increases the harm of the offence or when it directly incites further and unjustified instances of violence. And although violence may eloquently communicate a dissenter's seriousness and frustration, it changes the nature of the dialogue. It pushes authorities to respond in ways consonant with their stance on violence – responses which may be harsher than those they would otherwise wish to make toward acts of civil disobedience that defend values they can appreciate.

The final possible view is that civil disobedients should be dealt with more leniently than ordinary offenders are, at least when their disobedience is morally justified. These offenders are conscientiously motivated and often their protests serve the interests of society by forcing a desirable re-examination of moral boundaries. That said, moral justifications do not usually translate into legal justifications and disobedients have been notoriously unsuccessful at advancing a defence of necessity (a defence that their action was legally justified being the lesser of two evils). Whether the law should be more accommodating of their conscientious motivation and efforts to engage in moral dialogue with government and society is a topic for further debate.

5. Conclusion

Some theorists maintain that civil disobedience is an outdated, overanalysed notion that little reflects current forms of political activism, which tend toward more extreme modes of engagement. Herbert Storing has suggested that 'The most striking characteristic of civil disobedience is its irrelevance to the problems of today.' (Storing, 1991, 85). He said, shortly after the assassination of Martin Luther King Jr, that the fashion of civil disobedience is as likely to die out as it was to burst forth under the words of King. There is of course much evidence to show that Storing was mistaken in his predictions for the popularity of civil disobedience as a mode of dissent. Certainly though there have been shifts in the paradigm forms of civil disobedience in recent years; yet these shifts have occurred largely within the framework of conscientious communication discussed at the outset. The historical paradigms of Gandhi, King, the suffragettes, and Mandela are representative of that kind of civil disobedience which aims to guarantee legal protection for the basic rights of a specific constituency. Such disobedience contrasts with much contemporary civil disobedience, which focuses not on individuals' basic rights, but on broader issues or special interests such as the environment, animal rights, nuclear disarmament, globalisation, foreign policy, and so on.

Civil disobedience taken in support of concerns such as the environment or animal rights may be seen in part as a response to some breakdown in the mechanisms for citizen engagement in the decision-making process. This breakdown might be termed a democratic deficit (Markovits, 2005). Such deficits in that dialogue may be an inevitable part of real democracies, and disobedience undertaken to correct those deficits may be said to reflect, to varying degrees, dissenters' sensitivity to democratic ideals. Civil disobedience remains today very much a vibrant part of liberal democracies and there are significant issues concerning civil disobedience for philosophers to address, particularly in how this practice may be distinguished from more radical forms of protest and how this practice should be treated by the law.

CIVIL DISOBEDIENCE

8 LEGAL PUNISHMENT

The question of whether, and how, legal punishment can be justified is central to both legal and political philosophy: what could justify a state in using the apparatus of the law to inflict burdensome sanctions on its citizens? Radically different answers to this question are offered by consequentialist and by retributivist theorists—and by those who seek to combine consequentialist with retributivist considerations in 'mixed' theories of punishment; an important strand in recent theorising has been the idea of punishment as a communicative enterprise. Meanwhile, abolitionist theorists argue that we should aim to replace legal punishment rather than to justify it.

1. Legal Punishment and its Justification
2. Punishment, Crime and the State
3. Pure Consequentialism and Punishment
4. Limited Consequentialism and Punishment
5. 'Positive' Retributivism and the Meaning of Desert
6. Punishment as Communication
7. 'Restorative Justice' and Restitution
8. Further Issues

1. Legal Punishment and its Justification
The central question asked by philosophers of punishment is: What

can justify punishment? More precisely, since they do not usually talk much about punishment in such contexts as the family or the workplace (but see Zaibert 2006; Bennett 2008: Part II), their question is: What can justify formal, legal punishment imposed by the state on those convicted of committing criminal offences? We will also focus on legal punishment here: not because the other species of punishment do not raise important normative questions (they do), nor because such questions can be answered in terms of an initial justification of legal punishment as being the paradigm case (since it's not clear that they can be), but because legal punishment, apart from being more dramatically coercive and burdensome than other species of punishment usually are, raises distinctive issues about the role of the state and its relationship to its citizens, and about the role of the criminal law. Future references to 'punishment' should therefore be read, unless otherwise specified, as references to legal or criminal punishment.

What then are we to justify in justifying punishment? The search for a precise definition of punishment that exercised some philosophers (for discussion and references see Scheid 1980; Boonin 2008: 3–28; Zimmerman 2011: ch. 1) is likely to prove futile: but we can say that legal punishment involves the imposition of something that is intended to be both burdensome and reprobative, on a supposed offender for a supposed crime, by a person or body who claims the authority to do so. Two points are worth particular notice here.

First, what distinguishes punishments from taxes or mere 'penalties' (see Feinberg 1970) is their reprobative or condemnatory character. Taxes might be imposed to discourage certain kinds of conduct; penalties might likewise be imposed to deter the penalised conduct (or to recoup some of the costs that it causes): but even if a primary purpose of punishment is deterrence (see ss. 3–4 below), its imposition (the conviction and formal sentence that the offender receives in court, the administration of the punishment itself) also expresses the censure or condemnation that the offender's crime is taken to warrant.

Second, punishment involves material impositions or exactions that are in themselves typically unwelcome: they deprive people of things that they value (liberty, money, time); they require people to do things that they would not normally want to do or do voluntarily (to spend time on unpaid community labour, to report to a probation officer regularly, to undertake demanding programmes of various kinds). What distinguishes punishment from other kinds of coercive imposition is that punishment is precisely intended to ...: but to what? Some would say that punishment is intended to inflict pain or suffering: but that suggests that what matters is pain or suffering as such (and invites the familiar criticism that we and the state should not be in the business of trying to inflict pain or suffering on people; see Christie 1981 on 'pain-delivery'), which some penal theorists would reject as a distortion. Others would say that punishment is intended to cause harm to the offender — adding, if they are careful (see Hanna forthcoming: s. 2) that what is intended is 'prima facie harm' rather than 'all-things-considered harm', to allow for the possibility that punishment might be, or might be intended to be, on balance beneficial to the offender. But some theorists would deny even this, since they would deny that punishment must be intended to be 'intrinsically bad' for the person punished. It is safer to say that punishment must be intended to be burdensome, and that is how punishment will be understood in what follows.

How then can the practice of criminal punishment, which infringes the freedom of those subjected to it, which not only burdens them but aims to burden them, be justified?

We should not assume, however, that there is only one question of justification, which can receive just one answer. As Hart famously pointed out (Hart 1968: 1–27), we must distinguish at least three justificatory issues. First, what is the 'general justifying aim' of a system of punishment: what justifies the creation and maintenance of such a system—what good can it achieve, what duty can it fulfil, what moral demand can it satisfy? Second, who may properly be punished: what principles or aims should determine the allocations of punishments to individuals? Third, how should the appropriate amount of punishment be determined: how should sentencers go about deciding what sentence to impose? (One dimension of this third question concerns the amount or severity of punishment; another, which is insufficiently discussed by philosophers, concerns the concrete modes of punishment that should be available, in general or for particular crimes.) It might of course turn out that answers to all these questions will flow from a single theoretical foundation—for instance from a unitary consequentialist principle specifying the good that punishment should achieve, or from some version of the retributivist principle that the sole proper aim of punishment is to impose on the guilty the punitive burdens they deserve. But, in this as in other matters of normative political theory, matters might not be as easy and simple as that: we might find that quite different and conflicting values are relevant to different issues about punishment; and that any complete normative account of punishment will have to find a place for these values—and to help us find some no doubt uncomfortable compromises between them when they conflict.

Even this way of putting the matter oversimplifies it, by implying that we can hope to find a 'complete normative account of punishment': an account, that is, of how punishment can be justified. That is certainly an implicit assumption of much philosophical and legal discussion: punishment can—of course—be justified, and the theorists' task is to establish and explicate that justification. But it is an illegitimate assumption: normative theorists must be open to the possibility, startling and disturbing as it might be, that this pervasive human practice cannot be justified. Nor is this merely the kind of fantastical scepticism that moral philosophers are sometimes prone to imagine ('suppose someone denied that killing for pleasure was wrong'): there is a significant strand of 'abolitionist' penal theorising (to which insufficient attention is paid in the philosophical literature) which argues precisely that legal punishment cannot be justified and should be abolished. The abolitionist claim is not merely that our existing penal practices are not justified: viewed in the light of many normative penal theories (one might almost say, of any plausible normative penal theory) our existing penal practices, especially those involving imprisonment (given the actual nature of our prisons) or execution, are not merely imperfect, but so radically inconsistent with the values that should inform a practice of punishment that they cannot claim to be justified. For those who think that punishment can in principle be justified, this means simply (and hardly surprisingly) that our penal practices need radical reform if they are to become justified: but the abolitionist critique goes much deeper than that, to argue that legal punishment cannot be justified even in principle.

We will attend to some abolitionist arguments in what follows. Even if those arguments can be met, even if legal punishment can be justified, at least in principle, the abolitionist challenge is one that must be met, rather than ignored; and it will help to remind us of the ways in which any practice of legal punishment is bound to be morally problematic.

2. Punishment, Crime and the State

Legal punishment presupposes crime as that for which punishment is imposed, and a criminal law as that which defines crimes as crimes; a system of criminal law presupposes a state, which has the political authority to make and enforce the law and to impose punishments. A normative account of legal punishment and its justification must thus at least presuppose, and should perhaps make explicit, a normative account of the criminal law (why should we have a criminal law at all?) and of the proper powers and functions of the state (by what authority or right does the state make and declare law, and impose punishments on those who break it?).

How far it matters, in this context, to make explicit a political theory of the state depends on how far different plausible political theories will generate very different accounts of how punishment can be justified and should be used. We cannot pursue this question here (for two sharply contrasting views on it, see Philips 1986, Davis 1989; for more recent contributions showing the importance of political theory, see Pettit 1997; Matravers 2000; Dolovich 2004; Garvey 2004; Dagger 2007; Brettschneider 2007; Markel 2012), save to note one central point. For any political theory (most obviously any version of liberalism or republicanism) that takes seriously the idea of citizenship as full membership of the polity, the problem of punishment takes a particularly acute form, since we have now to ask how punishment can be consistent with citizenship (how citizens can legitimately punish each other): if we are not to say that those who commit crimes thereby forfeit their status as citizens (see s. 4 below), we must—if we are to justify punishment at all—show how the imposition of punishment can be consistent with, or even expressive of, the respect that citizens owe to each other. Some recent versions of retributivism claim, as we will see, to offer a more satisfactory answer to this question than can any consequentialist theory. (Punishments are also, of course, imposed on non-citizens who commit crimes within a state's territory: on the primacy of citizenship in understanding criminal law and its authority, and on the status of non-citizens, see Duff forthcoming.)

Before we tackle such theories of punishment, however, we should look briefly at the concept of crime, since that is one focus of the abolitionist critique of punishment.

On a simple positivist view of law, crimes are kinds of conduct that are prohibited, on pain of threatened sanctions, by the law; and for positivists like Bentham, who combine positivism with a normative consequentialism, the questions of whether we should maintain a criminal law at all, and of what kinds of conduct should be criminalised, are to be answered by trying to determine whether and when this method of controlling human conduct is likely to produce a net increase in good. Such a perspective seems inadequate, however: inadequate both to the claims of the criminal law, which presents its demands as something other or more than those of a gunman writ large—as something other or more than 'Behave thus, or else!'; and to the normative issues at stake when we ask what kinds of conduct should be criminalised. For the criminal law portrays crime not merely as conduct which has been prohibited, but as a species of wrongdoing: whether our inquiry is analytical (into the concept of crime) or normative (as to what kinds of conduct, if any, should be criminal), we must therefore focus on that notion of wrongdoing.

Crimes are, at least, socially proscribed wrongs—kinds of conduct which are condemned as wrong by some purportedly authoritative social norm. That is to say that they are wrongs which are not merely 'private' affairs, which properly concern only those directly involved in them: the community as a whole—in this case the political community speaking through the law—claims the right to declare them to be wrongs. But crimes are 'public' wrongs in a sense that goes beyond this. Tort law, for instance, law deals in part with wrongs which are non-private in that they are legally and socially declared as wrongs—with the wrong constituted by libel, for instance: but they are still treated as 'private' wrongs in the sense that it is up to the person who was wronged to seek legal redress (see Theories of Tort Law, esp. s. 3). She must decide to bring, or not to bring, a civil case against the person who wronged her; and although she can appeal to the law to protect her rights, the case is still between her and the defendant. By contrast, a criminal case is between the whole political community—the state or the people—and the defendant: the wrong is 'public' in the sense that it is one for which the wrongdoer must answer not just to the individual victim, but to the whole polity through its criminal courts.

It is notoriously difficult to give a clear and plausible account of the distinction between civil and criminal law, between 'private' and 'public' legal wrongs, whether our interest is in the analytical question of what the distinction amounts to, or in the normative question of which kinds of wrong should fall into which category (see Murphy & Coleman 1984, ch. 3; a symposium in Boston University Law Review vol. 76 (1996): 1–373; Lamond 2007). It might be tempting to say that crimes are 'public' wrongs in the sense that they injure the whole community: they threaten social order, for instance, or cause 'social volatility' (Becker 1974); or they involve taking unfair advantage over those who obey the law (Murphy 1973); or they undermine the trust on which social life depends (Dimock 1997). But such accounts distract our attention from the wrongs done to the individual victims that most crimes have, when it is those wrongs that should be our central concern: we should condemn the rapist or murderer, we should see the wrong he has done as our concern, because of what he has done to his victim. Another suggestion is that 'public' wrongs are those which flout the community's essential or most basic values, in which all members of the community should see themselves as sharing: the wrong is done to 'us', not merely to its individual victim, in the sense that we identify ourselves with the victim as a fellow citizen (see Marshall & Duff 1998; Duff 2007, ch. 6; and see further Theories of Crime s.6).

Some abolitionists, however, argue that we should seek to eliminate the concept of crime from our social vocabulary: we should talk and think not of 'crimes', but of 'conflicts' or 'troubles' (Christie 1977; Hulsman 1986). One motivation for this might be the thought that 'crime' entails punishment as the appropriate response: but that is not so, since we could imagine a system of criminal law without punishment. To define something as a 'crime' does indeed imply that some kind of public response is appropriate, since it is to define it as a kind of wrong that properly concerns the whole community; and it implies that that response should be a condemnatory one, since to identify wrongs as wrongs is to mark them out as apt for condemnation: but that public, condemnatory response could consist in nothing more than, for instance, some version of a criminal trial which calls the alleged wrongdoer to answer for her alleged wrongdoing, and condemns her for it, through a criminal conviction, if she is proved guilty. One can of course count a criminal conviction as a kind of punishment: but it does not entail the kind of materially burdensome punishment, imposed after conviction, with which penal theorists are primarily concerned.

Another possible motivation for the abolitionist objection to the concept of crime is a kind of moral relativism which objects to the 'imposition' of values on those who might not share them (Bianchi 1994: 71–97): but since abolitionists are very ready to tell us, insistently, how we ought to respond to conflicts or troubles, and how a state ought or ought not to treat its citizens, such an appeal to relativism reflects serious confusion (see Williams 1976: 34–39). More plausibly, the abolitionist claim could be that rather than take wrongdoing as our focus, we should focus on the harm that has been done, and on how it can be repaired; we will return to this suggestion in s.7 below.

Another abolitionist concern is that by defining and treating conduct as 'criminal', the law 'steals' the conflicts which crime involves from those to whom they properly belong (Christie 1977): instead of allowing, and helping, those who find themselves in conflict to resolve their trouble, the law takes the matter over and translates it into the professionalised context of the criminal justice system, in which neither 'victim' nor 'offender' is allowed any appropriate or productive role. Now it is a familiar and disturbing truth that our existing criminal processes—both in their structure and in their actual operations—tend to preclude any effective participation by either victims or offenders, although an adequate response to the criminal wrong that was done should surely involve them both. One response is to argue, as some abolitionists do, that our response to crime should consist not in punishment, but in a process of mediation or 'restoration' between victim and offender (see further s 7 below); but another is to insist that we should retain a distinctive criminal process of trials, and punishments, in which the polity as a whole, acting on behalf of the victim as well as on its own behalf, calls the criminal wrongdoer to account—but that victims and offenders should be given a more active role in that process (see further Duff et al 2007, esp. chs. 3–5, 7). Such an insistence on the need for a public criminal process reflects two aspects of the concept of crime: first, it is sometimes important to recognise that a situation involves not just people in 'conflict', but a victim who has been wronged and an offender who has done the wrong; second, some such wrongs are 'public' wrongs in the sense sketched above—

wrongs that properly concern not just those directly affected, but all members of the political community. Faced, for instance, by feuding neighbours who persistently accuse each other of more or less trivial wrongs, it might indeed be appropriate to suggest that they should forget about condemning each other and look for a way of resolving their conflict. But faced by a rapist and the person he raped, or by a violent husband and the wife he has been beating up, it would a betrayal both of the victim and of the values to which we are supposedly committed to portray the situation merely as a 'conflict' which the parties should seek to resolve: whatever else or more we can do, we must recognise and declare that here is a victim who has been seriously wronged; and we must be collectively ready to censure the offender's action as a wrong (for a useful discussion of the significance of criminal law in the context of domestic violence, see Dempsey 2009).

However, to argue that we should retain the concept of crime, that we should maintain a criminal law which defines and condemns a category of 'public' wrongs, is not yet to say that we should maintain a penal system which punishes those who commit such wrongs; as I have noted, while a system of criminal law might require something like a system of criminal trials which will authoritatively identify and condemn criminal wrongdoers, it does not of its nature require the imposition of further sanctions on such wrongdoers. So we must turn at last to the question of what could justify such a system of punishment.

3. Pure Consequentialism and Punishment

Many people, including those who do not take a consequentialist view of other matters, think that any adequate justification of punishment must be basically consequentialist. For we have here a practice which inflicts, indeed seeks to inflict, significant hardship or burdens: how else could we hope to justify it than by showing that it brings consequential benefits sufficiently large to outweigh, and thus to justify, those burdens? We need not be Benthamite utilitarians to be moved by Bentham's famous remark that "all punishment in itself is evil. ... [I]f it ought at all to be admitted, it ought only to be admitted in as far as it promises to exclude some greater evil" (Bentham 1789: ch. XIII.2). However, when we try to flesh out that simple consequentialist thought into something closer to a full normative account of punishment, problems begin to appear.

A consequentialist must justify punishment (if she is to justify it at all) as a cost-effective means to certain independently identifiable goods. Whatever account she gives of the final good or goods at which all action ultimately aims, the most plausible immediate good that a system of punishment can bring is the prevention of crime: a rational consequentialist system of law will define as criminal only conduct that is in some way harmful; in preventing crime we will thus be preventing the harms that crime causes; and punishment can prevent crime by incapacitating, or deterring, or reforming potential offenders. (There are of course other goods that a system of punishment can bring. It can reassure those who fear crime that the state is taking steps to protect them— though this is a good that, in a well-informed society, will be achieved only insofar as the more immediate preventive goods are achieved. It can also bring satisfaction to those who want to see wrongdoers suffer—though to show that to be a genuine good, rather than merely a means of averting vigilantism and private revenge, we would need to show that it involves something more than mere vengeance, which would be to make sense of some version of retributivism.)

It is a contingent question whether punishment can be an efficient method of preventing crime in any of these ways, and some objections to punishment rest on the empirical claim that it cannot be—that there are other and more efficient methods of crime-prevention, for instance those involving a therapeutic approach to offenders (see Wootton 1963; Menninger 1968). Our focus here, however, must be on the moral objections to consequentialist accounts of punishment—on objections to the effect that crime-preventive efficiency does not suffice to justify a system of punishment.

The most familiar objections to consequentialist penal theories are objections to purely consequentialist theories which hold that only the consequences are relevant to question of justification (for two simple examples of such theories, see Wilson 1983; Walker 1991). For, critics argue, quite apart from the difficult question of whether punishment is or could be a cost-effective way of securing its intended benefits, consequentialists would have to regard manifestly unjust punishments (the punishment of those known to be innocent, for instance, or excessively harsh punishment of the guilty) to be in principle justified if they would efficiently serve the aim of crime prevention: but such punishments would be wrong, just because they would be unjust (see e.g., Hart 1968, chs. 1–2; Ten 1987; Primoratz 1999, chs. 2–3; Boonin 2008: ch. 2).

There are some equally familiar consequentialist responses to this familiar objection. One is to argue that such 'unjust' punishments would be justified if they would really produce the best consequences (see e.g., Smart 1973: 69–72; Bagaric & Amarasekara 2000)—to which the critic will reply that we cannot thus put aside the moral significance of injustice. Another is to argue that in the real world it is extremely unlikely that such punishments would ever be for the best, and even less likely that the agents involved could be trusted reliably to pick out those rare cases in which they would be: thus we, and especially our penal officials, will do best if we think and act as if such punishments are intrinsically wrong and unjustifiable (see e.g., Rawls 1955; Hare 1981, chs. 3, 9.7)—to which the critic will respond that this still makes the wrongness of punishing a known innocent contingent on its effects, and fails to recognise the intrinsic wrong that such punishment does (see e.g., Duff 1986: 151–64; Primoratz 1999, chs. 3.3, 6.5). Another response is to argue that a richer or subtler account of the ends that the criminal law should serve will generate suitable protection against unjust punishments (see Braithwaite & Pettit 1990, especially 71–6, on 'dominion' as the end of criminal law): but the objection remains that any purely consequentialist account will make the protection of the innocent against injustice contingent on its instrumental contribution to the system's aims (on Braithwaite & Pettit, see von Hirsch & Ashworth 1992; Duff 1996: 20–25; Pettit 1997).

4. LimitedConsequentialism and Punishment
The most familiar response to such objections is to replace pure consequentialism by a limited or qualified consequentialism: to insist that the positive 'general justifying aim' (Hart 1968: 8–11) of a system of punishment must lie in its beneficial effects, but to argue that our pursuit of that aim must be constrained by non-consequentialist principles that preclude the kinds of injustice alleged to flow from a purely consequentualist account. A simple version of this approach identifies certain side-constraints to which our pursuit of the consequential benefits of punishment must be subject: constraints that forbid, for instance, the deliberate punishment of the innocent, or the excessively harsh punishment of the guilty. (See most famously Hart 1968, and Scheid 1997

for a sophisticated Hartian theory; on Hart see Lacey 1988: 46–56; Morison 1988; Primoratz 1999, ch. 6.6.)

One question about such accounts concerns the grounding of these side-constraints. If they are derived from a 'negative' retributivism which insists that punishment is justified only if it is deserved (see Dolinko 1991: 539–43), they face the problem of explaining this retributivist notion of desert (see s. 5 below): but it is not clear whether they can be justified without such an appeal to retributivist desert (see Hart 1968: 44–48; Feinberg 1988: 144–55; Walker 1991, ch. 11). Even if such side-constraints can be securely grounded, however, consequentialist theories of punishment face further objections, focused on the moral character of punishment within those constraints. For the side-constrained consequentialist, so long as punishment is deserved it may and should be used to serve consequentialist ends—most obviously the end of crime prevention: but, the critic now objects, to use punishment thus is to use those who are punished 'merely as means' to those further ends, which is to deny them the respect, the moral standing, that is their due as responsible agents (see Murphy 1973: 218). Objections to purely consequentialist theories often focused on the rights of the innocent: the objections to side-constrained consequentialism, which clearly protects the rights of innocent, focus on the rights or moral standing of the guilty.

The Kantian prohibition on treating each other 'merely as means' is admittedly unclear in its implications (for a useful discussion of how we should understand 'the means principle', see Tadros 2011: ch. 6); and it can be argued that if punishment is reserved for those who voluntarily break the law, it does not treat them merely as means (see Walker 1980: 80–85; Hoskins 2011). But a version of it does seem to have force against purely reformative punishments that aim simply so to modify offenders' dispositions that they will in future willingly obey the law; against purely incapacitative punishments that aim simply to prevent offenders from committing further crimes; and against purely deterrent punishments that aim simply to give potential offenders prudential reason to obey the law. For, the Kantian can argue, if we are to treat another 'as an end', with the respect due to her as a rational and responsible agent, we must seek to modify her conduct only by offering her good and relevant reasons to modify it for herself. These modes of consequentialist punishment, however, do not satisfy that demand. A purely reformative system treats those subjected to it not as rational, self-determining agents, but as objects to be re-formed by whatever efficient (and humane) techniques we can find. A purely incapacitative system does not leave those subjected to it free, as responsible agents should be left free, to determine their own future conduct, but seeks to pre-empt their future choices by incapacitating them. And although a purely deterrent system does, unlike the others, offer potential offenders reason to obey the law, it offers them the wrong kind of reason: instead of addressing them as responsible moral agents, in terms of the moral reasons which justify the law's demands on them, it addresses them as merely self-interested beings, in the coercive language of threat; deterrence treats 'a man like a dog instead of with the freedom and respect due to him as a man' (Hegel 1821: 246. For these objections see Lewis 1953; H Morris 1968; Duff 1986: 178–86; von Hirsch 1993: 9–14; von Hirsch & Ashworth 1998, chs. 1, 3).

Such objections leave many people unpersuaded. One strategy for dealing with them is to posit a two-step justification of punishment. The first step, which typically appeals to non-consequentialist values, shows how the commission of a crime renders the offender eligible for, or liable to, the kinds of coercive treatment that punishment involves: such treatment, which is normally inconsistent with the respect due to us as rational agents or as citizens, and inconsistent with the Kantian means principle, is rendered permissible by the commission of the offence. The second step is then to offer positive consequentialist reasons for imposing punishment on those who are eligible for it or liable to it: we should punish if and because this can be expected to produce sufficient consequential benefits to outweigh its undoubted costs. (Further non-consequentialist constraints might also be placed on the severity and modes of punishment that can be permitted: constraints either flowing from an account of just what offenders render themselves liable to, or from other values external to the system of punishment.)

Thus, for instance, some argue that those who voluntarily break the law thereby forfeit at least some of the rights that citizens can normally claim: their wrongdoing therefore legitimises kinds of treatment (reformative or incapacitative treatment, for instance, or deterrent punishment) that would normally be wrong as violating citizens' rights (see Goldman 1982; C Morris 1991; Wellman 2012; for criticisms see Lippke

2001a; Boonin 2008: 103–19). We must ask, however, whether we should be so quick to exclude fellow citizens from the rights and status of citizenship, or whether we should not look for an account of punishment (if it is to be justified at all) on which punishment can still be claimed to treat those punished as full citizens. (The common practice of denying imprisoned offenders the right to vote whilst they are in prison, and perhaps even after they leave prison, is symbolically significant in this context: those who would argue that punishment should be consistent with recognised citizenship should also oppose such practices; see Lippke 2001b; Journal of Applied Philosophy 2005.)

Others portray punishment (in particular deterrent punishment) as a species of societal (self-) defence—and it seems clear that to defend oneself against a wrongful attack is not to use the attacker 'merely as a means', or to fail to show him the respect that is his due.(For versions of this kind of argument see Alexander 1980; Quinn 1985; Farrell 1985, 1995; Montague 1995; Ellis 2003. For criticism, see Boonin 2008: 192–207. For a particularly intricate development of this line of thought, grounding the justification of punishment in the duties that we incur by commtting wrongs, see Tadros 2011: for critical responses, see Law and Philosophy 2013.) Others offer contractualist or contractarian justifications of punishment, grounded in an account of what rational agents or reasonable citizens would agree to: the punishment of those who commit crimes is then, it is argued, rendered permissible by the fact that the offender himself would, as a rational agent or reasonable citizen, have consented to a system of law that provided for such punishments (see e.g., Brettschneider 2007; Finkelstein 2011; for criticism see Dagger 2011; see also Matravers 2000).

Yet others argue that the the Hegelian objection to a system of deterrent punishments is at least seriously overstated, and that it can be met if punishment is only threatened against, and only imposed on, those who commit crimes. For deterrent punishment does not treat people like 'dogs' who must be cowed into obedience by waving a big stick: it offers people prudential reasons to refrain from crime—reasons of a kind that can be expected to appeal to self-interested agents; and such reasons are intended to dissuade from crime those who are not sufficiently moved by the law's moral appeal (see Baker 1992; Hoskins 2011; in partial response see Duff 2001: chs. 1.3, 3.1–3).

All the theories noted in this section could be called 'retributivist': for even if they do not appeal to the idea of desert that is central to many retributivist accounts, they ground an essential part of their justifications of punishment on the claim that it is a permissible response to the commission of a crime: the justification of punishment must thus look not only to the future (to the consequential benefits that it is intended to bring), but also to the past—to the justificatory relationship between crime and punishment which renders the offender liable to be punished. They are, however, versions of 'negative' retributivism (see Dolinko 1991: 539–43): they do not posit a notion of retribution as the positive justifying aim of punishment; they rather take the commission of the crime to remove what would otherwise be a conclusive reason against punishment, thus clearing the way for the consequentialist reasons that are to provide punishment's positive justification. A 'negative' retributivist insists that we must not punish the innocent, or punish the guilty more than their crimes warrant: this does not imply that we ought to punish the guilty; it implies only that we may punish the guilty, if we have other good (presumably consequentialist) reasons to do so. We must now turn to 'positive' retributivist accounts, which find punishment's positive justification in its relationship to the past commission of a crime (but see Berman 2011 for an argument that some recent versions of retributivism actually turn it into a consequentialist theory).

5. 'Positive' Retributivism and the Meaning of Desert

'Positive' retributivism is typically expressed in the language of penal desert. The guilty, those who commit criminal offences, deserve to be punished: which is to say, for the positive retributivist, not merely that we must not punish the innocent, or punish the guilty more than they deserve, but that we should punish the guilty, to the extent that they deserve: penal desert constitutes not just a necessary, but an in principle sufficient reason for punishment (only in principle, however, since there are very good reasons—to do with the costs, both material and moral, of punishment—why we should not even try to punish all the guilty). A striking feature of penal theorising during the last three decades of the twentieth century was a revival of positive retributivism—of the idea that the positive justification of punishment is to be found in its intrinsic character as a deserved response to crime (see H. Morris 1968; N. Morris 1974; Murphy 1973; von Hirsch 1976; two useful collections of contemporary papers on retributivism are White 2011 and Tonry 2012).

Positive retributivism comes in very different forms (Cottingham 1979). All can be understood, however, as attempting to answer the two central questions faced by any retributivist theory of punishment. First, what is the justificatory relationship between crime and punishment that the idea of desert is supposed to capture: why do the guilty 'deserve to suffer' (see L. Davis 1972)—and what do they deserve to suffer (see Ardal 1984; Honderich 2005, ch. 2)? Second, even if they deserve to suffer, or to be burdened in some distinctive way, why should it be for the state to inflict that suffering or that burden on them through a system of criminal punishment (Murphy 1985; Husak 1992; Shafer-Landau 1996)?

One retributivist answer to these questions which was popular for a time was that crime involves taking an unfair advantage over the law-abiding, and that punishment removes that unfair advantage. The criminal law benefits all citizens by protecting them from certain kinds of harm: but this benefit depends upon citizens accepting the burden of self-restraint involved in obeying the law. The criminal takes the benefit of the self-restraint of others, but refuses to accept that burden herself: she has gained an unfair advantage, which punishment removes by imposing some additional burden on her. (See H. Morris 1968; Murphy 1973; Sadurski 1985; Sher 1987, ch. 5; Adler 1992, chs. 5–8; Dagger 1993, 2008, 2011: for criticism, see Burgh 1982; Duff 1986, ch. 8; Falls 1987; Dolinko 1991; Anderson 1997; Boonin 2008: 119–143).

This kind of account does indeed answer the two questions noted above. What the criminal deserves to suffer is the loss of her unfair advantage, and she deserves that because it is unfair that she should get away with taking the benefits of the law without accepting the burdens on which those benefits depend; it is the state's job to inflict this suffering on her, because it is the author or guarantor of the criminal law. However, such accounts have internal difficulties: for instance, how are we to determine how great was the unfair advantage gained by a crime; how far are such measurements of unfair advantage likely to correlate with our judgements of the seriousness of crimes? (For a detailed defence of the 'unfair advantage' theory as a theory of sentencing, see M. Davis 1992, 1996; for criticism see Scheid 1990, 1995; von Hirsch 1990.) Furthermore, they seem to misrepresent what it is about crime that makes it deserving of punishment: what makes murder, or rape, or theft, or assault a criminal wrong, deserving of punishment, is surely the wrongful harm that it does to the individual victim—not (as on this kind of account) the supposed unfair advantage that the criminal takes over all those who obey the law.

A different retributivist account appeals not to the abstract notion of unfair advantage, but to our (normal, appropriate) emotional responses to crime: to, for instance, the resentment or 'retributive hatred', involving a desire to make the wrongdoer suffer, that crime may arouse (see Murphy & Hampton 1988, chs. 1, 3); or to the guilt, involving the judgement that I ought to be punished, that my own wrongdoing would arouse in me (see Moore 1997, ch. 4). Such accounts try to answer the first of the two questions noted above: crime deserves punishment in the sense that it makes appropriate certain emotions (resentment, guilt) which are satisfied by or expressed in punishment. However, they do not yet show why it should be the state's task to satisfy or provide formal expression for such emotions (but see Stephen 1873: 152); and their answers to the first question are also problematic. Criminal wrongdoing should, we can agree, provoke certain kinds of emotion, such as self-directed guilt and other-directed indignation; and such emotions might typically involve a desire to make those at whom they are directed suffer. But just as we can agree that anger is an appropriate response to wrongs done to me, whilst also arguing that we should resist the desire to hit back which anger often, even typically, involves (see Horder 1992:194–7): so we could argue that although guilt, resentment and indignation are appropriate responses to our own and others' wrongdoing, we should resist the desire for suffering that they so often involve. At the least we need to know more than we are told by these accounts about just what wrongdoers deserve to suffer, and why the infliction of suffering should be an appropriate way to express such proper emotions. (For critical discussions of Murphy, see Murphy & Hampton 1988, ch. 2; Duff 1996: 29–31; Murphy 1999. On Moore, see Dolinko 1991: 555–9; Knowles 1993; Murphy 1999. See also Murphy 2003, 2012.)

A third kind of account seeks the meaning and justification of punishment as a deserved response to crime in its expressive or communicative character. (On the expressive dimension of punishment, see generally Feinberg 1970, Primoratz 1989: for critical discussion see Hart 1963: 60–69; Skillen 1980; M. Davis 1996: 169–81.)

Consequentialists can of course portray punishment as useful partly in virtue of its expressive character (see Lacey 1988; Braithwaite & Pettit 1990): but a portrayal of punishment as a mode of moral communication has been central to some recent versions of retributivism.

6. Punishment as Communication

The central meaning and purpose of punishment, on such accounts, is to communicate to offenders the censure or condemnation that they deserve for their crimes. Once we recognise, as we should, that punishment can serve this communicative purpose, we can see how such accounts begin to answer the two questions that retributivists face. First, there is an obviously intelligible justificatory relationship between wrongdoing and censure—as a response which is intended to impose a burden (the burden of condemnation by one's fellows) on an offender for his offence: whatever puzzles there might be about other attempts to explain the idea of penal desert, the idea that wrongdoers deserve to suffer censure is surely unpuzzling. Second, it is appropriate for the state to ensure that such censure is formally administered through the criminal justice system: if crimes are public wrongs, breaches of the political community's authoritative code; as such, they merit public censure by the community. Furthermore, whilst internal to censure is the intention, or hope, that the person censured will accept the censure as justified and will thus be motivated to avoid crime in future, this kind of account can avoid the charge (as brought against consequentialist theories) that it seeks to coerce or manipulate offenders into obeying the law. For censure addresses, and respects, the person censured as a rational and responsible agent: it constitutes an appropriate, deserved response to the wrong that she did, and seeks to bring her to modify her future conduct only by reminding her of the good moral reasons that she has for refraining from crime; it is an appropriate way for citizens to treat and respond to each other. (For different kinds of communicative account, see especially von Hirsch 1993, ch.2; Duff 2001, chs. 1.4.4, 3.2; Bennett 2008; Markel 2011, 2012. For critical discussion, see Davis 1991; Boonin 2008: 171–80; Hanna 2008; Matravers 2011).

However, an obvious and crucial question faces any such justification of punishment as a communicative enterprise. Censure can be communicated through a formal conviction in a criminal court; or it could be communicated by some further formal denunciation issued by a judge or some other representative of the legal community, or by a system of purely symbolic punishments which were burdensome only in virtue of their censorial meaning. It can, of course, also be communicated by 'hard treatment' punishments of the kinds imposed by our courts—by imprisonment, by compulsory community service, by fines and the like, which are burdensome independently of their censorial meaning (on 'hard treatment', see Feinberg 1970): but why should we choose such methods of communication, rather than methods that do not involve hard treatment (see Christie 1981: 98–105)? Is it because they will make the communication more effective (see Falls 1987; Primoratz 1989; Kleinig 1991)? But why is it so important to make the communication effective—and is there not a serious danger that the hard treatment will conceal, rather than highlight, the moral censure it should communicate (see Mathiesen 1990: 58–73)?

One kind of answer to this question brings consequentialism and deterrence back into the picture: we should communicate censure through penal hard treatment because this will give those who are insufficiently impressed by the moral appeal of censure prudential reason to refrain from crime; because, that is, the prospect of such punishment might deter those who are not susceptible to moral persuasion. (See Lipkin 1988, Baker 1992. For a sophisticated revision of this idea, which makes deterrence firmly secondary to censure, see von Hirsch 1993, ch. 2; Narayan 1993: for critical discussion see Bottoms 1998; Duff 2001, ch. 3.3. For another subtle version of this kind of account, see Matravers 2000.) This kind of account differs from the side-constrained consequentialist accounts discussed earlier, since the (retributivist) imposition of deserved censure is now part of the positive justifying aim of punishment; and it can claim, in response to the Hegelian objection to deterrence, that it does not address potential offenders merely 'like dogs', since the law's initial appeal to the citizen is in the appropriate moral terms: the prudential, coercive reasons constituted by penal hard treatment as deterrence are relevant only to those who are deaf, or at least insufficiently attentive, to the law's moral appeal. It might be objected that on this account the law, in speaking to those who are not persuaded by its moral appeal, is still abandoning the attempt at moral communication in favour of the language of threats, and thus ceasing to address its citizens as responsible moral agents: to which it might be replied, first, that the law is addressing us, appropriately, as fallible moral agents who know that we need the additional spur of prudential deterrence to persuade us to act as we should; and second, that we cannot clearly separate the (merely) deterrent from the morally communicative dimensions of punishment—that the dissuasive efficacy of legitimate punishment still depends crucially on the moral meaning that the hard treatment is understood to convey.

A different answer to the 'Why hard treatment?' question explains penal hard treatment as an essential aspect of the enterprise of moral communication itself. Punishment, on this view, should aim not merely to communicate censure to the offender, but to persuade the offender to recognise and repent the wrong he has done, and so to recognise the need to reform himself and his future conduct, and to make apologetic reparation to those whom he wronged. His punishment then constitutes a kind of secular penance that he is required to undergo for his crime: its hard treatment aspects, the burden it imposes on him, should serve both to assist the process of repentance and reform, by focusing his attention on his crime and its implications, and as a way of making the apologetic reparation that he owes (see Duff 2001, 2011; see also Garvey 1999, 2003; Tudor 2001; Bennett 2008; for a sophisticated discussion see Tasioulas 2006). This kind of account has some relation to accounts that portray punishment as a kind of moral education (see H. Morris 1981; Hampton 1984; for criticism see Deigh 1984; Shafer-Landau 1991). It faces serious objections (see Bickenbach 1988; Ten 1990; von Hirsch 1999; Bagaric & Amarasekara 2000; von Hirsch & Ashworth 2005, ch. 7): in particular that it cannot show penal hard treatment to be a necessary aspect of a communicative enterprise which is still to respect offenders as responsible and rational agents who must be left free to remain unpersuaded; that apologetic reparation must be voluntary if it is to be of any real value; and that a liberal state should not take this kind of intrusive interest in its citizens' moral characters. We cannot discuss these objections here, but must turn to some themes in contemporary abolitionist thought (one of which can be connected to the communicative conception of punishment.

7. 'Restorative Justice'and Restitution

Abolitionist theorising about punishment takes many different forms, united only by the insistence that we should seek to abolish, rather than merely to reform, our practices of punishment. (Classic abolitionist texts include Christie 1977, 1981; Hulsman 1986, 1991; de Haan 1990; Bianchi 1994; see also Golash 2005.) In this section we will attend to just two types of abolitionist theory.

Many abolitionists look to 'restorative justice' as an alternative to punishment. ('Restorative' practices and programmes also play an increasingly significant, although still somewhat marginal, role within the criminal process of trial and punishment; but our concern here is with restorative justice as an alternative to punishment.) The restorative justice movement has been growing in strength: although there are different and conflicting conceptions of what 'restorative justice' means or involves, one central theme is that what crime makes necessary is a process of reparation or restoration between offender, victim and other interested parties; and that this is achieved not through a criminal process of trial and punishment, but through mediation or reconciliation programmes that bring together the victim, offender and other interested parties to discuss what was done and how to deal with it (see generally Matthews 1988; Daly & Immarigeon 1998; von Hirsch & Ashworth 1998, ch. 7; Braithwaite 1999; Walgrave 2002; von Hirsch et al 2003; von Hirsch, Ashworth & Shearing 2005; London 2011; Johnstone 2011, 2012).

Now advocates of restorative justice often contrast it with 'retributive' justice, and argue that we should look for restoration rather than retribution or punishment, and seek to repair harms caused rather than to inflict punitive suffering for wrongs done. But it could be argued that this is a mistake. For when we ask what it is that requires 'restoration' or repair, the answer must refer not only to whatever material harm was caused by the crime, but to the wrong that was done: that was what fractured the relationship between offender and victim (and the broader community), and that is what must be recognised and 'repaired' or made up for if a genuine reconciliation is to be achieved. A restorative process that is to be appropriate to crime must therefore be one that seeks an adequate recognition, by the offender and by others, of the wrong done—a recognition that must for the offender, if genuine, be repentant; and that seeks an appropriate apologetic reparation for that wrong from the offender. But those are also the aims of punishment as a species of secular penance, as sketched above. A system of criminal punishment, however improved it might be (see s. 8 below), is of course not well designed to bring about the kind of personal reconciliations and transformations that advocates of restorative justice sometimes seek; but it could be apt to secure the kind of formal, ritualised reconciliation that is the most that a liberal state should try to secure between its citizens. If we focus only on imprisonment, which is still often the preferred mode of punishment in many penal systems, this suggestion will appear laughable; but if we think instead of punishments such as Community Service Orders (now part of what is called Community Payback) or probation, it might seem more plausible.

This argument does not, of course, support that account of punishment against its critics. What it might suggest, however, is that whilst we can learn much from the restorative justice movement, especially about the role that processes of mediation and reparation can play in our responses to crime, its aim should not be the abolition or replacement of punishment: 'restoration' is better understood, in this context, as the proper aim of punishment, not as an alternative to it (see further Duff 2001, ch. 3.4–6, but also Zedner 1994).

A similar issue is raised by the other kind of abolitionist theory that we should note here: the argument that we should replace punishment by a system of enforced restitution (see e.g., Barnett 1977; Boonin 2008: ch. 5—which also cites and discusses a number of objections to the theory). For we need to ask what restitution can amount to, what it should involve, if it is to constitute restitution not merely for any harm that might have been caused, but for the wrong that was done; and it is tempting to answer that restitution for a wrong must involve the kind of apologetic moral reparation, expressing a remorseful recognition of the wrong, that communicative punishment (on the view sketched above) aims to become.

More generally, advocates of restorative justice and of restitution are right to highlight the question of what offenders owe to those whom they have wronged—and to their fellow citizens (see also Tadros 2011 for a focus on the duties that offenders incur). Some penal theorists, however, especially those who connect punishment to apology, will reply that what offenders owe precisely includes accepting, undertaking, or undergoing punishment.

8. Further Issues

The previous sections sketched the central contemporary accounts of whether and how legal punishment can be justified—and some of the objections and difficulties that they face. A number of further important questions face any theory of punishment, which can only be noted here.

First, there are questions about sentencing. (On sentencing see generally Robinson 1987; Morris & Tonry 1990; von Hirsch 1993; Tonry 1996; von Hirsch & Ashworth 2005; Ashworth, von Hirsch and Roberts 2009; Frase 2012.) Who should decide what kinds and what levels of sentence should be attached to different offences or kinds of offence: what should be the respective roles of legislatures, of sentencing councils or commissions, of appellate courts, of trial judges, of juries? By what criteria should such decisions be made: how far should they be guided by a retributivist principle of proportionality, requiring punishments to be 'proportionate' in their severity to the seriousness of the crime; how far by consequentialist considerations of efficient crime-prevention? What kinds of punishment should be available to sentencers, and how should they decide which mode of punishment is appropriate for the particular offence (see e.g., Lippke 2007; considerations of the meaning of different modes of punishment should be central to this question)?

Second, there are questions about the relation between theory and practice—between the ideal, as portrayed by a normative theory of punishment, and the actualities of existing penal practice. Suppose we have come to believe, as a matter of normative theory, that a system of legal punishment could in principle be justified—that the abolitionist challenge can be met. It is, to put it mildly, unlikely that our normative theory of justified punishment will justify our existing penal institutions and practices: it is far more likely that such a theory will show our existing practices to be radically imperfect—that legal punishment as it is now imposed is far from meaning or achieving what it should mean or achieve if it is to be adequately justified. If our normative theorising is to be anything more than an empty intellectual exercise, if it is to engage with actual practice, we then face the question of what we can or should do about our current practices. The obvious answer is that we should strive so to reform them that they can be in practice justified, and that answer is certainly available to consequentialists, on the plausible assumption that maintaining our present practices, whilst also seeking their reform, is likely to do more good or less harm than abandoning them. But for retributivists who insist that punishment is justified only if it is just, and for communicative theorists who insist that punishment is just and justified only if it communicates an appropriate censure to those who deserve it, the matter is harder: for to maintain our present practices, even while seeking their radical reform, will be to maintain practices which perpetrate serious injustice (see Murphy 1973; Duff 2001, ch. 5).

Third, the relation between the ideal and the actual is especially problematic in the context of punishment partly because it involves the preconditions of just punishment. That is to say, what makes an actual system of punishment unjust(ified) might be not its own operations as such (what punishment is or achieves within that system), but the absence of certain political, legal and moral conditions on which the whole system depends for its legitimacy (see Duff 2001, ch. 5.2). For instance, a just system of criminal law must convict and punish only those who are responsible, in the sense of being answerable for their crimes: only those who have the capacities necessary to answer for their actions, who are bound by this criminal law, and who are answerable to the political community whose law it is and whose courts call them to answer. We can highlight some of the issues that arise here by noting that criminal punishment, at least or especially if it involves the kind of moral communication discussed in s. 6 above, must treat and address those who are punished as citizens—as full members of the polity by whose values they are both bound and protected. One question then is whether and how punishment itself can achieve this: can it reaffirm, or at least be consistent with, a recognition of fellow citizenship (compare Garland 2001, on criminologies 'of the self' and 'of the other')? Another question, concerning the preconditions of punishment, is whether those who appear before the criminal courts have been treated as citizens by the polity that now seeks to call them to account for their wrongdoing, and what the implications are if they have not. There is much work to be done in spelling out such preconditions of just punishment: but it is at least arguable that they are far from satisfied for many of those who are convicted and punished by our own systems of criminal justice (see Heffernan & Kleinig 2000). To the extent that they are not satisfied, however, those systems lack legitimacy, and the punishments they inflict are unjustified. This conclusion should not surprise us: but it challenges any comfortable assumption that we can support and rely on our existing systems of criminal justice with a clear conscience.

Fourth, theorists of punishment should also attend to various kinds of coercive measure that can be imposed on those who have committed, or are thought likely to commit, crimes: these include, for instance, the kinds of formally non-punitive 'measure' (including detention) that can be imposed on offenders in the Netherlands and other European countries (see de Keijer 2012); the provisions that many countries have for continued 'civil' detention, after the end of their formal punishment, for offenders judged to be dangerous (see e.g., Ramsay 2012); and the many kinds of restriction that may be imposed on people suspected of involvement in terrorism. Such measures might not be formally classed as punishments (one effect of which is that they often escape the constraints of justice and proportionality to which punishment is subject), and are avowedly imposed for 'preventive' rather than 'punitive' purposes: but as modes of state coercion, aimed at the prevention of future crimes, they clearly fall within the same normative field as punishment, and are as much in need of critical theorising as are our formally punitive institutions and practices (see Ashworth and Zedner 2011, 2012; Ashworth, Zedner and Tomlin 2013).

Finally, theoretical discussions of criminal punishment and its justification typically focus, as this discussion has focused, on criminal punishment in the context of domestic criminal law. But a theory of punishment must also have something to say about its aims and justification in the context of international criminal law—about how we should understand, and whether and how we can justify, the punishments imposed by such tribunals as the International Criminal Court: for we cannot assume that a normative theory of domestic criminal punishment can simply be read across into the context of international criminal law. That, however, is a topic that we cannot tackle here (see Drumbl 2007).

LEGAL PUNISHMENT

9 AFFIRMATIVE ACTION

"Affirmative action" means positive steps taken to increase the representation of women and minorities in areas of employment, education, and culture from which they have been historically excluded. When those steps involve preferential selection—selection on the basis of race, gender, or ethnicity—affirmative action generates intense controversy.

The development, defense, and contestation of preferential affirmative action has proceeded along two paths. One has been legal and administrative as courts, legislatures, and executive departments of government have made and applied rules requiring affirmative action. The other has been the path of public debate, where the practice of preferential treatment has spawned a vast literature, pro and con. Often enough, the two paths have failed to make adequate contact, with the public quarrels not always very securely anchored in any existing legal basis or practice.

The ebb and flow of public controversy over affirmative action can be pictured as two spikes on a line, the first spike representing a period of passionate debate that began around 1972 and tapered off after 1980, and the second indicating a resurgence of debate in the 1990s leading up to the Supreme Court's decision in the summer of 2003 upholding certain kinds of affirmative action. The first spike encompassed controversy about gender and racial preferences alike. This is because in the beginning affirmative action was as much about the factory, the firehouse, and the corporate suite as about the college campus. The second spike represents a quarrel about race and ethnicity. This is because the burning issue at the turn of the twentieth-first century is about college admissions. In admissions to selective colleges, women need no boost; African-Americans and Hispanics do.[1]

1. In the Beginning
2. The Controversy Engaged
3. Rights and Consistency
4. Real World Affirmative Action: The Workplace
5. Real World Affirmative Action: The University
6. Equality's Rule
7. Diversity's Dominion
8. The Integration Argument
9. A Blip
10. Desert Confounded, Desert Misapplied

1. In the Beginning
In 1972, affirmative action became an inflammatory public issue. True enough, the Civil Rights Act of 1964 already had made something called "affirmative action" a remedy federal courts could impose on violators of the Act. Likewise, after 1965 federal contractors had been subject to President Lyndon Johnson's Executive Order 11246, requiring them to take "affirmative action" to make sure they were not discriminating. But what did this 1965 mandate amount to? The Executive Order assigned to the Secretary of Labor the job of specifying rules of implementation. In the meantime, as the federal courts were enforcing the Civil Rights Act against discriminating companies, unions, and other institutions, the Department of Labor mounted an ad hoc attack on the construction industry by cajoling, threatening, negotiating, and generally strong-arming reluctant construction firms into a series of region-wide "plans" in which they committed themselves to numerical hiring goals. Through these contractor commitments, the Department could indirectly pressure recalcitrant labor unions, who supplied the employees at job sites.

While the occasional court case and government initiative made the news and stirred some controversy, affirmative action was pretty far down the list of public excitements until the autumn of 1972, when the Secretary of Labor's Revised Order No. 4, fully implementing the Executive Order, landed on campus by way of directives from the Department of Health, Education, and Welfare. Its predecessor, Order No. 4, first promulgated in 1970, cast a wide net over American institutions, both public and private. By extending to all contractors the basic apparatus of the construction industry "plans," the Order imposed a one-size-fits-all system of "underutilization analyses," "goals," and "timetables" on hospitals, banks, trucking companies, steel mills, printers, airlines—indeed, on all the scores of thousands of institutions, large and small, that did business with the government, including a special set of institutions with a particularly voluble and articulate constituency, namely, American universities.

At first, university administrators and faculty found the rules of Order No. 4 murky but hardly a threat to the established order. The number of racial and ethnic minorities receiving PhDs each year and thus eligible for faculty jobs was tiny. Any mandate to increase their representation on campus would require more diligent searches by universities, to be sure, but searches fated nevertheless largely to mirror past results. The 1972 Revised Order, on the other hand, effected a change that punctured any campus complacency: it included women among the "protected classes" whose "underutilization" demanded the setting of "goals" and "timetables" for "full utilization" (Graham 1990, 413). Unlike African-Americans and Hispanics, women were getting PhDs in substantial and growing numbers. If the affirmative action required of federal contractors was a recipe for "proportional representation," then Revised Order No. 4 was bound to leave a large footprint on campus. Some among the professoriate exploded in a fury of opposition to the new rules, while others responded with an equally vehement defense of them.[2]

As it happened, these events coincided with another development, namely the "public turn" in philosophy. For several decades Anglo-American philosophy had treated moral and political questions obliquely. On the prevailing view, philosophers were suited only to do "conceptual analysis"—they could lay bare, for example, the conceptual architecture of the idea of justice, but they were not competent to suggest political principles, constitutional arrangements, or social policies that actually did justice. Philosophers might do "meta-ethics" but not "normative ethics."

This viewed collapsed in the 1970s under the weight of two counter-blows. First, John Rawls published in 1971 A Theory of Justice, an elaborate, elegant, and inspiring defense of a normative theory of justice (Rawls 1971). Second, in the same year Philosophy & Public Affairs, with Princeton University's impeccable pedigree, began life, a few months after Florida State's Social Theory and Practice. These journals, along with a re-tooled older periodical, Ethics, became self-conscious platforms for socially and politically engaged philosophical writing, born out of the feeling that in time of war (the Vietnam War) and social tumult (the Civil Rights Movement, Women's Liberation), philosophers ought to do, not simply talk about, ethics. In 1973, Philosophy & Public Affairs published Thomas Nagel's "Equal Treatment and Compensatory Justice" (Nagel 1973) and Judith Jarvis Thomson's "Preferential Hiring" (Thomson 1973), and the philosophical literature on affirmative action burgeoned forth.[3]

In contention was the nature of those "goals" and "timetables" imposed on every contractor by Revised Order No. 4. Weren't the "goals" tantamount to "quotas," requiring institutions to use racial or gender preferences in their selection processes? Some answered "no" (Ezorsky 1977, 86). Properly understood, affirmative action did not require (or even permit) the use of gender or racial preferences. Others said "yes" (Goldman 1976, 182–3). Affirmative action, if it did not impose preferences outright, at least countenanced them. Among the yea-sayers, opinion divided between those who said preferences were morally permissible and those who said they were not. Within the "morally permissible" set, different writers put forward different justifications.

2. The Controversy Engaged

The essays by Thomson and Nagel defended the use of preferences but on different grounds. Thomson endorsed job preferences for women and African-Americans as a form of redress for their past exclusion from the academy and the workplace. Preferential policies, in her view, worked a kind of justice. Nagel, by contrast, argued that preferences might work a kind of social good, and without doing violence to justice. Institutions could for one or another good reason properly depart from standard meritocratic selection criteria because the whole system of tying economic reward to earned credentials was itself indefensible.

Justice and desert lay at the heart of subsequent arguments. Several writers took to task Thomson's argument that preferential hiring justifiably makes up for past wrongs. Preferential hiring seen as redress looks perverse, they contended, since it benefits individuals (African-Americans and women possessing good educational credentials) least likely harmed by past wrongs while it burdens individuals (younger white male applicants) least likely to be responsible for past wrongs (Simon 1974, 315–19; Sher 1975, 162; Sher 1979, 81–82; and Goldman 1976, 190–1).[4] Instead of doing justice, contended the critics, preferential treatment violated rights. What rights were at issue? The right of an applicant "to equal consideration" (Thomson 1973, 377; Simon 1974, 312),the right of the maximally competent to an open position (Goldman 1976, 191; Goldman 1979, 24–8), or the right of everyone to equal opportunity (Gross 1977a, 382; Gross 1978, 97). Moreover, according to the critics, preferential treatment confounded desert by severing reward from a "person's character, talents, choices and abilities" (Simon 1979, 96), by "subordinating merit, conduct, and character to race" (Eastland and Bennett 1979, 144), and by disconnecting outcomes from actual liability and damage (Gross 1978, 125–42).

Defenders of preferences were no less quick to enlist justice and desert in their cause. Mary Anne Warren, for example, argued that in a context of entrenched gender discrimination, gender preferences might improve the "overall fairness" of job selections. Justice and individual desert need not be violated.

If individual men's careers are temporarily set back because of...[job preferences given to women], the odds are good that these same men will have benefited in the past and/or will benefit in the future—not necessarily in the job competition, but in some ways—from sexist discrimination against women. Conversely, if individual women receive apparently unearned bonuses [through preferential selection], it is highly likely that these same women will have suffered in the past and/or will suffer in the future from...sexist attitudes. (Warren 1977, 256)

Likewise, James Rachels defended racial preferences as devices to neutralize unearned advantages by whites. Given the pervasiveness of racial discrimination, it is likely, he argued, that the superior credentials offered by white applicants do not reflect their greater effort, desert, or even ability. Rather, the credentials reflect their mere luck at being born white. "Some white...[applicants] have better qualifications...only because they have not had to contend with the obstacles faced by their African-American competitors" (Rachels 1978, 162). Rachels was less confident than Warren that preferences worked uniformly accurate offsets. Reverse discrimination might do injustice to some whites; yet its absence would result in injustices to African-Americans who have been unfairly handicapped by their lesser advantages.

Rachels' diffidence was warranted in light of the counter-responses. If racial and gender preferences for jobs (or college admissions) were supposed to neutralize unfair competitive advantages, they needed to be calibrated to fit the variety of backgrounds aspirants brought to any competition for these goods. Simply giving blanket preferences to African-Americans or women seemed much too ham-handed an approach if the point was to micro-distribute opportunities fairly (Sher 1975, 165ff).

3. Rights and Consistency
To many of its critics, reverse discrimination was simply incoherent. When "the employers and the schools favor women and blacks," objected Lisa Newton, they commit the same injustice perpetrated by Jim Crow discrimination. "Just as the previous discrimination did, this reverse discrimination violates the public equality which defines citizenship" (Newton 1973, 310).[5]

William Bennett and Terry Eastland likewise saw racial preferences as in some sense illogical:

To count by race, to use the means of numerical equality to achieve the end of moral equality, is counterproductive, for to count by race is to deny the end by virtue of the means. The means of race counting will not, cannot, issue in an end where race does not matter (Eastland and Bennett 1979, 149).[6]

When Eastland and Bennett alluded to those who favored using race to get to a point where race doesn't count, they had in mind specifically the Supreme Court's Justice Blackmun who, in the famous 1978 Bakke case (discussed below), put his own views in just those simple terms. For Blackmun, the legitimacy of racial preferences was to be measured by how fast using them moves us toward a society where race doesn't matter (a view developed in subtle detail by the philosopher Richard Wasserstrom in Wasserstrom 1976). While the critics of preferences feigned to find the very idea of using race to end racism illogical and incoherent, they also fell back on principle to block Blackmun's instrumental defense should it actually prove both reasonable and plausible. "The moral issue comes in classic form," wrote Carl Cohen. "Terribly important objectives...appear to require impermissible means." Cohen asked, "might we not wink at the Constitution this once" and allow preferences to do their good work (Cohen 1995, 20)? Neither he nor other critics thought so. Principle must hold firm. "[I]n the distribution of benefits under the laws all racial classifications are invidious" (Cohen 1995, 52).

But what, exactly, is the principle—constitutional or moral—that always bars the use of race as a means to "terribly important objectives"? Alan Goldman did more than anyone in the early debate to formulate and ground a relevant principle. Using a contractualist framework, he surmised that rational contractors would choose a rule of justice requiring positions to be awarded by competence. They would choose this rule because it instantiates a principle of equal opportunity which in turn instantiates a broad right to equal consideration of interests, this last principle springing from the basic condition of the contracting parties as rational, self-interested, and equally situated choosers. On its face, the rule of competence would seem to preclude filling positions by reference to factors like race and gender that are unrelated to competence. However, Goldman's "rule" blocked preferences only under certain empirical conditions. Goldman explained the derivation of the rule and its consequent limit this way:

The rule for hiring the most competent was justified as part of a right to equal opportunity to succeed through socially productive effort, and on grounds of increased welfare for all members of society. Since it is justified in relation to a right to equal opportunity, and since the application of the rule may simply compound injustices when opportunities are unequal elsewhere in the system, the creation of more equal opportunities takes precedence when in conflict with the rule for awarding positions. Thus short-run violations of the rule are justified to create a more just distribution of benefits by applying the rule itself in future years. (Goldman 1979, 164–165).

In other words, if "terribly important objectives" having to do with equalizing opportunities in a system rife with inequality could in fact be furthered by measured and targeted reverse discrimination, justice wouldn't stand in the way. Goldman's principle did not have the adamantine character Cohen and other critics sought in a bar to preferences. Where can such an unyielding principle be found? I postpone further examination of this question until I discuss the Bakke case, below, whose split opinions constitute an extended debate on the meaning of constitutional equality.

4. Real-World Affirmative Action: The Workplace

The terms of the popular debate over racial and gender preferences often mirrored the arguments philosophers and other academics were making to each other. Preference's defenders offered many reasons to justify them, reasons having to do with compensatory or distributive justice, as well as reasons having to do with social utility (more African-Americans in the police department would enable it better to serve the community, more female professors in the classroom would inspire young women to greater achievements). Critics of preferences retorted by pointing to the law. And well they should, since the text of the Civil Rights Act of 1964 seemed a solid anchor even if general principle proved elusive. Title VI of the Act promised that "[n]o person...shall, on the ground of race, color, or national origin, be excluded from participation in, be denied the benefits of, or be subjected to discrimination under any program or activity receiving Federal financial assistance."[7] Title VII similarly prohibited all employment practices that discriminated on the basis of race, gender, religion, or national origin.[8]

In face of the plain language of Titles VI and VII, how did preferential hiring and promotion ever arise in the first place? How could they be justified legally? Part of the answer lies in the meaning of "discrimination." The Civil Rights Act did not define the term. The federal courts had to do that job themselves, and the cases before them drove the definition in a particular direction. Many factories and businesses prior to 1964, especially in the South, had in place facially discriminatory policies and rules. For example, a company's policy might have openly relegated African-Americans to the maintenance department and channeled whites into operations, sales, and management departments, where the pay and opportunities for advancement were far better. If, after passage of the Civil Rights Act, the company willingly abandoned its facially segregative policy, it could still carry forward the effects of its past segregation through other already-existing facially neutral rules. A company policy, say, that required workers to give up their seniority in one department if they transferred to another would have locked in place older African-American maintenance workers as effectively as the company's prior segregative rule that made them ineligible to transfer at all. Consequently, courts began striking down facially neutral rules that carried through the effects of an employer's past discrimination, regardless of the original intent or provenance of the rules. "Intent" was effectively decoupled from "discrimination." In 1971, the Supreme Court ratified this process, giving the following construction of Title VII:

The objective of Congress in the enactment of Title VII...was to achieve equality of employment opportunities and remove barriers that have operated in the past to favor an identifiable group of white employees over other employees. Under the Act, practices, procedures, or tests neutral on their face, and even neutral in terms of intent, cannot be maintained if they operate to "freeze" the status quo of prior discriminatory employment practices.

What is required by Congress is the removal of artificial, arbitrary, and unnecessary barriers to employment when the barriers operate invidiously to exclude on the basis of racial or other impermissible classification.[9]

In a few short paragraphs the Court advanced from proscribing practices that froze in place the effects of a firm's own past discrimination to proscribing practices that carried through the effects of past discrimination generally. The Court characterized statutory discrimination as any exclusionary practice not necessary to an institution's activities. Since many practices in most institutions were likely to be exclusionary, rejecting minorities and women in greater proportion than white men, all institutions needed to reassess the full range of their practices to look for, and correct, discriminatory effect. Against this backdrop, the generic idea of affirmative action took form:

Each institution should effectively monitor its practices for exclusionary effect and revise those that cannot be defended as "necessary" to doing business. In order to make its monitoring and revising effective, an institution ought to predict, as best it can, how many minorities and women it would select over time, were it successfully nondiscriminating. These predictions constitute the institution's affirmative action "goals," and failure to meet the goals signals to the institution (and to the government) that it needs to revisit its efforts at eliminating exclusionary practices.There may still remain practices that ought to be modified or eliminated.[10]

The point of such affirmative action: to induce change in institutions so that they could comply with the nondiscrimination mandate of the Civil Rights Act.

However, suppose this self-monitoring and revising fell short? In early litigation under the Civil Rights Act, courts concluded that some institutions, because of their past exclusionary histories and continuing failure to find qualified women or minorities, needed stronger medicine. Courts ordered these institutions to adopt "quotas," to take in specific numbers of formerly excluded groups on the assumption that once these new workers were securely lodged in place, the institutions would adapt to this new reality.[11]

Throughout the 1970s, courts and government enforcement agencies extended this idea across the board, requiring a wide range of firms and organizations—from AT&T to the Alabama Highway Patrol—temporarily to select by the numbers. In all these cases, the use of preferences was tied to a single purpose: to prevent ongoing and future discrimination. Courts carved out this justification for preferences not through caprice but through necessity. They found themselves confronted with a practical dilemma that Congress had never envisaged and thus never addressed when it wrote the Civil Rights Act. The dilemma was this: courts could impose racial preferences to change foot-dragging or inept defendants (and by doing so apparently transgress the plain prohibition in Title VII) or they could order less onerous steps they knew would be ineffective, thus letting discrimination continue (and by doing so violate their duty under Title VII). Reasonably enough, the federal courts resolved this dilemma by appeal to the broad purposes of the Civil Rights Act and justified racial preferences where needed to prevent ongoing and future discrimination.[12]

Thus, preferential affirmative action in the workplace served the same rationale as the non-preferential sort. Its purpose was not to compensate for past wrongs, offset unfair advantage, appropriately reward the deserving, or yield a variety of social goods; its purpose was to change institutions so they could comply with the nondiscrimination mandate of the Civil Rights Act.

5. Real-World Affirmative Action: The University

In the 1970s, while campuses were embroiled in debate about how to increase African-Americans and women on the faculty, universities were also putting into effect schemes to increase minority presence within the student body. Very selective universities, in particular, needed new initiatives because only a handful of African-American and Hispanic high school students possessed test scores and grades good enough to make them eligible for admission. These institutions faced a choice: retain their admissions criteria unchanged and live with the upshot—hardly any African-Americans and Hispanics on campus—or fiddle with their criteria to get a more substantial representation. Most elected the second path.

The Medical School of the University of California at Davis was typical. It reserved sixteen of the one hundred slots in its entering classes for minorities. In 1973 and again in 1974, Allan Bakke, a white applicant, was denied admission although his test scores and grades were better than most or all of those admitted through the special program. He sued. In 1977, his case, Regents of the University of California v. Bakke, reached the Supreme Court. The Court rendered its decision a year later (438 U.S. 265 [1978]).[13]

An attentive reader of Title VI of the Civil Rights Act might have thought this case was an easy call. So, too, thought four justices on the Supreme Court, who voted to order Bakke admitted to the Medical School. Led by Justice Stevens, they saw the racially segregated, two-track scheme at the Medical School (a recipient of federal funds) as a clear violation of the plain language of the Title.

Four other members of the Court, led by Justice Brennan, wanted very keenly to save the Medical School program. To find a more attractive terrain for doing battle, they made an end-run around Title VI, arguing that, whatever its language, it had no independent meaning itself. It meant in regard to race only what the Constitution meant.[14] Thus, instead of having to parse the stingy and unyielding language of Title VI ("no person shall be subjected to...on the ground of race"), the Brennan group could turn their creative energies to interpreting the broad and vague language of the Fourteenth Amendment ("no person shall be denied the equal protection of the laws"), which provided much more wiggle-room for justifying racial preferences. The Brennan group persuaded one other member, Justice Powell, to join them in their view of Title VI. But Powell didn't agree with their view of the Constitution. He argued that the Medical School's policy was unconstitutional and voted that Bakke must be admitted. His vote, added to the four votes of the Stevens group, meant that Allan Bakke won his case and that Powell got to write the opinion of the Court. The Brennan strategy didn't reap the fruit it intended.

Against the leanings of the Brennan group, who would distinguish between "benign" and "malign" uses of race and deal more leniently with the former, Powell insisted that the Fourteenth Amendment's promise of "equal protection of the law" must mean the same thing for all, black and white alike. To paraphrase Powell:

The Constitution can tolerate no "two-class" theory of equal protection. There is no principled basis for deciding between classes that deserve special judicial attention and those that don't. To think otherwise would involve the Court in making all kinds of "political" decisions it is not competent to make. In expounding the Constitution, the Court's role is to discern "principles sufficiently absolute to give them roots throughout the community and continuity over significant periods of time, and to lift them above the pragmatic political judgments of a particular time and place" (Bakke, at 295–300 [Powell quoting Cox 1976, 114]).

What, then, was the practical meaning of a "sufficiently absolute" rendering of the principle of equal protection? It was this: when the decisions of state agents "touch upon an individual's race or ethnic background, he is entitled to a judicial determination that the burden he is asked to bear on that basis is precisely tailored to serve a compelling governmental interest (Bakke, at 300).

Powell, with this standard in hand, then turned to look at the four reasons the Medical School offered for its special program: (i) to reduce "the historic deficit of traditionally disfavored minorities in medical schools and the medical profession;" (ii) to counter "the effects of societal discrimination;" (iii) to increase "the number of physicians who will practice in communities currently underserved;" and (iv) to obtain "the educational benefits that flow from an ethnically diverse student body" (Bakke, at 307). Did any or all of them specify a compelling governmental interest? Did they necessitate use of racial preferences?

As to the first reason, Powell dismissed it out of hand.

If [the School's] purpose is to assure within its student body some specified percentage of a particular group merely because of its race or ethnic origin, such a preferential purpose must be rejected not as insubstantial but as facially invalid. Preferring members of any one group for no reason other than race or ethnic origin is discrimination for its own sake.

As to the second reason, Powell allowed it more force. A state has a legitimate interest in ameliorating the effects of past discrimination. Even so, contended Powell, the Court,

has never approved a classification that aids persons perceived as members of relatively victimized groups at the expense of other innocent individuals in the absence of judicial, legislative, or administrative findings of constitutional or statutory violations (Bakke, at 308).

And the Medical School does not purport to have made, and is in no position to make, such findings. Its broad mission is education, not the formulation of any legislative policy or the adjudication of particular claims of illegality....[I]solated segments of our vast governmental structures are not competent to make those decisions, at least in the absence of legislative mandates and legislatively determined criteria (Bakke, at 309).

As to the third reason, Powell found it, too, insufficient. The Medical School provided no evidence that the best way it could contribute to increased medical services to underserved communities was to employ a racially preferential admissions scheme. Indeed, the Medical School provided no evidence that its scheme would result in any benefits at all to such communities (Bakke, at 311).

This left the fourth reason. Here Powell found merit. A university's interest in a diverse student body is legitimated by the First Amendment's implied protection of academic freedom. This constitutional halo makes the interest "compelling." However, the Medical School's use of a racial and ethnic classification scheme was not "precisely tailored" to effect the School's interest in diversity, argued Powell.

The diversity that furthers a compelling state interest encompasses a far broader array of qualifications and characteristics of which racial or ethnic origin is but a single though important element. [The Medical School's] special admissions program, focused solely on ethnic diversity, would hinder rather than further attainment of genuine diversity (Bakke, at 316).

The diversity which provides an educational atmosphere "conducive to speculation, experiment and creation" includes a nearly endless range of experiences, talents, and attributes that students might bring to campus. In reducing diversity to racial and ethnic quotas, the Medical School wholly misconceived this important educational interest.

In sum, although the last of the Medical School's four reasons encompassed a "compelling governmental interest," the School's special admissions program was not necessary to effect the interest. The special admissions program was unconstitutional. So concluded Justice Powell.

6. Equality's Rule

This was a conclusion Justice Brennan tried vigorously to forestall. Brennan agreed with Powell that "equal protection" must mean the same thing—that is, remain one rule—whether applied to blacks or whites. But the same rule applied to different circumstances need not yield the same results. Racial preferences created for different reasons and producing different outcomes need not all be judged in the same harsh, virtually fatal, manner. This point was the crux of Brennan's defense of the Medical School's policy.

Powell thought there was no principled way to distinguish "benign" from "malign" discrimination, but Brennan insisted there was. He argued that if the Court looked carefully at its past cases striking down Jim Crow laws, it would see the principle at work. What the Court found wrong in Jim Crow was that it served no purpose except to mark out and stigmatize one group of people as inferior. The "cardinal principle" operating in the Court's decisions condemned racial classifications "drawn on the presumption that one race is inferior to another" or that "put the weight of government behind racial hatred and separation" (Bakke, at 358 [Brennan, dissenting]). Brennan agreed with Powell that no public racial classification motivated by racial animus, no classification whose purpose is to stigmatize people with the "badge of inferiority," could withstand judicial scrutiny. However, the Medical School's policy, even if ill-advised or mistaken, reflected a public purpose far different from that found in Jim Crow. The policy ought not be treated as though it were cut from the same cloth.

Brennan granted that if a state adopted a racial classification for the purpose of humiliating whites, or stigmatizing Allan Bakke as inferior and confining him to second-class citizenship, that classification would be as odious as Jim Crow. But the Medical School's policy had neither this purpose nor this effect. Allan Bakke may have been upset and resentful at losing out under the special plan, but he wasn't "in any sense stamped as an inferior by the Medical School's rejection of him." Nor did his loss constitute a "pervasive injury," in the sense that wherever he went he would be treated as a "second-class citizen" because of his color (Bakke, at 376 [Brennan, dissenting]).

In short, argued Brennan, the principle embedded in the Equal Protection Clause should be viewed as an anti-caste principle, a principle that uniformly and consistently rejects all public law whose purpose is to subject people to an inferior and degraded station in life, whether they are black or white.[15] Of course, given the asymmetrical position of whites and blacks in our country, we are not likely to encounter laws that try to stigmatize whites as an inferior caste (much less succeed at it). But this merely shows that a principle applied to different circumstances produces different results. Because the Medical School's program sought to undo the effects of a racial caste system long-enduring in America, it represented a purpose of great social importance and should not be found Constitutionally infirm: so maintained Brennan (Bakke, at 363 [Brennan, dissenting]).

Justice Powell never successfully engaged this way of reading "constitutional equality." His insistence on clear, plain, unitary, absolute principle did not cut against the Brennan view. The issue between Powell and Brennan was not the consistency and stringency of the principle but its content. If the Constitution says, "The state cannot deliberately burden someone by race if its purpose is to create or maintain caste," then constitutional law doesn't block any of the Medical School's justifications.[16]

If we turn away from exegesis of the Constitution, are we likely to find in political theory itself any principle of equality implying that every use of racial preferences in every circumstance works an intolerable injustice? There is reason to think not. To see why, consider John Rawls' theory of justice-as-fairness. For our purposes, what is striking about the theory is the division of labor it embraces. Its very broadest principles of liberty and equality are themselves unable to single out proper micro-allocations of social benefits and burdens. This is not a defect; this is their nature. What they can do is structure roles and institutions which then create the social and legal machinery for assigning benefits and burdens. Rawls' principles oblige a constitution to protect equality of citizenship but leaves most other matters to legislative judgment. Thus, law that in form and in fact makes some people "second-class citizens" would be unjust, clearly, but this limitation doesn't bar government from asking people to bear unequal burdens for the common good, not even unequal burdens premised on race or ethnicity. Nor does Rawls' principle of fair equality of opportunity block such burdens, either, for, while ordinarily discouraging selection based on race or ethnicity, it can itself be limited in the name of achieving greater equality of opportunity (the point noted by Goldman). To reformers in a society that has grievously failed to secure equal citizenship and fair equality of opportunity for most of its history, Rawls' principles of equality supply few guideposts.[17]

Will looking farther afield yield an understanding of general equality adamantly inhospitable to every use of preferences? The prospects seem dim. As Georgia Warnke has argued (1998), any very general notion of equality can be employed as much to defend affirmative action (and the social inclusion it effects) as to condemn it (and the racial non-neutrality it involves). The challenge here is well-illustrated by Carl Cohen's most recent effort, in a debate with James Sterba, to extract a strict prohibition on racial preferences from the Aristotelian principle that "equals should be treated equally" (Cohen and Sterba 2003, 23). This principle, urges Cohen, "certainly entails at least this: It is wrong, always and everywhere, to give special advantage to any group simply on the basis of physical characteristics that have no relevance to the award given or the burden imposed" (Cohen and Sterba 2003, 25). Whether anything interesting follows from this proposition depends on how we construe "relevance." Cohen admits that public policy may rightly treat some people differently because of their physical characteristics. For example, the state might offer special assistance to the old or disabled. As it happens, this example suggests that the "relevance" of physical differences is something independent of social policy. Age and disability it seems are real features of persons and public policy simply tracks them. However, the difference that differences make is not something itself given by nature; it is determined by public purposes. Age and disability are made "relevant" in this manner—in the one case, by the social purpose of assuring that people do not have to live in poverty when they can no longer work; in the other case, by the social purpose of assuring that people are not foreclosed from developing and marketing their talents by impediments in the (largely constructed) physical environment.

Purpose determines relevancy, and this is true whether or not the relevant differences are physical. For example, if the nation thinks the public interest is served by maintaining a domestic sugar industry through subsidies, then a Michigan farmer who grows sugar beets is relevantly different from his neighbor across the road who grows tomatoes. If the nation thinks a modest program of redistributing income is legitimate, then it uses a social security payout formula that gives disproportionate return to low wage-earners over high wage-earners. Similarly, if the nation thinks it desirable to change white institutions so that they are less uniformly white, that purpose links skin color to recruitment.

Because the Aristotelian principle by itself doesn't rule out racial preferences (since blacks and whites may be relevantly different with respect to certain legitimate public purposes), it is not surprising that Cohen also invokes a substantive conception of equality: "All members of humankind are equally ends in themselves, all have equal dignity—and therefore all are entitled to equal respect from the community and its laws" (Cohen and Sterba 2003, 24). This principle, however, brings us back to the interpretive questions about "equal protection of the laws" played out in the Powell-Brennan exchange in Bakke. By Justice Brennan's lights, Allen Bakke's basic dignity was not violated. The Medical School's two-track policy that resulted in Bakke's rejection did not, by intent or effect, stigmatize him as inferior, or mark him off as a member of a despised caste, or turn him into a second-class citizen. Bakke arguably had to bear a particular burden because of his race but the burden was not significantly different objectively from others that public policy might have thrown his way. If the Medical School had reserved sixteen of its seats for applicants from economically deprived backgrounds, no one would have suggested that it had violated the equal protection clause of the Fourteenth Amendment. Yet under this hypothetical policy Allan Bakke could have lost out as well—lost out to low-income applicants whose college grades and MCAT scores were inferior to his own. Allen Bakke may have felt aggrieved at losing out under the Medical School's policy of racial preferences, but it is not enough to show that those who lose out under some public scheme feel offended or disgruntled. Cohen needs to specify a conception of dignity in which bearing unequal burdens on behalf of urgent social ends invariably amounts to an assault on dignity if the burdens happen to be assigned by race. This specification remains unfinished in his work so far.

7. Diversity's Dominion

How, if it held the Medical School's policy unconstitutional, did Justice Powell's Bakke opinion become the basis upon which universities across the land enacted—or maintained—racially preferential admissions policies?

If Powell had concluded with his assessment of the Medical School's four justifications, Bakke would have left university affirmative action in a precarious situation. However, he didn't stop there. In an earlier ruling on Bakke's lawsuit, the California Supreme Court had forbidden the Medical School to make any use of race or ethnicity in its admissions decisions. Powell thought this went too far. Given higher education's protected interest in "diversity," and given that a student's race or ethnicity might add to diversity just in the same way that her age, work experience, family background, special talents, foreign language fluency, athletic prowess, military service, and unusual accomplishments might, Powell vacated that portion of the California Supreme Court's order.

Then he added some dicta for guidance. If universities want to understand diversity and the role that race and ethnicity might play in achieving it, they should look to Harvard, proposed Powell, and he appended to his opinion a long statement of Harvard's diversity program. In such a program, Powell contended, racial or ethnic background might

be deemed a "plus" in a particular applicant's file, yet it does not insulate the individual from comparison with all other candidates for the available seats....This kind of program treats each applicant as an individual in the admissions process. The applicant who loses out on the last available seat to another candidate receiving a "plus" on the basis of ethnic background will not have been foreclosed from all consideration for that seat simply because he was not the right color or had the wrong surname. It would mean only that his combined qualifications...did not outweigh those of the other applicant. His qualifications would have been weighed fairly and competitively, and he would have had no basis to complain of unequal treatment under the Fourteenth Amendment (Bakke, at 318, 319).

In these off-hand comments, universities saw a green light for pushing ahead aggressively with their affirmative action programs. Justice Powell's basic holding could not have been plainer: any system like the Medical School's that assessed applications along two different tracks defined by race or that used numerical racial quotas must fail constitutional muster. Yet by the mid-1980s universities across the land had in place systems of admissions and scholarships that exhibited one or both of these features. When the University of Maryland's Banneker scholarships—awarded only to African-American students—were held in violation of the Constitution in 1994, the house of cards forming university affirmative action began to fall.[18] In 1996, the Court of Appeals for the Fifth Circuit struck down the University of Texas Law School's admissions program. In 1998, the Court of Appeals for the First Circuit struck down a Boston plan assigning students to selective high schools by race.[19] In 2001, two more schools saw their admissions programs invalidated by federal courts: the University of Georgia[20] and the University of Michigan Law School.[21] In many of these cases, educational institutions were using schemes that made race something very much more than Justice Powell's "plus" factor.[22] The Fifth Circuit Court's ruling in the University of Texas case (Hopwood v. Texas, 78 F 3d 932 [Fifth Circuit, 1996]) threw a cloud even over this small window for affirmative action, boldly asserting that the Bakke holding was now dead as law and that race could not be used at all in admissions.

Given Justice Powell's singular opinion, supported by no one else on the Court, and given the drift of Supreme Court decisions on racial preferences since 1978,[23] the Hopwood court was not outlandish, if a bit presumptuous, in declaring Powell's holding in Bakke dead. As it happened, Powell's opinion was far from dead. In the University of Michigan Law School case, Grutter v. Bollinger, eventually decided by the

Supreme Court in June 2003, Justice Sandra Day O'Connor's lead opinion declared: "today we endorse Justice Powell's view that student body diversity is a compelling state interest that can justify the use of race in university admissions" (Grutter v. Bollinger, 539 U.S. 306 [2003], at 330). Diversity was alive after all. But how it worked its affirmative action elixir remained as unclear in 2003 as it had been in 1978.

To see why, consider how in Grutter Justice O'Connor posed the issue:

The [Law School's] policy aspires to "achieve that diversity which has the potential to enrich everyone's education and thus make a law class stronger than the sum of its parts." [...] The policy does not restrict the types of diversity contributions eligible for substantial weight in the admissions process, but instead recognizes "many possible bases for diversity admissions." [...] The policy does, however, reaffirm the Law School's longstanding commitment to "one particular type of diversity," that is, "racial and ethnic diversity with special reference to the inclusion of students from groups which have been historically discriminated against" (Grutter, at 325).

Now, posing the issue this way and allowing the Law School to assert a special interest in "one particular type of diversity" invites the conflation of general diversity—a diversity of opinions, experiences, backgrounds, talents, aspirations, and perspectives—with ethnic and racial diversity that Justice Powell appeared strongly to resist. After all, the Medical School too had asserted in its defense a similar special interest.

Diversity is many things insisted Powell; it cannot be reduced to one thing. But why not? This question—and Justice O'Connor's acquiescence in the Law School's way of framing its affirmative action goal—spotlights a crucial gap in Powell's Bakke opinion. Diversity is many things—so many things, in fact, that institutions will think it worthwhile to concentrate on some diversity factors rather than others. One college may emphasize admitting foreign students; another may make its mission to educate poor students; a third may specialize in getting science students who have shown unusual promise in high school. If colleges have a legally protected interest in choosing a diverse student body, why don't they have a legally protected interest in deciding which part of the diversity spectrum to single out for special attention? If they can single out a part of the spectrum, why can't they use a simple device like set-asides to effect their purpose?

Recall Justice Powell's principal objection to the Medical School's set-asides. In making the race or ethnicity of an applicant a "plus," as in the Harvard Plan, an admissions scheme does

not insulate the individual from comparison with all other candidates for the available seats. The file of a particular African-American applicant may be examined for his potential contribution to diversity without the factor of race being decisive when compared, for example, with that of an applicant identified as an Italian-American if the latter is thought to exhibit qualities more likely to promote beneficial educational pluralism....In short, an admissions program operated in this way is flexible enough to consider all pertinent elements of diversity in light of the particular qualifications of each applicant.... This kind of program treats each applicant as an individual in the admissions process (Bakke, at 318–19).

By contrast, Allan Bakke was not able to compete for all one hundred seats at the Medical School; sixteen were reserved for candidates not like him.

It is Powell's resistance to this reservation that underpins Justice O'Connor's opinion in Grutter, where she observed:

We find that the Law School's admissions program bears the hallmark of a narrowly tailored plan. As Justice Powell made clear in Bakke, truly individualized consideration demands that race be used in a flexible, non-mechanical way. It follows from this mandate that universities cannot establish quotas for members of certain racial groups (Grutter, at 337).

What vindicated the Law School in O'Connor's eyes was its "highly individualized, holistic review of each applicant's file, giving serious consideration to all the ways an applicant might contribute to a diverse educational environment" (Grutter, at 339).[24] This "individualized consideration" is crucial; in Gratz v. Bollinger, decided the same day as Grutter, Justice O'Connor switched sides to hold unconstitutional the undergraduate admissions process at the University of Michigan. The undergraduate admissions office operated differently than the Law School. It computed an index score for each applicant by assigning numerical points for academic factors such as high school grades, admissions test scores, quality of high school, strength of curriculum; and for nonacademic factors such as being a resident of Michigan, a child of an alumnus, a recruited athlete, or a member of "an underrepresented minority group." An applicant falling in this last category automatically received 20 points (Gratz v. Bollinger, 539 U. S. 244 [2003], at 287). In O'Connor's view, this "mechanical" procedure meant that the undergraduate admissions office did not fully take account in each application "of all factors that may contribute to student body diversity (Gratz, at 288).

But O'Connor's conclusion here simply draws us back to the lacuna in Justice Powell's Bakke opinion. Why should the undergraduate admissions office take account of all the factors that may contribute to student body diversity if it especially wants to select from certain parts of the diversity spectrum? Why can't it, like the Law School, claim a special interest in "one particular type of diversity"? Why bar the undergraduate admissions office from using an effective tool to promote its interest even if the tool is "mechanical"? In fact, the Law School's "non-mechanical" procedure differed from the undergraduate admissions policy only on its face, not in its results. During admissions season, the Law School's director of admissions frequently consulted the "daily reports" that "kept track of the racial and ethnic composition" of the incoming class. He did so to make sure a "critical mass" of minority students was included (Grutter, at 326). In short, the Law School "managed" its admissions process so that roughly 6 to 7 percent of each entering class was African-American. The undergraduate admissions procedure, with its index scores, yielded a similar outcome (Grutter, at 367–69 [Rehnquist, dissenting] and 374 [Kennedy, dissenting]). Only surface appearance distinguished the two procedures. Justice Scalia called the Law School's "holistic" admissions process "a sham," and not without reason (Grutter, at 375 [Scalia, dissenting]).

In any case, the Law School's affirmative action program was vindicated by the Supreme Court and "diversity" securely established as its basis. Nevertheless, diversity hardly seems the right basis. When the University of Michigan was first challenged in federal court it insisted that it had a compelling educational interest in achieving racial and ethnic diversity and put into evidence findings by one of its psychology professors, Patricia Gurin, showing that

students learn better in a diverse educational environment, and they are better prepared to become active participants in our pluralistic, democratic society once they leave such a setting....[S]tudents who experienced the most racial and ethnic diversity in classroom settings and in informal interactions with peers showed the greatest engagement in active thinking processes, growth in intellectual engagement and motivation, and growth in intellectual and academic skills (Gratz v Bollinger, 122 F. Supp. 2d 811 [2000], at 823).

But suppose Patricia Gurin's findings had turned out differently. Can we imagine that the University would have abandoned affirmative action?[25]

8. The Integration Argument

In fact, the main reason the University of Michigan strives for a reasonable representation of minorities on campus is because of the way it conceives of its mission: to prepare Michigan's future leaders.

The argument is straightforward:

The leadership of the state ought roughly to represent the state's population, ethnically and racially.

As the state's premier training ground for leadership, the University ought to graduate rising generations of future leaders that conform to this representational goal.

To graduate such rising generations, it needs to admit racially and ethnically representative classes.

This is the "Michigan Mandate" (Gratz v. Bollinger, 135 F. Supp. 2d 790 [2001], at 796–797). Racial and ethnic diversity aren't incidental contributors to a distinct academic mission; they are part of the mission of the University, just as educating young people from Michigan is part of it.

This "integration" rationale seems much more aligned with the actual practice of university affirmative action than the diversity rationale. Indeed, in the midst of her nominally Powell-like defense of the Law School, Justice O'Connor for a moment veered away from the "educational benefits of diversity" to go down a quite different path. Institutions like the University of Michigan and its Law School, she noted, "represent the training ground for...our Nation's leaders." She went on:

In order to cultivate a set of leaders with legitimacy in the eyes of the citizenry, it is necessary that the path to leadership be visibly open to talented and qualified individuals of every race and ethnicity. All members of our heterogeneous society must have confidence in the openness and integrity of the educational institutions that provide this training....Access.... must be inclusive...of every race and ethnicity, so that all members of our heterogeneous society may participate in the educational institutions that provide the training and education necessary to succeed in America (Grutter, at 336).

This "legitimacy" argument—not in any way about enriching the climate of opinion on campus—parallels the simple syllogism set out just above. It provides an oblique way of justifying the second premise. Justice O'Connor inserted this new rationale into the middle of her Grutter opinion—inserted it unexpectedly and then abandoned it just as quickly to resume tracing the byways of diversity.

Certainly, something in the spirit of the "Michigan Mandate" has animated the elite universities studied by William Bowen and Derek Bok in The Shape of the River: Long-Term Consequences of Considering Race in College and University Admissions. The primary aim of these institutions is not through vigorous affirmative action to enhance the liberal learning of their students (although they welcome this gain for all students). Their main motive for assuring that the percentage of African-Americans and Hispanics on their campuses is more than token derives from their self-conceptions as institutions training individuals who will some day take up national and international leadership roles in the professions, arts, sciences, education, politics, and government (Bowen and Bok 1998, 7). Society, they believe, will be stronger and more just if the ranks of its leading citizens include a racially and ethnically broader range of people than it does now (and than it did twenty-five years ago).

Three recent works have developed versions of the integration argument. In a long article, "Integration, Affirmative Action, and Strict Scrutiny," published just before the Supreme Court's decisions in Grutter and Gratz, Elizabeth Anderson argues that an integration rationale is superior to the diversity rationale not only on its merits but as a plausible rending of what "compelling state interest"—the legal standard employed by the Supreme Court in racial classification cases—really demands. She concludes:

Current affirmative action debates have lost sight of the ideal of integration as a compelling moral and political goal. Unless disadvantaged racial groups are integrated into mainstream social institutions, they will continue to suffer from segregation and discrimination. But the loss is not only theirs. It is a loss suffered by the American public at large in its failure fully to realize civil society—extensive social spaces in which citizens from all origins exchange ideas and cooperate on terms of equality—which is an indispensable social condition of democracy itself. It is high time that institutions of higher education—the most ardent practitioners of integration today—forthrightly defend this ideal in its own right, and that the Supreme Court recognize integration as a compelling interest legitimately addressed through race-conscious means. (Anderson 2002, 1270–71)

Anderson has developed her thesis more elaborately in her recent book, The Imperative of Integration (Anderson 2010).

Robert Fullinwider and Judith Lichtenberg, in their 2004 book, Leveling the Playing Field: Justice, Politics, and College Admissions, present an integration argument for affirmative action centered around the little syllogism above (Fullinwider and Lichtenberg 2004, 165–188). A state like Michigan has strong reasons for wanting its leaders of commercial, financial, legal, cultural, and educational institutions to reflect to some practical degree the racial and ethnic variety of its population. One of the reasons is offered by Justice O'Connor: the very legitimacy of state institutions comes under a cloud if important segments of the population—long excluded from participating at the highest levels—remain on the outside looking in. Another reason is emphasized by Elizabeth Anderson: democratic governance draws nurture from inclusion rather than exclusion. If the leaders who frame the political agenda and shape public opinion remain uniformly white, the common good gets shortchanged; it isn't really common. Finally, racial and ethnic comity are harder to achieve when whites see a black or brown face in a position of leadership or power as a novelty rather than a commonplace.[26] Thus, if states like Michigan have strong reasons for creating an integrated stratum of leaders, they have strong reasons for making sure that the universities that feed this stratum are themselves integrated.

Lastly, Lesley Jacobs, in Pursuing Equal Opportunities (2004), sees affirmative action as a means of overcoming the structural exclusion of

African-Americans from major institutions: affirmative action assists structural integration, and structural integration serves the ideal of equal opportunity (Jacobs 2004, 124–142).

The integration argument, like the diversity argument, is straightforwardly instrumental. It points to hoped-for outcomes of affirmative action. If those outcomes don't materialize, then affirmative action's cause is weakened. Moreover, the little integration syllogism isn't complete as it stands. It needs to include another premise: that the gains from achieving racially and ethnically integrated classes don't come at a disproportionate cost.

Perhaps the cost is high, or even too high. Stephan and Abigail Thernstrom certainly think so. They contend that most of the cost falls on the very persons affirmative action is supposed to benefit. Under-prepared African-Americans are thrown into academic environments where they cannot succeed (Thernstrom and Thernstrom 1997, 395–411). In the Thernstroms' view, race-blind admissions policies will result in a desirable "cascading," with African-American and Hispanic students ending up at colleges and universities where the academic credentials of their fellow students match their own. However, the Bowen and Bok study provides some evidence that cascading isn't necessarily a valuable phenomenon. In fact, at the schools they studied, the better the institution a student entered, whatever his academic credentials, the more likely he was to graduate, go on to further education, and earn a good income (Bowen and Bok 1998, 63, 114, 144).[27]

Even so, the select schools Bowen and Bok studied may be quite unrepresentative of the full range of colleges and universities that resort to racial preferences and the cost-benefit picture that holds for these schools may not hold for the rest. Indeed, the picture drawn by Richard Sander in a lengthy review of affirmative action in law schools, published in the November 2004 Stanford Law Review, lends credence to the Thernstrom's academic mismatch thesis. Ranking law schools from best to worst, Sander found that affirmative action boosts African-American students 20 or more steps up the ladder, putting them in schools with white classmates who possess considerably better LSAT scores and undergraduate college grades. The upshot: "close to half of black students end up in the bottom tenth of their classes." This bad performance yields three bad consequences. First, African-American students suffer high attrition rates. Second, they fail the bar exam at a high rate (the principal predictor of a student's passing or failing is her grades, not the quality of her school). Third, they suffer a significant employment penalty for low grades "in all schools outside the top ten." Sander estimates that under a race-blind admissions system, American law schools would actually create more African-American lawyers than they do under affirmative action (Sander 2004, 449, 460, 478, 479).

Sander's article inspired a flurry of responses disputing his methodology and conclusions (e.g., Ayers and Brooks 2005, Chambers, et al. 2005, Wilkins 2005, Ho 2005, Barnes 2007, and Rothstein and Yoon 2008). Sander replied to his critics (Sander 2005); other writers found evidence of mismatch effects in educational domains outside law schools (Elliott et al. 1996, Smith and McArdle, 2004, Arcidiacono et al. 2012); yet other scholars presented independent confirmation of Sander's hypothesis (Arcidiacono et al. 2011b, Williams 2013); one critic, upon re-analysis, had to withdraw her refutation of Sander (Barnes 2007, Barnes 2011); and in 2012 Sander joined with co-author Stuart Taylor to publish Mismatch, a book-length treatment setting out old and new research supporting Sander's hypothesis.

One reason disputes persist about cause and effect is paucity of data. Sander was able to launch his study of mismatch in law schools because the Law School Admissions Council had undertaken a study in the 1990s tracking 27,000 law students from matriculation to bar passage. Likewise, Bowen and Bok were able to access a vast store of information about students and colleges collected by the Mellon Foundation. The Bowen and Bok information remained "in–house," not available to all researchers. The Sander information dwelt just on law students and only within a narrow time-frame. Much of the back–and–forth about the effects of affirmative action could be resolved if educational institutions disclosed information about their admissions processes, student grades, graduation rates, and the like. But institutional resistance makes this unlikely.[28]

9. A Blip

In 2004, after the Supreme Court's Grutter decision, the University of Texas revised its admissions policy to include race as one input to an applicant's Personal Achievement Index which, combined with her

Academic Index, qualifies her, or not, for admission. Prior to 2004, the University's admissions procedure had been governed by the Hopwood decision of the Fifth Circuit Court of Appeals, which barred the University from considering race; and by the Top Ten Percent policy created by the Texas legislature soon after the Hopwood decision[29]. The University had broadened the considerations making up the Personal Achievement Index in order to improve minority admissions but saw Grutter as opening a way for a more direct and effective approach. In 2008, Abigail Fisher, an unsuccessful applicant to the University, sued. As her case proceeded toward the Supreme Court, her plea, among other things, asked the Court to overturn Grutter. Instead, by a 7–1 vote in June, 2013, the Court left the Grutter framework in place but sent the case back to the lower courts, arguing that they had been too deferential in accepting the University's argument that using race was "necessary" to achieving a "critical mass" of minority students on campus (Fisher v. Texas, 133 S. Ct. 2411 [2013], at 2417–2422).

10. Desert Confounded, Desert Misapplied

The affirmative action debate throws up many ironies but one in particular should be noted. From the time in 1973 when Judith Jarvis Thomson conjectured that it was "not entirely inappropriate" that white males bear the costs of the community's "making amends" to African-Americans and women through preferential affirmative action, the affirmative action debate has been distracted by intense quarrels over who deserves what. Do the beneficiaries of affirmative action deserve their benefits (Allen 2011)? Do the losers deserve their loss?

Christopher Edley, the White House assistant put in charge of President Clinton's review of affirmative action policy in 1994–95, speaks of how, during the long sessions he and his co-workers put in around the conference table, the discussion of affirmative action kept circling back to the "coal miner's son" question.[30]

Imagine a college admissions committee trying to decide between the white [son] of an Appalachian coal miner's family and the African American son of a successful Pittsburgh neurosurgeon. Why should the black applicant get preference over the white applicant? (Edley 1996, 132ff)

Why, indeed? This is a hard question if one defends affirmative action in terms of compensatory or distributive justice. If directly doing justice is what affirmative action is about, then its mechanisms must be adjusted as best they can to reward individual desert and true merit. The "coal miner's son" example is meant to throw desert in the defender's face: here is affirmative action at work thwarting desert, for surely the coal miner's son—from the hard scrabble of Harlan County, say—has lived with far less advantage than the neurosurgeon's son who, we may suppose, has reaped all the advantages of his father's (or mother's) standing. Why should the latter get a preference?

A defender might answer in the way that Charles Lawrence and Mari Matsuda do in their 1997 book, We Won't Go Back: "All the talk about class, the endless citings of the 'poor white male from Appalachia,' cannot avoid the reality of race and gender privilege" (Lawrence and Matsuda 1997, 190–191). Because white privilege persists, racial preferences really do balance the scales. Because male privilege persists, gender preferences really do make selections fairer. There must be no concession: in every case the loser in affirmative action is not the more deserving.[31]

Even Justice Brennan tried his hand at this argument, writing in Bakke:

If it was reasonable to conclude—as we hold that it was—that the failure of minorities to qualify for admission at [the University of California at] Davis [Medical School] under regular procedures was due principally to the effects of past discrimination, then there is a reasonable likelihood that, but for pervasive racial discrimination,...[Bakke] would have failed to qualify for admission even in the absence of Davis' special admissions program (Bakke, at 365–6 [Brennen, dissenting].
Bakke was not denied anything to which he had moral claim in the first place.[32]

Just as Mary Anne Warren and James Rachels in the 1970s thought that the losers under affirmative action were losing only illicit privileges, and the gainers merely gaining what should have been theirs to start with, so Michel Rosenfeld in the 1990s, in his extended "dialogic" defense of affirmative action, echoes the same thought:

Although affirmative action treats innocent white males unequally, it need not deprive them of any genuine equal opportunity rights. Provided an affirmative action plan is precisely tailored to redress the losses in prospects of success [by African-Americans and women] attributable to racism and sexism, it only deprives innocent white males of the corresponding undeserved increases in their prospects of success.... [R]emedial affirmative action does not take away from innocent white males anything that they have rightfully earned or that they should be entitled to keep (Rosenfeld 1991, 307–8, emphasis added).

However, programs that give blanket preferences by race or gender are hardly "precisely tailored" to match desert and reward since, as Lawrence and Matsuda themselves acknowledge at one place, the white male "privilege" is "statistical" (Lawrence and Matsuda 1997, 252). Yet it is individuals, not statistical averages, who gain or lose in admissions determinations and employment selections.

The persistence of this strategy of defense reflects a residual feeling that the fruits of affirmative action are somehow spoiled if they are not deserved (Harris 2003). Nevertheless, it is the wrong strategy for defending real world affirmative action. The programs legitimated under the Civil Rights Act, in both their nonpreferential and preferential forms, had—and have—a clear aim: to change institutions so that they can meet the nondiscrimination mandate of the Act. Selection by race or gender was—and is—a means to such change. To the extent that such selection also compensates individuals for past wrongs or puts people in places they really deserve, these are incidental by-products of a process aimed at something else.

The same is true with university admissions policy. When the Medical School of the University of California at Davis offered four reasons in defense of the special admissions program that left Bakke on the outside, none of these reasons said anything about matching admissions and desert. The criteria of the special admissions program—race and ethnicity—were instruments to further ends: integrating the classroom, the profession, and the delivery of medical services, and breaking the chain of self-reproducing societal discrimination. Likewise, when the University of Michigan and the University of Texas defended their programs they pointed not to desert rewarded but educational value generated.

Now, if the neurosurgeon's son because of his race can advance each of these goals and the coal miner's son, because of his race, cannot, then isn't the selection decision easy? Pick the African-American neurosurgeon's son (however advantaged he may be) over the white coal miner's son (even if he is the most deserving creature imaginable). The aims of real world affirmative action make race and ethnicity (and sometimes gender) salient, not personal desert or merit. The test of real world affirmative action lies in the urgency of its ends (preventing discrimination, promoting diversity or integration) and the aptness (moral and causal) of its means (racial, ethnic, and gender preferences). Both remain much in dispute..

AFFIRMATIVE ACTION

ABOUT THE AUTHOR

Tafadzwa Mahachi is a Mathematician and a teacher with a creative arts background. He is a devout Christian and a former missionary. At the time of the writing of this book, he is a member of BTTC debate society and a high school debate coach. Tafadzwa proved his prowess in debates that has managed to get him to be the ZNDC 2015 debates semi-finalist, PAUDC Ghana 2015 public speaking semi-finalist (although circumstances disturbed him from participating in the semi-finals), Debate Open Tournament 2016 quarter-finalist and hDot 2016 debate quarter-finalist. This book is his first in the Debater Reads series with hope to cover topics such as politics, economics and debate basics. This work is meant for trainings and grooming of debaters. However, the principles of justice as outlined here are usable in the learning of the justice system and therefore a good textbook for law students.